INSTRUCTOR'S MANUAL

Issues for Today, 3rd Edition

and

Concepts for Today, 2nd Edition

and

Topics for Today, 3rd Edition

Lorraine C. Smith • **Nancy Nici Mare**
Nancy Hubley

THOMSON
™
HEINLE

Australia • Canada • Mexico • Singapore • United Kingdom • United States

Instructor's Manual with Answer Key
for *Issues for Today*, *Concepts for Today*, and *Topics for Today*

Lorraine C. Smith, Nancy Nici Mare, Nancy Hubley

Publisher, Adult and Academic ESL: *James W. Brown*
Senior Acquisitions Editor: *Sherrise Roehr*
Director of Product Development: *Anita Raducanu*
Development Editor: *Sarah Barnicle*
Editorial Assistants: *Katherine Reilly, John Hicks*
Editorial Intern: *Sarah Bilodeau*
Senior Production Editor: *Maryellen E. Killeen*
Academic Marketing Manager: *Laura Needham*
Director, Global ESL Training & Development: *Evelyn Nelson*
Senior Print Buyer: *Mary Beth Hennebury*
Project Manager: *Tünde A. Dewey*
Contributing Editor: *Tania Maundrell-Brown, Kate Briggs*
Compositor: *Parkwood Composition Service*
Cover Designer: *Ha Ngyuen*
Text Designer: *Parkwood Composition Service*
Printer: *WestGroup*

ISBN   0-7593-9816-X

CONTENTS

TO THE TEACHER

The updated **Reading for Today** series features a broad range of reading materials and resources to prepare students for academic success. The core of the series consists of reading passages of general and academic interest that provide a context for vocabulary development. The student books also contain a wealth of visual materials and nonlinear texts such as graphs, charts, maps and photographs. In addition, each unit is accompanied by a CNN® video clip and Internet activities that provide thematically related, current, and authentic materials for expanding reading skills and strategies. A Web site gives teachers and students access to further resources for Internet exploration and vocabulary review. Lastly, assessment materials are provided in two forms. Reproducible quizzes for each chapter appear in the Instructor's Manuals. The *ExamView® Pro* computerized Test Bank assists instructors in building tests and quizzes, which emphasize vocabulary and grammar in context using fresh materials related to the unit themes.

The introduction to each student book presents strategies by the authors for using the sections for each chapter. In addition to providing chapter prereading activities, culture and background notes, and follow-up activities, this Instructor's Manual focuses on ways to make the most of the video and assessment materials in the **Reading for Today** series.

Videos

Use the video clips *after* students have worked through unit chapters so that concepts and vocabulary in the text provide background scaffolding for viewing. "Reading videos"—actively watching videos for information—is different from passive watching for entertainment. Explain that students will employ many of the same skills they do in reading a text passage. They will engage in "pre-reading" by brainstorming what they already know about a subject, and they will predict what the video will show. During the video, they will identify the main ideas and supporting details.

They will also look for contextual information and differentiate between fact and opinion. After viewing, they should be able to answer comprehension questions. Here are some specific suggestions for helping your students become active viewers:

- Prepare students by giving the title of the video. Have students predict what it will be about.
- The video clips are very short (averaging 2–3 minutes per clip) so students may benefit from viewing them several times. First, "skim the video" for an overview of the topic and coverage. In other words, view for general comprehension. Then watch again for details. Students can "scan the video" for particular information, perhaps to answer comprehension questions in the book. Repeated viewings can be used to identify opinions or interpretations. These can be compared and contrasted with views from the text readings.
- The videos are authentic material from CNN® and therefore speech is at a natural speed. Moreover, speakers occasionally use regional dialects. This presents a contrast to video materials made especially for English language learners where the content, pace and varieties of English are tightly controlled. Let students know that they are not expected to understand every word. Instead, have them initially focus on main points.
- Since the videos use authentic language, the speech often contains idioms and new vocabulary words. These are identified in the video script. You may choose to pre-teach some of these before showing the video to enhance comprehension.
- The video segments share a particular structure. Usually a reporter introduces the topic by interviewing knowledgeable people. Sometimes several people are presented as supporting examples for the topic. At the end, the reporter concludes the segment, often with a summary or personal opinion. Check on comprehension of this structure by asking about the reporter, the setting, and the people who are inter-

To the Teacher

viewed. Where does this take place? Why were people chosen for this video? Are some of these people "authorities"? How do we know that?

Internet Resources

Internet sites change often, so relatively few URLs or Internet addresses are given in the book. Instead, students are encouraged to develop search strategies using key words and search engines such as Netscape™, Google™, or Yahoo™. There are several ways in which exploring Internet sites fosters the development of good reading skills. First, students need to consider what words to use with the search engine. This leads naturally to a discussion of key terms and their relationships. If a term is too broad, the search results in too many sites. Conversely, a narrow key word search will produce a limited range of sites. Use graphic organizers to show specific and more general terms in a hierarchy.

Secondly, the Internet provides a full range of texts from the simplest and most straightforward (often intended for young learners but equally accessible to beginning English language learners) to sites meant for technical specialists. For learners using *Issues, Concepts* and *Topics,* it may be appropriate to pre-identify sites that use language that stretches their comprehension skills slightly.

Third, Internet resources vary enormously in terms of accuracy and reliability. Early in the course, find sites with very different perspectives on a topic to illustrate this point. Attune students to investigating the source of a site. For example, if the domain in the site address is *.edu,* the source is academic—from a college or university. With experience, students will learn to rely on dependable sites.

Lastly, using the Internet effectively is a giant exercise in critical thinking. Encourage students to treat online material the same way they would evaluate print material. From the beginning, require students to identify their sources. Expect students to paraphrase information in their own words and you'll reinforce good summarizing and vocabulary skills.

Reading for Today Web Site

A list of useful search words and Web sites related to topics in the *Reading for Today* series appear on the Heinle Web site at www.heinle.com.

Vocabulary review resources such as chapter glossaries, flashcards, and crossword puzzles may be found on the individiual book sites. The Web site also provides access to other materials for teacher and student use, such as guidelines and worksheets for self-evaluation of reading strategies, for new vocabulary review, as well as for group project worksheets. Answers for the assessment found in this instructor's manual may also be found on the *Reading for Today* Web site.

Assessment

This Instructor's Manual contains sets of quizzes for each chapter in the *Reading for Today* series. The first section emphasizes reading comprehension and recall. Encourage students to do this from memory instead of referring to the text passages. The second section uses key vocabulary from each chapter in a cloze passage similar to the text. Each text chapter has grammatical exercises and extensive work on vocabulary in context. These sections should make students aware of the function and relationship of words within sentences. When students do the cloze exercises, they should pay close attention to parts of speech as well as collocations.

Separate from the Instructor's Manual, the ExamView® Test Bank builds on all aspects of skill development presented in the *Reading for Today* series. Some sections focus on major reading skills such as skimming, scanning, and finding the main idea. Vocabulary from the textbooks is recycled in new readings on the same topics to provide students with further opportunity to recognize the meaning of recently learned words in context. Reflecting the text, there are assessment sections on grammar in context since accurate comprehension rests on understanding structure. Visual material and graphics are presented for analysis and interpretation. Other assessments focus on inference and drawing conclusions. Teachers can quickly generate tests from material in the test bank or they can use the ExamView® software to create their own custom assessments.

Reading for Today provides an integrated package of resources that enables every teacher to tailor the course to the needs of particular students. We hope you enjoy exploring all five levels of the *Reading for Today* series.

Issues for Today
TEACHER NOTES

| Unit 1 | Trends in Living |

Chapter 1   **A Cultural Difference: Being on Time**   **Audio CD, Track 1**

An American professor teaching in Brazil discovered that his students had different ideas about being on time. He learned that promptness depends on social factors in Brazil. Eventually, he adapted his own behavior to fit local expectations.

Suggestions for Prereading Activity

Direct students' attention to the unit title and photograph on Student Book ("SB") page 1 as well as the chapter title and photograph on page 2. Before referring to the table on SB page 3, elicit what *on time* means to your class. Instruct students to look at the table. Ask what the differences are between the types of appointments. What happens in each case if someone is late? Discuss any cultural differences that your students may be aware of.

Culture Notes

Issues for Today introduces the use of graphic organizers for analyzing the organization of texts and the relationships between parts or components of the reading passage. Many different types of graphic organizers will be used throughout the book, but Chapter 1 uses a flowchart to make the sequence of the reading passage more apparent. Students will need to differentiate between main ideas and supporting details in the reading passage, then fill in the flowchart on page 10. With practice, students will naturally use graphic organizers, but, at first, they may need explicit instruction. Before they attempt to fill in the flowchart, you can help them be aware that they will only use the most important terms and phrases; they will not write details or complete sentences. One effective method for presenting this task is to ask students to use colored highlighters to mark what they consider the most important ideas and words as they read the text. You may first want to model a paragraph for them, using an overhead projector. Then ask students to work in pairs to identify the most important concepts and terms of a new paragraph. Go over choices with the entire class. Explain to students that the flowchart can help them answer the comprehension questions on SB pages 11 and 12. It can also assist them with writing their summary. As a result, the flowchart becomes an instructional tool for organizing the main points and the essential structure of the reading.

As the passage indicates, promptness or perception of time varies from culture to culture and sometimes even within one culture. For example, promptness and speed of response vary considerably from one part of the United States to another. One of the most important studies of cultural perceptions of time is Edward Hall's *The Hidden Dimension* (Garden City, N.Y.: Doubleday, 1966).

The distinction between formal and informal settings provides a natural opportunity to discuss registers in language. Be sure to bring up the differences between formal and colloquial stylistic variety. Ask students for examples from their own culture and explain differences in an English-speaking context.

Suggestions for Follow-Up Activities

If students want to know more about cultural differences in promptness, enter the words *intercultural communication* in an Internet search engine such as Google or Yahoo.

Alternatively, if your college or university community is multicultural, have students survey people in the community about being "on time" in their culture for the types of appointments given on SB page 3.

Chapter 2   **Changing Lifestyles and New Eating Habits**   **Audio CD, Track 2**

Changes in American lifestyles have had an adverse effect on eating habits. There has been an increase in the number of people living alone, single parents, and double-income families, resulting in less time for cooking and eating meals. Greater knowledge of nutrition results in different food choices, as do ideas about appropriate foods for different occasions.

Suggestions for Prereading Activity

Ask questions about the family in the photograph on SB page 20 to elicit ideas about working parents and the challenge of multitasking. Ask where these people probably live and why they seem to be in a hurry. Note that in North America long commutes to work are common.

Also look at the photographs on SB pages 22 and 34. Who are these people and what are they doing? What do the three photographs have in common? How are they different?

Culture Notes

The *Newbury House Dictionary,* 4th Edition, (Boston, M.A.: Thomson/Heinle, 2004) defines *lifestyle* as "the manner in which one lives." This very general definition covers a range of factors that people usually mean when they use the term *lifestyle.* The reading passage uses the word to refer to demography or household size, marital status, and employment. It can also refer to where a person lives, an individual's tastes and belongings, and their leisure activities. Lifestyle correlates with socioeconomic background, education, and type of employment or occupation. A college-educated professional who is earning $90,000 a year and living in an upscale neighborhood will have a very different lifestyle from an unemployed laborer who is struggling to pay his or her rent.

In the past 50 years in the United States, development has extended out from cities in what is known as *urban sprawl.* It is in areas of sprawl that most malls or shopping centers are located as well as fast-food outlets, services, and sports facilities. In addition, historical patterns and availability of land have led to most people living in single-family homes in the suburbs. Lifestyle for many Americans means having sufficient income to buy various consumer goods, including cars, advertised heavily in the media. Typically, families own more than one car and depend on driving to reach their jobs, shopping, and recreational activities. Vehicles have become larger and more expensive at the same time that roadways have become more congested. In fact, the most popular car is a SUV, a suburban utility vehicle.

Note that there are some contradictions in the reading passage. While it is true that Americans are better informed about nutrition than they were in the past, they often choose to ignore sound information. For example, they know the dangers of too much cholesterol, yet prefer shrimp and lobster for romantic meals. Both seafoods are high in cholesterol. Similarly, health awareness of obesity and diabetes has not reduced the consumption of greasy, high-calorie snacks and sweets such as donuts, nor has it slowed the merchandising of "super-sized" fast food which has far more calories than any person needs.

In the Fact-Finding Exercise on SB page 22, note that some statements are negative. That means that if they are false, double negatives cancel each other out. For example, in the second item, the result is "Americans eat increasing amounts of sweets now." In Word Forms on SB page 29, point out that sometimes paired sentences are linked in meaning. For example, 4b makes it clear that the answer to 4a is "didn't employ." Students should also be aware that the second sentence can also clarify tense use.

Suggestions for Follow-Up Activities

In the Follow-Up Activity on SB page 33, items d and e pertain to the increase in the number of nontraditional American households. The answers to these questions can be presented either in percentages or numbers. If you use percentages, single-parent households increased the most (by 166% as contrasted to 109% for one-person or 36% for dual-income households). However, if numbers are used, one-person households increased the most, by 11 million during the 20-year period.

Ask students to keep a food diary or journal for a week. They should write down what they eat, where they eat (home, type of restaurant, work), why they are eating (snack, regular meal, perhaps boredom), and who they are eating with (family, friends, alone). Suggest that students indicate why they have made particular food choices (a celebration of some kind, diet, taking part in sports).

| **Chapter 3** | **Dreams: Making Them Work for Us** | **Audio CD, Track 3** |

A man named Joseph had the same bad dream for months. Dream researchers believe we can remember our dreams and change the bad ones. Through the use of dream therapy techniques, Joseph eventually stopped having nightmares and started having more positive dreams.

Suggestions for Prereading Activity

Pairwork is an effective way for students to successfully prepare for this reading. Ask students to recall and share a dream that they have had. Explain that they can discuss both good and bad dreams, if they wish. Teachers should be sensitive to the possibility that some students' dream experiences may be rather personal and best discussed only with a partner.

Culture Notes

Dreams have fascinated people throughout history. Some people believe that dreaming is a supernatural state. A century ago, the psychoanalyst Sigmund Freud thought that dreams were keys to the unconscious mind. He believed that when we sleep, we are in a primitive state where aggressive and sexual feelings from childhood come to the surface. Although scientists still don't agree on what dreams really mean, within the last two decades they have learned a great deal about what physically happens to the body during sleep.

Sleep researchers have based their understanding on laboratory studies of humans and animals while they sleep and dream. Scientists attach measuring devices to monitor changes in brain activity, eye movement, breathing, and blood pressure. Based on thousands of studies, they know that there are two basic types of sleep. The names are related to what happens to the eye during these sleep periods. During NREM (non-rapid eye movement) sleep, blood circulation occurs at a lower rate but there is no dreaming. By contrast, dreams happen during REM (rapid eye movement) sleep. Most of our sleep is the NREM type, but it alternates during the night with four or five periods of dreaming during REM sleep. In all, we dream for about one-quarter of each night's sleep time.

Although scientists can track what happens to the body during sleep, they disagree about the function of sleep. Some researchers think that dreams are meaningless themselves; they only provide a way of getting rid of unused information so we don't overload our brain. Other scientists think that dreams help us integrate new information with old memories. Still others think dreaming is an important way of unconsciously expressing feelings and, therefore, can be used to treat problems.

In Chapter 3, students will be using material from the reading to complete the chart on SB page 44. Ask them to work with a partner to highlight the main ideas, preferably in color. Before they complete the chart, have each pair of students compare their highlighted sentences with another pair of students.

Suggestions for Follow-Up Activities

Ask students if they have ever had a dream that actually came true later. If they have, they could write about their dream in their journal. If they haven't, ask students to write about the most interesting dream they can remember.

Another interesting topic for discussion is whether animals dream. If your students have pets or have worked closely with animals, perhaps they could share their opinions with the class. Ask students what they think animals dream about.

Unit 1 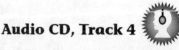 Video Report

Have students watch the Unit 1 video, *Nutrition Survey*. Since the video is about eating habits and nutrition, you might want to show it for the first time after completing Chapter 2. Ask students how the information in the video supports and differs from what they have read in the reading passage. Is it true that knowing more about nutrition results in people eating a healthier diet? Why or why not? Have your students ever stopped eating a favorite food because it isn't as healthy as other foods? Ask students what they consider to be a *balanced diet*.

After students have discussed the issues presented in the video, ask them to answer the Video Report questions on SB page 58.

Unit 2	Issues in Society

Chapter 4	**Language: Is It Always Spoken?**	**Audio CD, Track 4**

Linguists believe language ability is inborn, although the development of communication in deaf babies has only recently been studied. Both hearing and deaf infants make

hand motions, but the motions of deaf infants are more patterned and soon become complex enough to communicate messages. In order to learn more about spoken and signed language, future research will focus on babies with one hearing parent and one deaf parent.

Suggestions for Prereading Activity

Ask students if they know any people who are deaf or hearing-impaired. How do these people communicate? How did they learn to do this? Then have students look at the American Sign Language (ASL) chart on SB page 60 and the photographs on SB pages 62 and 73. What's happening in those photographs?

The Newbury House Dictionary defines *language* as "human communication by systems of written symbols, spoken words, and movements."

Culture Notes

Many interesting issues arise in the reading passage. They include the theory that language ability is innate, the use of signs and ASL in communication, and the development of communication in hearing and deaf babies.

It is now generally accepted that the ability to use language as defined above is innate or inborn. Since language is symbolic communication, it can be accomplished with signs or body movements and does not always depend on speech. Scientists have conducted a number of experiments with nonhuman primates to see if they can use symbolic communication. These have had some degree of success, so it is not certain that language is unique to humans, although speech is. There is a huge amount of literature available on these topics which may be of interest to your students. The library is a good place to start further research.

Since the Middle Ages, people have developed systems of signs to communicate with hearing-impaired persons. Today there are three major systems of manually spelling the alphabet. The chart on SB page 60 shows the one most common in America. There is also a Swedish system, plus a two-handed British one. Alphabet signs are used as the equivalent of writing systems for teaching reading as well as for spelling out words not included in the lexicon of ASL. ASL is a fully developed system of symbols that many people consider to be a language in itself. Research on deaf and hearing-impaired infants shows that they can develop communication skills in much the same way that hearing infants do. However, early identification and intervention (focused attention) is very important so that communication development is not delayed. Many doctors believe all babies should be screened for hearing and vision problems soon after birth. They think that the first six months of life—before babies start babbling—is a very important period in preparation for communication.

Intervention often takes the form of teaching mothers and fathers of deaf infants to pay particular attention to when their babies are watching them. Parents should start sign language early, use dramatic facial expressions, and also use touch as a way of getting their baby's attention. Deaf parents do these things naturally, but it is also possible for hearing parents to adapt these techniques.

Suggestions for Follow-Up Activities

There are already a number of excellent follow-up suggestions on SB page 73, but if your students are interested in exploring other aspects of nonverbal communication, they might want to explore lip-reading. Locate a videotape that shows a close-up of a person talking. If you can't locate one, record a short segment of yourself speaking. The second option would be the most effective because your students will be familiar with your communication style. Play the video without sound and ask students to take notes. Have them work in small groups to discuss and interpret your communication. After playing the video without sound several times, play the video with sound. Have students determine the accuracy of their interpretation.

Chapter 5   **Loneliness: How Can We Overcome It?**   **Audio CD, Track 5**

For most people, loneliness lasts for only a short time. Psychologists have identified three types of loneliness, but they are most concerned about chronic loneliness that lasts longer than two years. Chronically lonely people are more prone to health problems and unhappiness, so doctors are trying to find ways to help them.

Suggestions for Prereading Activity

Make sure students understand the distinction between being *alone*—a natural and normal condition—and *loneliness*—a sad, negative condition. You may also want to introduce the word *lonesome*. You can then explain the term *loner* means a person who actually prefers solitude—or being alone—to being social with other people.

Culture Notes

Loneliness is a state affected by both personality and cultural values. Some people are *extroverts*—people who are most comfortable when surrounded by other people with whom they intensively interact. Others are *introverts*—much shyer, quieter people who are more reserved. Psychologists believe these two descriptions are fundamental elements of personality and influence one's approach to life. On the other hand, psychologists disagree about how personality traits are formed. Some believe that they are innate, but others say they are heavily influenced by experiences after birth. This basic disagreement is known as the nature-nurture controversy.

Swiss psychologist Carl Jung is among the most famous researchers of personality traits. In his book *Psychological Types* (Princeton, N.J.: Princeton University Press, 1971) first published in 1921, Jung was the first to propose the extrovert and introvert types, along with other contrast sets such as sensing and intuiting, and feeling and thinking. Other psychologists built on his work to develop Myers-Briggs Trait Inventory in 1942. This test breaks down basic personality traits into 16 categories and suggests that people function according to the particular combination of traits that are dominant for them. The test is widely used in business and academia.

Different cultures and subcultures can also emphasize and influence solitary or social behavior. Anthropologist Margaret Mead, whose life and work was featured in Chapter 7 of *Themes for Today,* was a principal scholar in the field of culture and personality. Mead emphasized the value of looking carefully and openly at other cultures to better understand the complexities of being human. She noted that attitudes toward spending time alone and relating closely to other people vary enormously between cultures, and even within the same culture at different times or under certain conditions.

The process of *enculturation* is the training that occurs in childhood to ensure that a person understands the approved ways of behaving in a particular culture. Parents, teachers, and other important figures model the way people are supposed to behave and use various ways to punish people who behave differently. In American culture, sending badly behaved children for "time-out" (short amounts of time spent alone) is a common punishment. In other cultures, young people have to go through a long period by themselves to prove that they are ready to be adults. As the reading suggests, individuals often perceive loneliness even though they are surrounded by other people, so it is not always just a matter of being alone. Ask students about attitudes toward being alone and loneliness in their cultures.

Suggestions for Follow-Up Activities

Although the reading mentions that young adults are at particular risk for loneliness, it does not talk about all of the social factors that can contribute to an individual's loneliness. Peer approval and acceptance are particularly important to young adults, and an absence of these can compound and heighten feelings of loneliness. Ask students to identify situations where a young person may feel lonely because they don't feel accepted by their peers.

What services exist at your institution for students experiencing loneliness? Is there a counselor they can visit? Are there peer hotlines or support groups? This is a great opportunity for students to explore what support resources are available.

Suggest students consider other groups of people who may experience loneliness. Chapter 2 mentioned changing lifestyles whereby more people live alone and there are more single parents raising children by themselves. In addition, as people live longer, more elderly people live alone. Do these groups experience loneliness?

Chapter 6

The Importance of Grandmothers

Audio CD, Track 6

Anthropologists recently held a conference at which they presented research on how grandmothers influence the survival rate of grandchildren in some cultures. Generally, they found that maternal grandmothers increase the chances that children will survive childhood. In other cultures, grandmothers may not necessarily increase the survival rate of their grandchildren, although they still play an important role in their grandchildren's lives.

Suggestions for Prereading Activity

The prereading activities focus on differences between maternal and paternal grandmothers. These distinctions are important in the reading passage. In many cultures, extended families—those including more than two generations—live together with a set of grandparents. Ask if your students have ever lived with their grandparents.

In countries where it is not unusual for families to relocate or for parents to divorce, you may find that children do not live near their grandparents and may not see them often. If this is evident in your class, you can modify the chart on SB page 90, substituting the word *contact* for *treat*. For example, someone might have received a birthday card from one distant grandmother, but a telephone call from the other.

Also, be sensitive to the possibility that some students may not have known any or all of their grandparents. You may wish to explain that this is not uncommon, especially in today's society. Perhaps a student may consider another adult in a similar capacity a grandparent. Suggest that they complete the activities with this person in mind.

Remind students how important it is for them to apply critical reading and thinking skills. Students should be active participants in their reading experiences. Encourage students to question sources of information and any generalizations that may be implied to the reader.

Culture Notes

Anthropologists have studied the influence of grandmothers for at least 75 years, so this in itself is not a new area of research. In addition, the studies cited are somewhat controversial. Research is guided by *hypotheses,* which are not theories or facts. They are, according to *The Newbury House Dictionary,* "working theories" or "unproved assumptions." In this case, the reading passage reports recent findings of evolutionary biologists and anthropologists about the "Grandmother Hypothesis." This is a working theory about the roles of postmenopausal women in societies where older women help with the care of grandchildren in their households. Other scientists who have worked with different groups have debated the "Grandmother Hypothesis." It is a controversial topic and not everyone accepts the ideas presented in the reading.

Since much of the research presented in the reading is based on historical records, encourage students to explore the crucial role that grandmothers continue to play in many modern intergenerational families. For instance, in African-American families in the Caribbean, parents often leave their young children in the care of their own mothers when they go overseas for employment. The grandmothers become the heads of households who provide all the essential child care. Similar patterns occur in the United States, where grandparents raise children as depicted in the video for this unit. Furthermore, as older people have more active lifestyles than they did in the past, some stereotypes of grandparents may not be relevant to modern families.

Suggestions for Follow-Up Activities

Point out to students that the outline on SB page 97 and the graphs on SB pages 104 and 105 focus on particular case studies. Explain that students' answers and conclusions should be limited to these specific studies, and therefore will not be applicable to all cultures.

To expand upon this chapter's reading passage and activities, students may also enjoy an opportunity to discuss their paternal and maternal grandfathers. Like grandmothers, grandfathers often play an active role in the lives of their grandchildren, especially during childhood. Ask students to write a paragraph or two about their grandfathers. How were their maternal and paternal grandfathers the same? How were they different? In what ways are grandfathers different from grandmothers? Have students share their ideas in pairs.

Unit 2 CNN Video Report

Have students watch the Unit 2 video, *Grandparents as Parents.* Since the video features grandparents, students may find the video most beneficial after completing Chapter 6. After viewing the video, ask if students understand why the two boys are living with their grandparents. Explain that in the United States, the state government can remove children from their parents if their parents are unfit to care for them. If grandparents are willing and able to care for their grandchildren, usually the state will oblige. Otherwise, children are placed with foster parents. Only rarely do children go to an *orphanage,* an institution for children without parents.

Ask students why the grandmother in the support group isn't allowed to see her grandson. What rights does a parent have? What rights does a former caregiver have?

After discussing the video, have students answer the Video Report questions on SB page 112.

Unit 3 | Justice and Crime

Chapter 7 | Innocent Until Proven Guilty: The Criminal Court System   Audio CD, Track 7

The American court system protects people's rights by maintaining that someone is innocent until a court process finds him or her guilty. An arrested person must be told about his rights, and a series of procedures must take place before a trial. Evidence is presented in a trial and a jury decides whether the person is innocent or guilty.

Suggestions for Prereading Activity

Each country has its own legal system, but many people are familiar with the American legal system through television programs and famous trials that have been reported in the media. Brainstorm all the words students know that refer to the legal system and write them on the board. Ask students to look at the photographs on SB pages 114, 116, and 120. What can they tell you about the photographs? Add important words to the class list.

Inform students that Chapter 7 introduces Dictionary Skills, a component of each of the remaining chapters of *Issues for Today*. Refer students to SB page 126 and draw their attention to the fact that each dictionary entry has several definitions, sometimes with different parts of speech. Their task is to select the most appropriate meaning for the word as it is used in each sentence.

Culture Notes

The reading passage describes the steps or process in American criminal courts, which operate within the justice system—a major branch of American government. In the United States, part of this system is national and covers people throughout the country, and part of it is specific to each of the 50 states. The whole system is based on English common law which dates back to the Middle Ages. Other countries have systems based on civil or religious law, or sometimes both. These systems vary greatly in how they regard the accused person and in the processes that are used to come to a decision about guilt (that the person did commit a crime) or innocence (that the person did not commit a crime).

In common law systems such as those in England, Canada, and the United States, the *adversarial system* is used. This means that there are two sides that oppose each other. The two sides are the *prosecution*—who argues on behalf of the party that has been wronged—and the *defense*—who represents the accused party. The two sides each present evidence (words or things that support their argument) and their own views of what the laws mean. Each side has the same number of turns and the same amount of time to make their case. The jury listens to both sides and eventually weighs all the evidence and testimony (what people say) and finally decides whether the accused person is guilty or not. The judge is in charge of the courtroom and makes important decisions about what laws apply, whether evidence can be admitted or not, and what the sentence will be if the defendant is found guilty.

The reading passage says that all arrested people must be informed of their rights, one of which is to be represented by a lawyer. Make sure that students read the footnotes in small print at the bottom of SB page 115. The first footnote gives further information about the Miranda rights. Unfortunately, even though everyone is entitled to be represented by a lawyer, people with more money can afford better lawyers than people without much money. The more expensive lawyers are likely to be more successful in the adversarial process in court.

Suggestions for Follow-Up Activities

The discussion topics mention the duty of jury service. In the American legal system, jury duty is an obligation—something that citizens are obligated to do. The court examines all potential jurors to make sure that they are not already biased in the case and that they fairly represent the citizens in the area where the crime occurred. Ask students if they can think of specific reasons why a person would not be chosen to serve on a jury.

If students are unable to attend an American trial, perhaps they could watch a trial on television as a small group and then report to the class on the participants and the steps in the process. Programs such as *Law and Order* are shown nightly on major channels that can be accessed via satellite.

Chapter 8

The Reliability of Eyewitnesses

Audio CD, Track 8

Eyewitnesses—people who actually see crimes firsthand—give important testimony in criminal trials. However, eyewitnesses are not always accurate and, as a result, people have been imprisoned because of mistaken identity. In an attempt to increase eyewitness reliability, researchers are learning about the factors that influence accuracy.

Suggestions for Prereading Activity

The photograph on SB page 131 shows a police lineup where people who fit the description of the crime suspect are shown together. The markings on the wall indicate height for comparison. The photograph shows the eyewitness pointing to someone she identifies as the suspect. Police often include innocent people, such as other police officers, in a lineup to check on the reliability of the witness.

In the photograph on SB page 133, police are interviewing or questioning an eyewitness at the scene of a crime. Two officers are asking questions while the third is writing down what the witness says.

Culture Notes

The term *witness*—someone who observes or experiences an incident and is able to report on it—was essential in the reading in Chapter 7, but the term also pertains to this chapter. A *witness* sees something take place, overhears a conversation, or swears that certain conditions existed at the time of a crime. In a legal sense, *swear* means to take an oath on a sacred book, such as the Bible, to ensure that a person is telling the truth. An *eyewitness* is someone who actually sees what goes on at the scene of a crime.

Some people cannot be witnesses. For instance, people who are mentally insane or who have a record of lying are, by definition, unreliable witnesses. Very young children are seldom good witnesses. Aside from these instances, people who have witnessed a crime not only can be called as witnesses, but sometimes are required to appear in court. In this case, the court issues a legal document called a *subpoena*. This document commands a person to appear in court to testify as a witness. However, there are limits to an individual's legal obligation. A person does not have to say things against themselves (self-incrimination) or against their husband or wife. During a criminal trial, the lawyers for both sides may examine the witnesses (ask them questions).

Police use a variety of tools to help eyewitnesses identify criminals. The reading mentions photographs, and it is common for police departments to maintain a book with photographs of known suspects. In the past, police artists drew sketches based on descriptions of eyewitnesses. Today, police use computerized programs to produce more sophisticated composite pictures. Using computers, they can quickly change features such as hair color and style, eye color, and facial hair (beards and mustaches), as well as add or remove eyeglasses. These pictures may appear in the media or on posters where the public can easily see them in the hope that someone will recognize the suspected criminal and give a useful lead about where to find him or her.

These days, surveillance cameras often monitor public places such as airports, banks, and subway platforms. These cameras run all the time. Law enforcement officers compare sketches from eyewitnesses with the film taken by surveillance cameras to find a match.

Suggestions for Follow-Up Activities

To prove that different people who witness an event often remember very different details, work with a colleague to set up a "surprise event" for your students. Ask your colleague to dress with a great deal of detail, such as patterned clothing, a lot of makeup, accessories, or jewelry, and perhaps a wig! Be sure that your students do not see them in costume before the event.

Do not alert your class that something is going to happen. Catch them by surprise. Have your colleague burst into the room and quickly do something to catch the students' attention. Perhaps they could yell something peculiar like: "Do you know there are flying elephants and singing monkeys outside?" Make sure the person makes fast movements and is only in the room for ten seconds or less. The event should be startling, but certainly not criminal. As soon as your colleague exits the room, ask your students to write down every detail they remember. Compare details and see how people agree and disagree. What things did no one notice at all? Did some people focus on clothing and others on physical descriptions? Did some eyewitnesses hear what was said while others only saw actions?

| Chapter 9 | **Solving Crime with Modern Technology** | **Audio CD, Track 9** |

New types of technology help law enforcement officers solve crimes in ways that were previously impossible. DNA analysis, computerized fingerprint identification, and laser lights used to detect body fluids are examples of modern technological tools used by criminologists.

Suggestions for Prereading Activity

Publicity given to notorious crimes has made the public much more aware of advances in crime detection technology. DNA analysis has especially been featured in the news. During the prereading phase, elicit what your students know about modern methods of criminal investigation.

In addition to the chart on SB page 151, students may find it helpful to use a KWL chart. Instruct students to make three columns and label them as follows: What I **K**now Now, What I **W**ant to Know, and What I **L**earned. Have students write down what they already know about modern crime technology in the first column and what they want to know more about in the second. After students have completed the chapter, have them return to the KWL chart and complete the third column. If there are items in the second column that students have still not learned about, instruct students to pursue them by using Internet search engines.

Culture Notes

The type of crime that has taken place and the sort of evidence left behind are the factors that determine what kind of criminal analysis might be useful. For example, fingerprints are typically left on hard surfaces, although the reading passage explains that they can now be taken from fabric or cloth. Recently, the U.S. government has started to collect even more fingerprints to expand the bank of fingerprint samples. Basic fingerprint patterns are illustrated on SB page 165.

In a shooting, there is often a bullet that can be analyzed. Each time a gun fires a bullet, it leaves a unique pattern of scratches on it. Gun or firearms experts look at bullets under microscopes to find these patterns which they can later match to a particular gun. Sometimes, ballistics or firearms specialists can look at a bullet hole and determine how far away the gun was when the victim was shot.

From violent crimes such as murder or rape, police often have samples of blood, other body fluids, or pieces of human hair. All of these can be analyzed for patterns of DNA. Every person's DNA is a unique genetic pattern, so microscopic analysis of chromosomes will show slight differences from one person to another. By using DNA, it is possible to eliminate some suspects by finding that their blood or body fluid has a very different DNA pattern. This means that fewer innocent people will be mistakenly found guilty of crimes. However, when a violent crime suspect, such as a rapist, is faced with the definite evidence of DNA, they sometimes plead guilty.

The branch of crime detection that deals with using science to establish if laws have been broken is called *forensic science*. In the U.S. legal system, the main person in forensic investigations is the medical examiner, a doctor who specializes in analyzing medical evidence from crimes. The medical examiner collects evidence at the scene of a crime, does an autopsy or examination of dead victims, coordinates laboratory investigations, and finally, reports the results to the court.

Suggestions for Follow-Up Activities

Ask students to track crimes reported in the media for a one-week period. Explain that students are to follow radio, television, and newspaper crime reports, paying particular attention to any mention of the modern technology described in this chapter. How is this technology used to gather evidence? Have students present their findings in the form of a report.

As an alternative, students could study the role technology played in solving a crime by watching an appropriate film or television program, or by reading a short mystery novel.

Unit 3 CNN Video Report

Have students watch the Unit 3 video, *Forensic Animation*. While this video supports all three readings in Unit 3, students will benefit from viewing this clip after studying the role technology plays in solving crimes (Chapter 9). Before watching the video, review the meaning of *forensic*, first introduced in the Student Book. *The Newbury House Dictionary* defines *forensic* as "related to using scientific, medical methods to get information about a crime." More recently, forensics is also used to reconstruct what happened in accidents that are not necessarily crimes.

The video points out that people are now accustomed to viewing videos of events and incidents. This is partially due to media news coverage, which attempts to get cameramen on the scene as soon as possible. Media agencies also try to find private citizens who might have filmed incidents with a video camera.

What do students think about the use of forensic animation in a courtroom? What could be some advantages and disadvantages of this technology?

After discussing the video, have students answer the Video Report questions on SB page 174.

Unit 4   Science and History

Chapter 10   Ancient Artifacts and Ancient Air

Audio CD, Track 10

In 1954, archaeologists opened an ancient king's tomb in Egypt. The chamber had been sealed so effectively that the air still smelled of cedar from the funeral boat within. Wanting to test the air and confirm the existence of a second funeral boat in an adjoining chamber, a team of scientists performed a nondestructive investigation in 1986. Through this investigation, archaeologists learned a great deal about historical preservation.

Suggestions for Prereading Activity

Students who have used *Themes for Today,* the first book in the *Reading for Today* series, will know that the photograph on SB page 176 depicts the Sphinx in the foreground and a pyramid in the background. These students will also know about the work of archaeologists. If students are not familiar with this topic, make sure they receive this background information.

As a way of discussing the term *ancient,* it might be appropriate to introduce a graphic organizer. Time lines give students a sense of important cultural events within a particular historical period. The tomb in the reading was constructed almost 5,000 years ago. Draw a long horizontal line and mark it off in 500-year intervals. See what background knowledge students have of past civilizations and when they existed. Initially, have students suggest items for the time line. If they need assistance, provide important dates within the history of your culture.

Culture Notes

Students often confuse anthropologists and archaeologists and what they do. Archaeologists are a special type of anthropologist who study cultures from the past. Some of these cultures existed before writing systems were developed, so interpretations of their culture must be made on the basis of what physically remains. These remains vary from place to place, depending on the culture, the climate, the conditions for preservation, as well as other factors such as whether warfare has taken place there, or whether more recent cultures have been built on the same site.

Ancient Egyptian civilization lasted from about 3300 B.C. to just before the birth of Christ (B.C. indicates "before Christ"). Some students may wish to use B.C.E. ("before the common era") to indicate dates on their time line. Egyptian civilization is the longest lasting of the world's great civilizations. Strategically located along the Nile River, this ancient civilization achieved great agricultural success. Annual flooding of the river, along with the warm, sunny climate of the region, ensured ideal conditions for agriculture. It was the Egyptians' success in agriculture that provided the economic basis for their civilization.

The natural environment provided the foundation for the development of a complex civilization that had a writing system known as *hieroglyphics*. Hieroglyphics enabled the Egyptians to make records on papyrus that included their knowledge of mathematics that made the construction of the Pyramids possible, and a religious system that emphasized life after death. The rulers of ancient Egypt—the pharaohs—were very wealthy and powerful. They created elaborate burial places such as the pyramids and the tombs described in the reading passage.

Since archaeologists have excavated so many Egyptian burial sites, and since there are written records that tell about burial customs, they have some idea of what to expect when they open a tomb. Still, there have been many surprises, and, as a result, archaeologists have had to develop their techniques by trial and error. In this chapter's reading, note that 32 years passed between the first and second excavations.

Suggestions for Follow-Up Activities

The follow-up activity on SB page 191 has students role-playing archaeologists. Another approach is to think of how archaeologists of the future will interpret present-day civilizations. Ask students to pretend that they live 3,000 years in the future. What would they find from life today? Would archaeologists of the future be able to make sense of our buildings, our important monuments, and our cities? What would happen if much of the information that now exists on computers disappears?

Students might also enjoy the opportunity to create a time capsule. Divide the class into groups of four or five students and have each group decide what items they will include. Explain that they should include items of cultural and historical significance. Each group should take turns explaining their choices to the rest of the class.

Chapter 11 How Lunar Eclipses Have Changed History

Audio CD, Track 11

Today, scientists understand and can predict lunar eclipses, but, in the past, people feared them or thought they were bad omens. In 1453, in Constantinople and in 1851, in Soochow, China, lunar eclipses influenced important military battles because the soldiers thought the darkened moon was an evil sign.

Suggestions for Prereading Activity

The key to understanding lunar eclipses is realizing that during a lunar eclipe, Earth comes between the moon and the sun. Earth therefore casts a shadow on the moon and it becomes dark. There are both full and partial eclipses, depending on whether the moon is in the full shadow of Earth, or just in a partial shadow. A full eclipse can last up to two hours.

It might be useful to use the citrus-fruit-with-flashlight routine to have students actually see how an eclipse occurs. Choose a large fruit, such as a grapefruit, for Earth and a small lemon or lime to represent the moon. The flashlight is the light from the sun. A darkened classroom will provide the greatest effect.

Culture Notes

A number of ancient civilizations developed complicated mathematical calculations that enabled them to predict lunar eclipses. For example, both Babylonian civilization in Mesopotamia (between the Tigris and Euphrates Rivers in present-day Iraq)

and Mayan civilization in Mexico were able to predict eclipses. These calculations were based on careful observation of the skies and equally careful record keeping over a long period of time. The Babylonians even realized that eclipses are not unique events; they occur as part of a cycle that astronomers called a *saros*.

Some ancient civilizations also had calendar systems for keeping track of time. To determine when an event actually occurred, historians use a combination of ancient calendar systems, records of important eclipses, records of historical events, and modern mathematical models. Historical study has revealed that solar eclipses often caught the attention of ancient people more than lunar ones, probably because solar eclipses are more dramatic. When they occur, day seems to turn to night, and animals are often confused and behave as they do at sunset.

There seem to have been at least two cultural responses with regard to eclipses. First, before the scientific era, people were more inclined to be influenced by *superstition,* defined by *The Newbury House Dictionary* as "the belief in magical or supernatural being and events." Superstition helped people explain events that were scientifically inexplicable at certain times in history. Thus, many cultures relied on superstition to explain what appeared to be the disappearance of the sun or the moon during an eclipse.

Another cultural response to inexplicable natural phenomena is known as the Chinese Mandate of Heaven, as described in the reading passage. This philosophy of history claims that there is a connection between astronomical events and politics, and that natural events should be interpreted as a comment on political leadership. Tables that show the co-occurrence of eclipses with other historical events identify how often this has happened.

In 1504, Christopher Colombus is reported to have used his scientific knowledge of a forthcoming eclipse to his advantage. He was bargaining for food with Indians near what is now Jamaica in the Caribbean. When the Indians refused to give him food, he said that God would show unhappiness by taking away the moon. When a lunar eclipse occurred, the Indians believed him and agreed to cooperate. For more details, you or your students may wish to enter the words "eclipse, Columbus, Indians" in an Internet search engine such as Google or Yahoo.

Suggestions for Follow-Up Activities

When doing the discussion and writing activity on SB page 210 and the follow-up activity on SB page 211, be sensitive to the difference between *superstition,* a word with a negative connotation, and *astrology,* a prediction system that is widely accepted in a number of cultures throughout the world.

If there is a planetarium nearby, perhaps your students would enjoy a field trip as an end-of-unit activity. Many planetariums have simulated eclipses and show films taken during them.

Chapter 12   **Mars: Our Neighbor in Space**   **Audio CD, Track 12**

Scientists believe that Mars and Earth began under similar conditions. Therefore, many scientists believe that it is possible that life once existed on Mars. Spacecraft were sent to Mars to explore the possibility of life, but not all missions were successful, and those that were found no evidence of life. Scientists are eager to conduct more missions to further explore Mars.

Suggestions for Prereading Activity

Mars exploration has been a frequent news item in recent history, so students should have enough knowledge of this topic to answer the prereading questions on SB page 214. Some students may benefit from refreshing their knowledge of the solar system and the relative positions of planets. Use the diagram on SB page 229 as a starting point. Further information is readily available in any encyclopedia or on the Internet.

Culture Notes

Mars, the red planet, has fascinated people for centuries. However, in the past, a number of myths or mistaken ideas about Mars arose. Actual exploration of the surface of Mars during the last 30 years has clarified some speculation about this planet, but further space missions are necessary to confirm or refute other ideas about Mars. In the 1800s, the Italian astronomer Giovanni Schiaparelli believed that he saw channels for water on Mars. Schiaparelli also believed that Mars had seasons similar to those on Earth. He based this idea on his observations that Mars seemed to change color at different times of the year. About 100 years ago, an American astronomer named Percival Lowell took Schiaparelli's idea one step further and claimed that man-made waterways in the form of canals were evident on the surface of Mars. Lowell popularized the canal idea by writing books and giving lectures. He claimed that the "canals" were part of an irrigation system that drew water from the polar ice caps to provide water for agriculture in the deserts of Mars. The public got very excited about the possibility that there were people who had an advanced civilization on Mars. In 1939, when a radio play called *The War of the Worlds* was broadcast, many people thought it was an actual news report of war with Mars, not just a fictional drama.

More powerful telescopes and actual exploration of Mars have shown that these earlier ideas were incorrect. The Hubble Space Telescope has played a vital role in revealing details about Mars. For instance, there are huge dust storms on Mars that give the planet its red color. These dust storms occur more frequently at some times than at others, so this explains the slight variations in the color of the planet's surface. The "canals" identified by some scientists turned out to be optical illusions, or tricks of the eye. Spacecraft have shown that Mars has neither canals nor any other man-made structures.

Sometimes, even scientific exploration can create false ideas. For a while, people thought they saw an image of a human face in a photograph that the 1976 Viking Orbiter took. However, in 2001, the Mars Global Surveyor showed that the "Face on Mars" was yet another optical illusion caused by shadows and dust.

Scientists know that water is necessary for life on Earth, and this is why they believe that finding water is the key to knowing whether Mars has ever sustained life in any form. In August, 2003, Mars and Earth were the closest that they have been since 1924. They will not be that close again until 2287. Scientists took advantage of this proximity to launch many space probes. In early 2004, NASA's two Mars rovers sent back photographs and information about the surface, and while circling around Mars, the European Space Agency's Mars Express orbiter sent back additional information.

Suggestions for Follow-Up Activities

Among the many topics to explore, the technology of space robots is essential to understanding what we are able to learn about Mars. For example, the rovers that landed on Mars are able to unfold from their landing gear and move around on the surface of this distant planet. They also contain spectrometers that can measure light coming from rocks, enabling scientists on Earth to identify various types of rocks and minerals.

Students may want to debate whether manned spacecraft should go to Mars instead of robotic spacecraft. Inform them that it takes seven months to travel to Mars. Astronauts would then have to stay there for two and a half years before they made the seven-month journey back to Earth, so as to ensure optimal alignment of Earth and Mars. In addition to Mars's thin atmosphere and extreme temperatures, what are some of the additional risks of going there? What could we learn from manned spacecraft that we cannot learn from "intelligent" robots?

Unit 4 CNN Video Report

Have students watch the Unit 4 video, *Water on Mars,* after they have completed Chapter 12. While the reading briefly mentions the existence of water on Mars (see lines 15 and 26), the video details explicit evidence of its existence. Scientists initially thought that there was a good possibility that there was ice—and therefore frozen water—at the north and south poles of Mars. However, they needed more evidence to support their theories. The NASA images from an unmanned spacecraft not only confirmed that there was indeed ice on Mars, but it showed ice in greater quantities than the scientists imagined.

Play the video several times and ask students to be precise about where the water and/or ice actually is. Why are the scientists so sure about what they have found? What technology are they using? What does the astronomer mean when he asks, "Are we alone?" Note that scientists are talking about life in general, not specifically whether humans lived on Mars.

After discussing the video, have students answer the Video Report questions on SB page 236.

Issues for Today
A N S W E R   K E Y

Unit 1	Trends in Living

Chapter 1   ## A Cultural Difference: Being on Time

Prereading Preparation (p. 2)
1. *On time* means arriving exactly at the agreed-upon time; it means prompt and punctual.
2–4. Answers will vary.

A. Fact-Finding Exercise (p. 5)
1. F. The professor arrived on time, but the students were late.   2. T   3. T   4. F. In a Brazilian class, most students do not leave immediately after the class is finished.   5. T   6. T   7. F. In Brazil, most successful people are not expected to be on time.   8. F. As a result of the study, the professor changed his own behavior.

B. Reading Analysis (p. 7)
1. c   **2.** b   **3.** on time / There is a comma and then the word *or* after the phrase on time which indicates that a synonym will follow.   **4.** b   **5.** a. 2   b. 1   **6.** a. lunch with a friend b. a university class   c. the use of *respectively*   d. 2   **7.** c   **8.** a   **9.** a   **10.** c   **11.** b

C. Information Organization (p. 10)
Professor arrived on time.
Students arrived late. They did not apologize for being late.
Professor decides to study students' behavior.
Professor gives students examples of: *an informal situation:* lunch with a friend, and *a formal situation:* a university class
American and Brazilian students define lateness.
Lunch with a friend: Americans: 19 minutes
Brazilians: 33 minutes
A university class: Americans: after scheduled time
Brazilians: up to one hour after the scheduled time.
Conclusions: 1. In the United States, lateness is disrespectful.   **2.** In Brazil, lateness means a person is important.
Result: The American professor was able to adapt his own behavior.

D. Information Recall and Summary (p. 11)
1. He decided to study the Brazilian students' behavior concerning time and lateness.
2. The professor gave American and Brazilian students examples of an informal situation—lunch with a friend, and a formal situation—a university class. The American and Brazilian students then defined lateness in both situations.
3. No, they didn't. In American culture, students or professors are late for class if they arrive any time after class is scheduled to begin, while in Brazilian culture, lateness is up to one hour after class is scheduled to begin.
4. The Brazilians felt that lateness began after 33 minutes; the Americans felt that lateness began after 19 minutes.
5. The Brazilian students thought that people who are late are important.
6. The American students thought that people who are late are disrespectful.
7. The professor learned to adapt his own behavior.

Summary

An American professor in Brazil studied the idea of lateness for both Brazilian and American students. His study enabled him to adapt his own behavior while living in Brazil.

E. Word Forms (p. 13)

Part 1

1. a. spelled b. spelling 2. a. understand b. understanding 3. a. ending b. ends
4. a. greetings b. greet 5. a. meetings b. don't meet

Part 2

1. a. will adapt b. adaptation 2. a. interpretation b. will interpret 3. a. expectations
b. do not expect 4. a. is observing b. observations 5. a. explanation b. explained

F. Vocabulary in Context (p. 15)

1. appropriate 2. unacceptable 3. prestige 4. greets 5. rude 6. punctual
7. adapt 8. In fact 9. apologized 10. behavior

G. Topics for Discussion and Writing (p. 16)

Answers will vary.

H. Follow-Up Activity (p. 17)

Answers will vary.

I. Cloze Quiz (p. 18)

1. punctual 2. difference 3. ended 4. greeted 5. rude 6. behavior 7. formal
8. appointment 9. hand 10. contrast 11. nor 12. only 13. neither 14. late
15. fact 16. status 17. unacceptable 18. misinterpret 19. instead 20. adapt

Chapter 2   Changing Lifestyles and New Eating Habits

Prereading Preparation (p. 20)

1. *Lifestyle* means the manner in which someone lives; the way that he or she chooses to spend his or her time.

2–3. Answers will vary.

A. Fact-Finding Exercise (p. 22)

1. F. Americans do not eat the same way they did in the past. *Or* Americans' eating habits are changing. **2.** F. Americans still eat sweets. **3.** T **4.** F. Red meat is not the most popular American choice for dinner anymore. **5.** T **6.** T **7.** F. It is not healthy to eat food with high cholesterol levels. **8.** F. Americans choose shrimp and lobster for romantic dinners.

B. Reading Analysis (p. 24)

1. a **2.** b **3.** a. 1 b. 3 **4.** b **5.** growers, processors, marketers, restaurateurs **6.** c
7. a. animal fat b. the use of the comma and the word *or* **8.** c **9.** a. 2 b. 1 **10.** b

C. Information Organization (p. 26)

Changes in Lifestyles

1. People who live alone 2. Single parents with children 3. Double-income families
1. 60 % of American homes have microwave ovens
2. Americans eat out nearly four times a week.
3. Americans have less time to prepare food.

Nutrition Awareness

High cholesterol food can be dangerous.
1. People eat less red meat.
2. People eat more chicken, turkey, and fish.
3. People eat special food for special situations.

Special Food for Special Situations

Physical Activity: pasta, fruit, vegetables

Breakfast: breads, cereals

Business Lunch: salads

Romantic Dinner: shrimp, lobster

D. Information Recall and Summary (p. 27)
1. Because they have different lifestyles than they had in the past.
2. a. Many people live alone. There are many single parents. There are many double-income families.
   b. Most Americans use microwave ovens at home. Americans eat out nearly four times a week.
3. They have learned that high-cholesterol food can be dangerous.
4. People eat less red meat, and more chicken, turkey, and fish.
5. Before or after physical activity, people eat pasta, fruit, and vegetables. For breakfast, people eat breads and cereal. During a business lunch, people eat salads. For a romantic dinner, people eat shrimp or lobster.

Summary
Because of changes in lifestyles and increased awareness of nutrition, Americans are changing their eating habits and eating healthier foods.

E. Word Forms (p. 29)
Part 1
1. a. does not grow b. growers 2. a. marketers b. will market 3. a. consumers
b. consume 4. did not employ b. employers 5. a. worker b. works
Part 2
1. a. broad b. will broaden 2. a. will not widen b. wide 3. a. sweet b. sweetens
4. a. short / shorter b. will shorten 5. a. lengthened b. long

F. Vocabulary in Context (p. 31)
1. variety 2. skip 3. rush 4. compile 5. favorite 6. survey 7. awareness
8. nutritional 9. alert 10. habit

G. Topics for Discussion and Writing (p. 32)
Answers will vary.

H. Follow-Up Activities (p. 33)
1. a. 11 b. 13 c. 8 d. one-person e. dual-income 2. Answers will vary.

I. Cloze Quiz (p. 35)
1. habits 2. nutrition 3. quantities 4. lifestyles 5. skip 6. consequence
7. nearly 8. average 9. consume 10. compile 11. favorite 12. recent
13. awareness 14. threat 15. survey 16. alert 17. example 18. however
19. along 20. variety

Chapter 3 # Dreams: Making Them Work for Us

Prereading Preparation (p. 37)
1. Dreams are fantasies that we experience as we sleep.
2–5. Answers will vary.

A. Fact-Finding Exercise (p. 40)
1. T 2. F. Milton Kramer believes that dreams are very important. 3. F. Many people feel discouraged after they have a bad dream. *Or* Many people feel optimistic after they have a good dream. 4. T 5. F. Our dreams are usually longer when we sleep a long time. 6. T 7. F. Joseph's bad dreams have finally stopped.

B. Reading Analysis (p. 41)
1. b **2.** remembered **3.** a **4.** a. 2 b. 3 c. 1 d. 3 **5.** a. 2 b. 2 c. 3 **6.** a **7.** a
8. Steps: 4, 2, 1, 3 Recognize when you are having a bad dream. Identify the part of the dream that makes you feel bad. Stop your bad dream. Change the negative part of the dream. **9.** a. 2 b. 1

C. Information Organization (p. 44)
How to Remember and Change Dreams

Ways to Remember a Dream
1. During the day:
   a. Keep a journal or diary of what you do when you are awake.
   b. Before going to sleep, review the day.
   c. As you fall asleep, remind yourself that you want to remember your dream.
2. When you wake up:
   a. Lie still while you try to remember your dream.
   b. Try to remember an important word or picture from the dream.
   c. If you have trouble remembering your dreams, try sleeping later.

How to Change a Dream: Dream Therapy
1. Recognize when you are having a bad dream that makes you feel helpless or upset the next morning.
2. When you wake up, identify what it is about the dream that makes you feel bad.
3. To stop any bad dream: remember that you are in charge.
4. Change the negative part of the dream:
   a. Wake yourself up and change the dream before you return to sleep.
   b. Change the dream while you are still asleep.

D. Information Recall and Summary (p. 45)

1. We can remember our dreams by keeping a journal of what we do when we're awake, and by reviewing the day before we go to sleep. As we begin to fall asleep, we should remind ourselves that we want to remember our dreams.
2. When we wake up, we should lie still while we try to remember our dreams. We should try to remember a word or picture from our dreams as soon as we wake up.
3. If we can't remember our dreams, we should try sleeping later.
4. The four steps in dream therapy are (1) recognize when we are having a bad dream; (2) identify what it is about the dream that makes us feel bad; (3) stop any bad dreams; (4) change the negative part of the dream.

Summary

With practice, we can learn to remember our dreams, and by following specific steps, we can stop bad dreams and change them.

E. Word Forms (p. 47)

Part 1
1. a. cheered b. cheerful 2. a. didn't help / did not help b. helpful 3. a. is going to rest / will rest b. discouraged 4. a. used b. useful 5. a. harmful b. harm
Part 2
1. a. frightening b. frightened 2. a. tiring b. tired 3. a. discouraging b. restful
4. a. refreshing b. refreshed 5. a. interested b. interesting

F. Vocabulary in Context (p. 49)

1. recall 2. journal 3. Gradually 4. cheerful 5. practice 6. dream 7. grown
8. altogether 9. harmful 10. discouraged

G. Topics for Discussion and Writing (p. 50)

Answers will vary.

H. Follow-Up Activity (p. 51)

Answers will vary.

I. Cloze Quiz (p. 52)

1. woke 2. dream 3. recall 4. continued 5. tired 6. hard 7. grown 8. changing
9. simple 10. step 11. upset 12. identify 13. Next 14. charge 15. negative
16. therapy 17. Gradually 18. altogether 19. positive 20. cheerful

Unit 1 Review

J. Crossword Puzzle (p. 54)

Across Answers

4. cheerful 6. sweeten 8. grown 11. gradually 14. rude 16. journal 17. up
20. quantity 22. skip 24. nightmare 26. employer 28. behavior 30. apologize

Down Answers

1. altogether 2. recall 3. one 5. harmful 7. image 9. while 10. but 12. discouraged
13. adapt 15. consumer 18. prestige 19. lifestyle 21. aware 23. instead 25. grow
27. are 29. to

Unit 1 Discussion (p. 57)

Answers will vary.

CNN Video Report: Nutrition Survey (p. 58)

1. Yes, Americans are aware of the importance of healthy eating habits. They don't want to give up their favorite foods, though.
2. 1. T 2. T 3. F 4. T 5. T
3. Answers will vary but may include: working long hours; walking less and driving more; more inexpensive and poor-quality food being available.

Unit 2   Issues in Society

Chapter 4   Language: Is It Always Spoken?

Prereading Preparation (p. 60)

1. *Language* is a system of human communication by means of written symbols, spoken words and movements.
2. Answers will vary but may include this information: after 6 months of age, and babies learn by imitating their parents speaking.
3. Answers will vary but may include this information: by motioning with their hands or communicating with facial expressions.
4. Answers will vary but may include this information: by using sign language or by writing.
5. Answers will vary but may include deaf people.
6. Answers will vary.

A. Fact-Finding Exercise (p. 63)

1. T 2. F. Dr. Petitto studied deaf babies and hearing babies. 3. F. The psychologist saw that deaf babies and hearing babies did not move their hands the same way. 4. T
5. F. Dr. Petitto believes that hearing babies who have one deaf parent and one hearing parent produce their first spoken word and signed word at about the same time.

B. Reading Analysis (p. 64)

1. a **2.** When a baby repeats the same sounds over and over again, this is called *babbling*. **3.** a. American Sign Language b. Deaf people use ASL to communicate because they cannot hear spoken language. **4.** a **5.** b **6.** a. 1 and 4 b. 3 **7.** b
8. a. A *linguist* is a person who studies language. b. This definition is between the dashes.
c. 2 d. 1 e. 2 **9.** a. We can express language by speech or by sign. b. 3 **10.** b

C. Information Organization (p. 67)

I.   How Babies Learn Language
    A. Hearing Babies
        1. Between the ages of 7 and 10 months, they begin to babble: to make sounds, repeating the same sounds over and over again.
        2. The sounds become words.

    B. Deaf Babies
       1. They make many different movements with their hands, but they make the same movements over and over again.
       2. The hand motions start to resemble some of the basic hand-shapes used in ASL.
  II. Experiment on How Babies Learn Language
    A. Who Conducted the Experiment: Dr. Laura Ann Petitto, a psychologist at McGill University in Montreal, Canada
    B. Who She Studied: 3 hearing infants and 2 deaf infants
    C. How She Studied Them: She watched and videotaped them three times: at 10, 12, and 14 months.
    D. Conclusion: the hearing children made varied motions with their hands, but there was no pattern to these motions. However, the deaf babies made the same hand movements over and over again.
  III. Future Experiments
    A. Theory: Humans' ability for language is innate.
    B. Who She Will Study: hearing children who have one deaf parent and one hearing parent
    C. Purpose of the Experiment: to see what happens when babies have the opportunity to learn both sign language and speech

D. Information Recall and Summary (p. 68)

1. a. Babbling is the repetition of the same sounds over and over again by infants.
2. b. Babbling occurs between the ages of 7 and 10 months.
3. Dr. Petitto studied three hearing infants and two deaf infants. She studied them to look at the differences between the ways in which they learn language.
4. After watching the videotapes, they discovered that the hearing children made varied hand motions with their hands, but there was no pattern to these motions. However, the deaf babies made the same hand movements over and over again.
5. She believes the theory that human language is innate.
6. She wants to study hearing children who have one deaf parent and one hearing parent. She wants to see what happens when babies have the opportunity to learn both sign language and speech.

Summary

Studies of hearing children and deaf children indicate that both seem to learn to communicate in similar ways at about the same time. The hearing children learn speech, while the deaf children learn sign language.

E. Word Forms (p. 69)

Part 1

1. a. talking b. talk 2. a. didn't begin / did not begin b. beginning 3. a. hearing b. doesn't hear / does not hear 4. a. babbles b. babbling 5. a. means b. meanings

Part 2

1. a. importance b. important 2. a. different b. differences 3. a. significant b. significance 4. a. dependence b. dependent 5. a. persistent b. persistence

F. Vocabulary in Context (p. 71)

1. persistent 2. If so 3. meaning 4. capacity 5. varied 6. observation 7. innate 8. motion 9. In other words 10. For instance

G. Topics for Discussion and Writing (p. 72)

Answers will vary.

H. Follow-Up Activities (p. 73)

Answers will vary.

I. Cloze Quiz (p. 74)

1. babies 2. psychologist 3. learn 4. deaf 5. observations 6. example 7. varied 8. pattern 9. movements 10. consistent 11. same 12. over 13. resemble 14. prefer 15. innate 16. words 17. capacity 18. matter 19. Language 20. speech

Chapter 5 Loneliness: How Can We Overcome It?

Prereading Preparation (p. 75)
1. *Loneliness* is defined as the condition of being alone and feeling sad.
2–5. Answers will vary.

A. Fact-Finding Exercise (p. 78)
1. F. There are three different kinds of loneliness. 2. F. Temporary loneliness lasts only a short time. 3. F. Temporary loneliness disappears quickly and does not require special attention. 4. T 5. T 6. T 7. F. Lonely people may have many social contacts.
8. F. The loneliest people are between 18 and 25. 9. T

B. Reading Analysis (p. 79)
1. a **2.** a. 3 b. 1 **3.** a. 2 b. habitual **4.** a. 1 b. 2 **5.** b **6.** It introduces the same information as in the previous sentence, but it explains it in a different way. **7.** b
8. a. 2 b. They were afraid to make new friends. **9.** c

C. Information Organization (p. 81)
Kinds of Loneliness

temporary
does not last a long time
disappears quickly
does not require any special attention
Problems
no problems
situational
does not last for more than a year
is a natural result of a particular situation
Problems
can cause physical problems, such as headaches and sleeplessness
chronic
usually lasts more than two years
Problems
causes problems in socializing and becoming close to others

Why psychologists want to help these people:
1. They are unhappy and unable to socialize.
2. There is a connection between chronic loneliness and serious illness such as heart disease.

D. Information Recall and Summary (p. 82)
1. a. There are three kinds of loneliness.
   b. Temporary loneliness does not last a long time, disappears quickly, and does not require any special attention. Situational loneliness is a natural result of a particular situation; it can cause physical problems, such as headaches and sleeplessness; and it does not last for more than a year. Chronic loneliness usually lasts more than two years and has no specific cause; chronically lonely people have problems socializing and becoming close to others.
2. Because it is the result of a particular situation.
2. Because chronically lonely people are unhappy and unable to socialize. (Secondly, researchers have found a connection between chronic loneliness and serious illnesses such as heart disease.)
4. There is a connection between chronic loneliness and serious illnesses such as heart disease.

Summary
There are three types of loneliness. Temporary and situational loneliness are not serious, but chronic loneliness is serious because it may cause serious illnesses.

E. Word Forms (p. 84)
Part 1
1. a. happy b. happiness 2. a. ill b. illness 3. a. loneliness b. lonely 4. a. shy b. shyness 5. a. sleeplessness b. sleepless

Part 2

1. a. complexity b. complex 2. a. popular b. popularity 3. a. similar b. similarities
4. a. rational b. rationality 5. a. equality b. equal

F. Vocabulary in Context (p. 86)

1. unlike 2. remain 3. temporary 4. overcame 5. chronic 6. shy 7. predicted
8. severe 9. factors 10. For instance

G. Topics for Discussion and Writing (p. 87)

Answers will vary.

H. Follow-Up Activity (p. 87)

Answers will vary.

I. Cloze Quiz (p. 88)

1. normal 2. phenomenon 3. temporary 4. loneliness 5. predict 6. severe
7. habitual / chronic 8. Unfortunately 9. factor 10. instance 11. interests
12. words 13. popularity 14. circumstances 15. shyness 16. rational
17. overcame 18. remained 19. connection 20. chronic / habitual

Chapter 6   The Importance of Grandmothers

Prereading Preparation (p. 90)

1–4. Answers will vary.

A. Fact-Finding Exercise (p. 93)

1. T 2. F. Many grandmothers have the time and energy to help with their
grandchildren. 3. F. Some people at the conference believe that having a grandmother
in the family may improve a child's survival rate. 4. F. In Gambia, the presence of a
grandmother improved a child's survival rate. 5. F. The death rate for boys in Japan
decreased when the maternal grandmother lived with the family. 6. T 7. T

B. Reading Analysis (p. 94)

1. b **2.** c **3.** a **4.** a. An *anthropologist* is a scientist who studies people, societies, and
cultures. b. 2 c. 2 **5.** a **6.** a. 3 b. death c. There is a comma and then the word *or*
after the word *mortality*, which indicates that a synonym will follow. **7.** a **8.** c
9. a. 2 b. 1 c. 1 d. 2 **10.** b

C. Information Organization (p. 97)

Name of Anthropologists: Dr. Ruth Mace and Dr. Rebecca Sear
Whom did they study? People in the countryside of Gambia, Africa. Children who were
about one to three years old.
What did they learn?
1. The presence or absence of the child's father did not affect the death rate.
2. The presence of a grandmother reduced the children's chances of dying by 50%.
3. The children were only helped by the presence of their maternal grandmother—their
   mother's mother.

Name of Anthropologist: Dr. Cheryl Jamison
Whom did she study? The people in a village in central Japan for the period 1671
through 1871
What did she learn?
1. The death rate for girls was not different whether or not a grandmother lived with
   them.
2. If a maternal grandmother lived in the household, boys were 52% less likely to die in
   childhood.
3. Boys were 62% more likely to die in childhood when a paternal grandmother lived in
   the household.
Conclusion:
Grandmothers still have an important role in their grandchildren's lives. Having a
grandmother in the family may improve a child's survival rate.

D. Information Recall and Summary (p. 98)

1. The presence of fathers did not affect the mortality rate of children in Gambia.
2. The presence of paternal grandmothers had no effect on the mortality rate in Gambia.
3. The presence of maternal grandmothers reduced the mortality rate of children in Gambia.
4. The mortality rate of children in Japan from 1671 through 1871 was 27.5%.
5. The presence of grandmothers did not affect the mortality rate of girls in Japan at this time.
6. If a maternal grandmother lived in the household, boys were 52% less likely to die in childhood in Japan.
7. Boys were 62% more likely to die in childhood when a paternal grandmother lived in the household.

Summary

Grandmothers may be the reason why human infants, who take so many years to grow up, are able to survive. Although grandmothers no longer have children, they are still young and active. As a result, they have the time and energy to help with their grandchildren. This extra help may be an important factor in reducing the mortality, or death, rate among young children.

E. Word Forms (p. 100)

Part 1

1. a. information   b. informed   2. a. populated   b. population   3. a. will examine
b. examination   4. a. explanation   b. couldn't explain / could not explain
5. a. reduced   b. reduction

Part 2

1. a. important   b. importance   2. a. different   b. differences   3. a. significant
b. significance   4. a. presence   b. present   5. a. absent   b. absences

F. Vocabulary in Context (p. 102)

1. treat   2. reduce   3. mortality   4. household   5. factor   6. significant   7. influence
8. absent   9. present   10. survive

G. Topics for Discussion and Writing (p. 103)

Answers will vary.

H. Follow-Up Activities (p. 104)

1. a. maternal grandmother
   b. paternal grandmother
   c. Answers will vary.
2. a. No
   b. Yes
   c. 2
3. Answers will vary.

I. Cloze Quiz (p. 107)

1. memories   2. treats   3. childhood   4. Anthropologists   5. factors   6. influence
7. examine   8. role   9. significant   10. survival   11. presence   12. absence
13. reduced   14. maternal   15. mortality   16. population   17. grandmothers
18. discovery   19. whether   20. household

Unit 2 Review

J. Crossword Puzzle (p. 109)

Across Answers

2. mortality   5. capacity   8. unlike   9. popular   10. paternal   11. did   13. chronic
15. babble   16. she   17. temporary   18. varied   22. anthropologist   23. the

Down Answers

1. complex   3. linguist   4. observation   6. influence   7. innate   9. papa   12. favorite
14. maternal   16. survive   19. have   20. grow   21. boy

Unit 2 Discussion (p. 111)
Answers will vary.

CNN Video Report: Grandparents as Parents (p. 112)
1. Answers will vary but may include these two answers: yes, because they can do all the things parents do; or no, because grandparents are aging and slowing down.
2. a. Jim and Fay, and their grandsons Brandon and Sean.
   b. No, it was easy. They loved the boys the first moment they held them as newborns.
   c. The grandparents in the support group share feelings and experiences.
   d. Answers will vary, but may include these possibilities: yes, because younger parents might be stronger and more vigorous than older parents; or no, because older parents may be wiser and more experienced.
3. Answers will vary.

Unit 3	Justice and Crime

Chapter 7   Innocent Until Proven Guilty: The Criminal Court System

Prereading Preparation (p. 114)
1–2. Answers may vary.
3. This representation of justice symbolizes the fair and just administration of the law. The blindfold represents the unprejudiced nature of ideal justice. The scales represent fairness and balance, and the sword represents the power of the law of the land.

A. Fact-Finding Exercise (p. 116)
1. F. The court must prove that a suspect is guilty.   2. F. A judge decides if a suspect stays in jail or can be released.   3. T   4. T   5. T   6. F. At a trial, a jury of 12 people decides if the suspect is guilty or innocent.   7. F. The judge gives the convicted person his punishment after the trial.

B. Reading Analysis (p. 118)
1. b   **2.** a   **3.** b   **4.** a   **5.** a. the Miranda rights   b. There is information at the bottom of the page that explains this.   c. 2   **6.** a. It means charging a person with a crime. b. 3   **7.** a. 3   b. 1   c. 2   **8.** A hearing is the time in court when a lawyer from the district attorney's office presents a case against the suspect.   **9.** sufficient evidence   **10.** c **11.** a. 3   b. 1   **12.** a. foundation   b. There is a comma and then the word *or* after the word *basis* which indicates that a synonym will follow.

C. Information Organization (p. 121)
The American Justice System
Police arrest suspect and read Miranda rights.
Police "book" suspect.
Suspect goes before a judge.

If Suspect has no criminal record, and
Suspect has family and home,
Then Suspect goes free until hearing.

If Suspect has a criminal record, and
Suspect has no family or home,
Then Judge asks Suspect for bail.
If Suspect puts up bail,
Then Suspect goes free until hearing.
If Suspect cannot put up bail,
Then Suspect waits in jail for hearing.
Judge appoints a court lawyer.

Suspect appears in court for hearing.
District Attorney presents case against suspect.

Judge decides:

Insufficient evidence: no trial
So Suspect is free.

Sufficient evidence: trial
If Suspect is convicted,
Then Suspect is sentenced: prison, fine, probation.
If Suspect is not convicted,
Then Suspect is free.

D. Information Recall and Summary (p. 122)
1. They must read the suspect his or her Miranda rights. Then they take the suspect to the police station and book the suspect.
2. The suspect goes before a judge. If the suspect has no criminal record and has a family and a home, he can go free until the hearing. If the suspect has a criminal record and / or has no family or home, the judge asks the suspect for bail. If the suspect puts up bail, he can go free until the hearing. If the suspect cannot put up bail, he waits in jail for the hearing and the judge appoints a court lawyer for the suspect. At the hearing, the district attorney presents a case against the suspect. If the judge feels that there is sufficient evidence, he or she calls for a trial.
3. At a trial, a jury of 12 people listens to the evidence from both attorneys and hears the testimony of the witnesses. Then the jury goes into a private room to consider the evidence and decide whether the defendant is guilty or innocent of the crime.
4. If a person is proven innocent, he goes free.
5. If a person is convicted, the judge sentences him to prison, a fine, or probation.

Summary
The American court system is very complex and was designed to protect the rights of the people. There are specific procedures that the police and judges must use during the legal process to make sure that an individual's rights are protected.

E. Word Forms (p. 124)
Part 1
1. a. will appoint b. appointment 2. a. punishment b. doesn't punish / didn't punish / wouldn't punish 3. a. establishment b. established 4. a. disagreements b. disagreed 5. a. judges b. judgments
Part 2
1. a. responsibilities b. responsible 2. a. formal b. formality a. complex b. Complexity a. individuality b. individual a. public b. publicity

F. Dictionary Skills (p. 126)
1. (4) The police list the statements of blame against a suspect in a book at the police station.
2. (3) The police may not have any history (written account) of criminal activity for a particular suspect.
3. (5) The judge's first action is to decide whether to keep the suspect in jail or allow him to go free until the hearing.
4. (1) The district attorney's office offers evidence against a suspect.
5. (1) The jury goes into a private room in order to think about the evidence against the suspect and decides whether the suspect is innocent or guilty.

G. Vocabulary in Context (p. 127)
1. record 2. establish 3. Otherwise 4. appoint 5. present 6. consider 7. basis
8. purpose 9. However 10. case

H. Topics for Discussion and Writing (p. 128)
Answers will vary.

I. Follow-Up Activities (p. 129)
Answers will vary.

J. Cloze Quiz (p. 130)

1. purpose 2. protect 3. people 4. crime 5. innocent 6. words 7. prove
8. guilty 9. responsibility 10. evidence 11. hears 12. witnesses 13. jury
14. consider 15. whether 16. defendant 17. However 18. appear 19. time
20. punishment

Chapter 8   The Reliability of Eyewitnesses

Prereading Preparation (p. 131)

1. Answers will vary, but may include this information: standing in a police lineup.
2. Answers will vary, but may include this information: fingerprints, pieces of clothing,
   security camera footage, eyewitnesses.
3–5. Answers will vary.

A. Fact-Finding Exercise (p. 134)

1. F. Bernard Jackson went to jail for five years even though he was innocent. 2. T 3. T
4. T 5. F. Police officers are not better witnesses than ordinary people. 6. T 7.
F. A jury must decide if a witness's story is accurate.

B. Reading Analysis (p. 135)

1. b. **2.** a, c, e, h **3.** a **4.** a. 1 b. 2 **5.** a. 3 b. The context of the sentence makes it
clear. **6.** b **7.** a. It is not true that police officers are more reliable witnesses than
ordinary people. b. 2 **8.** a. 3 b. 1 **9.** c **10.** a **11.** 1. A suspect in an armed robbery
2. A police artist 3. Robbed trucks full of designer clothing 4. Post office

C. Information Organization (p. 138)

I.   Bernard Jackson's Case
     A. His Crime: He was accused of raping two women.
     B. The Evidence: the eyewitness testimony of the two women
     C. Reason for His Conviction: The jury believed the women's testimony.
     D. The Problem: Jackson was innocent, but he was similar in appearance to the
        guilty man.
II. Factors Influencing the Accuracy of Eyewitness Testimony
     A. Witnesses sometimes see photographs of several suspects before they try to iden-
        tify the person they saw in a lineup of people.
     B. They can become confused by seeing many photographs of similar faces.
     C. The number of people in the lineup, and whether it is a live lineup or a photo-
        graph, may also affect a witness's decision.
     D. People sometimes have difficulty identifying people of other races.
     E. The questions the police ask witnesses have an effect on them.
III. Experiment to Test the Reliability of Police Officers and Ordinary People as Witnesses
     A. Experiment: Two psychologists showed a film of crimes to police officers and
        civilians.
     B. Results: The psychologists found no difference between the police and the civilians
        in correctly remembering the details of the crimes.
IV. Why Courts Cannot Exclude Eyewitness Testimony from a Trial
     A. Sometimes eyewitness testimony is the only evidence to a crime.
     B. Eyewitness testimony is often correct.

D. Information Recall and Summary (p. 139)

1. He went to prison because the two victims identified him. He was innocent.
2. The two witnesses testified that Jackson was with them in another location at the time
   of the crimes. The jury did not believe these two witnesses.
3. He was similar in appearance to the guilty man.
4. Witnesses sometimes become confused by seeing many photographs of similar faces.
   The number of people in the lineup, and whether it is a live lineup or a photograph,
   affects people. Witnesses sometimes have difficulty identifying people of different
   races. The questions the police ask witnesses also affect them.
5. a. No, they aren't.
   b. They showed a film of crimes to both police officers and civilians. They found no dif-
      ference between the police and civilians in correctly remembering the details of the
      crimes.

6. Sometimes it is the only evidence to a crime.

7. A jury of 12 people decides. It is valuable because many times it is right.

Summary

Eyewitness testimony is very important in the American legal system. Although witnesses sometimes make mistakes, very often they are correct and help to convict guilty people.

E. Word Forms (p. 141)

Part 1

1. a. depends b. dependence 2. a. do not differ / don't differ b. differences
3. a. occurrence b. does not occur / doesn't occur 4. a. appearance b. appeared
5. a. did not assist / will not assist / didn't assist / won't assist b. assistance

Part 2

1. a. influences (v.) b. influence (n.) 2. a. will not film (v.) / can't film (v.)
b. films (n.) 3. a. attacks (n.) b. attack (v.) 4. a. witness (n.) b. witnessed (v.)
5. a. mistake (v.) b. mistakes (n.) 6. a. did not question (v.) / didn't question (v.)
b. questions (n.)

F. Dictionary Skills (p. 144)

1. (3) The group of people in the row, placed side by side for identification, and whether it is a live lineup or a photograph, may affect a witness's decision.
2. (1) Courts cannot leave out eyewitness testimony from a trial.
3. (1) Eyewitness testimony continues to be of worth in the American judicial system.
4. (2) The two women were certain that Bernard Jackson had committed the crimes against them.

G. Vocabulary in Context (p. 145)

1. civilian 2. victims 3. guilty 4. testimony 5. evidence 6. bitter 7. innocent
8. Despite 9. similar 10. mistake

H. Topics for Discussion and Writing (p. 146)

Answers will vary.

I. Follow-Up Activities (p. 147)

Answers will vary, but students may decide to use the more general questions to avoid influencing eyewitnesses and victims. This will help avoid cases of mistaken identity.

J. Cloze Quiz (p. 149)

1. bitter 2. testimony 3. victims 4. appearance 5. mistake 6. yet 7. occurred
8. influence 9. instance 10. similar 11. questions 12. reliable 13. crimes
14. civilians 15. Despite 16. evidence 17. eyewitness 18. judges 19. innocent
20. guilty

Chapter 9   Solving Crime with Modern Technology

Prereading Preparation (p. 151)

1. Answers will vary, but may include magnifying glasses, DNA analysis, and microscopes.
2. Answers will vary, but may include police officers, medical examiners and detectives.

A. Fact-Finding Exercise (p. 154)

1. F. Fingerprints testing helps to solve crimes faster and more efficiently. 2. F. New fingerprint technology can reveal the age and sex of the owner. 3. T 4. F. Eric Berg spent years developing computer software in his own home to enhance, or improve, crime scene photos. 5. T 6. T 7. F. The laser system of lights can find evidence in daylight and in the dark.

B. Reading Analysis (p. 155)

1. b **2.** a. body fluids b. The phrase *such as* are used to introduce examples of body fluids. c. 1 d. 2 **3.** a. Blankets and curtains are examples of fabric. b. There is a comma and then the phrase *for example* after the word *fabric,* which indicates that types of fabrics will follow. **4.** evidence **5.** a. A forensic expert is a person who helps solve crimes. b. 3 c. To enhance is to improve. d. There is a comma and then the word *or* after the word *enhance,* which indicates that a synonym will follow. **6.** a. 3 b. They saved the evidence in case it could be used later when technology was improved.   **7.** a. A drop of sweat on the scissors.   b. a   **8.** b

C. Information Organization (p. 157)

1. Fingerprint Testing:
How can it help solve crimes?
It can record a fingerprint pattern. It can provide additional information about a fingerprint, such as the age and sex of its owner. The fingerprints can reveal if the person takes medication, too.
Which crime was it useful for?
The Tacoma, Washington, murder
Why was it useful?
It helped lead to finding the person who committed the crime.

2. DNA Testing:
How can it help solve crimes?
It can provide information based upon bodily fluids found at the scene of the crime.
Which crime was it useful for?
The Newport News, Virginia, murder
Why was it useful?
It provided DNA information where fingerprints couldn't be found.

3. Laser Lights:
How can it help solve crimes?
It helps detectives find evidence of body fluids at a crime scene in daylight and in the dark.

D. Information Recall and Summary (p. 158)

1. a. It can record a fingerprint pattern. It can provide additional information about a fingerprint, such as the age and sex of its owner. The fingerprints can reveal if the person takes medication, too. It can even get fingerprints from fabric, for example, blankets or curtains.
    b. In the past, fingerprint testing was only helpful if the fingerprints from the crime scene could be matched with "prints" that were already on file.
2. All the unique characteristics of fingerprints and palm prints can get lost in a fabric.
3. They can use DNA testing on the drop of sweat found on the scissors in order to identify the murderer.
4. Laser light technology is important because it helps detectives find evidence of body fluids at a crime scene in daylight and in the dark.

Summary

Solving crimes is one of the most important jobs of law enforcement. Improvements in crime technology help detectives solve crimes faster, and more efficiently, today. The invention of DNA testing and improvements made to fingerprint testing and laser lights allows for a better chance of solving crimes. By helping the police identify criminals, this new technology can help put more criminals in prison.

E. Word Forms (p. 160)

Part 1

1. a. improvements   b. do not improve / have not improved   2. a. enhances
b. enhancement   3. a. enforcement   b. enforces   4. a. development   b. do not develop / don't develop   5. a. required   b. requirement

Part 2

1. a. witnesses (n.)   b. witness (v.)   2. a. files (n.)   b. don't file (v.)   3. a. murder (n.)
b. murder (n.)   4. a. will arrest / are going to arrest (v.)   b. arrests (n.)   5. a. record (v.)
b. records (n.)

F. Dictionary Skills (p. 162)

1. (1) The latest technology can even get fingerprints from cloth material, for example, blankets or curtains.
2. (3) The newest kind of fingerprint testing can do much more than simply record a fingerprint design.
3. (3) In all crimes, detectives carefully take samples of evidence from the place where something happens.

G. Vocabulary in Context (p. 163)

1. enforce 2. evidence 3. file 4. scene 5. Clues 6. pattern 7. experts 8. fabric
9. Criminologists 10. arrests

H. Topics for Discussion and Writing (p. 164)

Answers will vary.

I. Follow-Up Activities (p. 165)

1. Answers will vary.
2. Answer included on Web site.
3. a. 3 b. 18–24 c. 50+ d. 2 4. a. 1 b. 2 c. 3 d. 2

J. Cloze Quiz (p. 168)

1. crime 2. efficiently 3. fluids 4. helpful 5. matched 6. criminals 7. file
8. solved 9. additional 10. reveal 11. technology 12. fabric 13. witnesses
14. clues 15. identify 16. evidence 17. expert 18. enhance 19. apparent
20. arrested

Unit 3 Review

K. Crossword Puzzle (p. 170)

Across Answers

3. testimony 5. innocent 8. bail 10. guilty 12. nonetheless 14. mistake 19. enhance
20. punishment 21. require 23. previously 25. witness

Down Answers

1. prints 2. pen 4. expert 6. evidence 7. fluids 8. book 9. victim 11. reliability
13. fabric 15. sentence 16. me 17. enforce 18. appoint 22. no 24. up

Unit 3 Discussion (p. 173)

Answers will vary.

CNN Video Report: Forensic Animation (p. 174)

Answers will vary.

1. a 2. b 3. b 4. d 5. b 3. Computer animations of accidents don't show faces or
graphic details because it would be too grisly, messy, or uncomfortable for the jury, and
might unfairly bias the jury. Answers will vary regarding the fairness of this technique.

Unit 4   Science and History

Chapter 10   Ancient Artifacts and Ancient Air

Prereading Preparation (p. 176)

1. Answers will vary but may include this information: archeologists study human life
   and civilizations through items of the past such as buried houses and statues.
2. Answers will vary but may include ancient cities and artifacts.
3. Answers will vary but may state that archeological discoveries show us how people
   lived, ate, and dressed in the past.
4. Answers will vary but may include the following: ancient air might be found in a box
   or bottle sealed tight and never opened since ancient times.
5. Answers will vary but may suggest that ancient air could help us study changes in the
   earth's atmosphere and conditions.

A. Fact-Finding Exercise (p. 179)

1. T 2. F. Archeologists recently discovered a boat in a crypt. 3. T 4. F. Archeologists
opened the second room in 1986. 5. T 6. F. The investigation team didn't go inside the
second chamber. 7. F. The Egyptian government is going to leave the boat in the chamber.

B. Reading Analysis (p. 180)

1. b **2.** a **3.** a tomb or burial place **4.** king **5.** c **6.** c **7.** b **8.** a. 1 b. 2 c. 1 **9.** b
10. a. 3 b. carbon dioxide c. The symbol CO_2 is in parentheses after *carbon dioxide*.
11. b **12.** a. 3 b. 2 **13.** c **14.** a

C. Information Organization (p. 183)

I. Archeological Discovery in Egypt
   A. Date: 1954
   B. Place: near the base of the Great Pyramid
   C. The Discovery: an ancient crypt of an Egyptian pharaoh

II. Historians' Belief About Egyptian Burial Customs
   A. Egyptians buried their pharaohs with two boats.
   B. The Purpose of the Boats: one to carry the body and one to carry the soul

III. The Excavation of the Crypt
   A. The archeologists broke the crypt open.
   B. They found a 4,600-year-old boat, very well preserved.
   C. They also found a second chamber.

IV. What the Archeologists and Historians Hoped to Learn
   A. Information about the Past: They would be sure about the religious custom of burying pharaohs with two boats.
   B. Information about Preserving Wood: They would find out if there was something special in the air that helped preserve the wood.
   C. Information about the Future: They would examine the air in the second chamber and compare it with the air of the present to be able to predict changes in the air of the future.

V. The Excavation of the Second Chamber
   A. Date: October 1986
   B. Method of Excavation:
     1. Scientists drilled a hole in the roof of the chamber. They kept the hole sealed.
     2. They took an air sample. The air was the same as the air outside.
     3. The scientists lowered a light and a camera into the hole and discovered the second boat.
     4. The scientists sealed the chamber again. They did not remove the second boat.

VI. The Significance of the Second Excavation
   A. Archeologists learned that the custom of burying a pharaoh with two boats is true.
   B. They practiced a new, nondestructive approach to archeology:
     1. investigate an ancient location
     2. photograph it
     3. leave it untouched
   C. They found out that when the Egyptian government built a museum for the first boat, vibrations from the machinery disturbed the second room and destroyed the seal.

D. Information Recall and Summary (p. 185)

1. Archeologists discovered the crypt in Egypt in 1954 near the base of the Great Pyramid.
2. Its purpose was to bury an Egyptian king, or pharaoh.
3. A custom is to bury a pharaoh with two boats: one to carry the body and one to carry the soul.
4. Because they would be sure about the religious custom of burying pharaohs with two boats; they would also have information about preserving wood.
5. They would examine the air in the second chamber and compare it with the air of the present to be able to predict changes in the air of the future.
6. a. Because the scientists sealed the room so that the air inside would not escape.
   b. Archeologists practiced a new nondestructive approach to archeology.
7. When the Egyptian government built a museum for the first boat, vibrations from the machinery disturbed the second room and destroyed the seal.
8. They sealed it up again.

Summary

In 1954 and in 1986, two boats were discovered in an ancient Egyptian pharaoh's tomb. This archeological discovery helped us understand the future and the past, and introduced new technology.

E. Word Forms (p. 187)

Part 1

1. a. did not predict b. prediction 2. a. corrects b. corrections 3. a. excavation
b. excavated 4. a. examination b. will not examine 5. a. is informing b. information

Part 2

1.a. recovered b. recovery 2. a. discovery b. will discover 3. a. does not deliver / doesn't deliver b. delivery 4. a. inquired b. inquiries 5. a. mastered b. mastery

F. Dictionary Skills (p. 189)

1. (1) In 1954, archeologists uncovered an ancient crypt near the foundation of the Great Pyramid.
2. (1) The ancient Egyptians had a special religious way.
3. (4) The air leaked out of the second chamber.
4. (1) The scientists let down a light and a camera into the second chamber.

G. Vocabulary in Context (p. 190)

1. Although 2. In fact 3. custom 4. sealed 5. If so 6. excavation 7. In addition
8. recover 9. predict 10. discovered

H. Topics for Discussion and Writing (p. 191)

Answers will vary.

I. Follow-Up Activity (p. 191)

Answers will vary.

J. Cloze Quiz (p. 192)

1. discovery 2. information 3. crypt 4. king 5. addition 6. so 7. custom
8. However 9. ancient 10. examining 11. recover 12. compare 13. predict
14. fact 15. sealed 16. air 17. chamber 18. Although 19. museum 20.excavations

Chapter 11   How Lunar Eclipses Have Changed History

Prereading Preparation (p. 195)

1. A lunar eclipse occurs when the earth is positioned between the moon and the sun.
2–3. Answers will vary.

A. Fact-Finding Exercise (p. 198)

1. F. Many people in the past thought that eclipses were bad signs. 2. T 3. F. The Taiping Rebellion of 1851 failed. 4. F. Gordon decided to make a night attack against Soochow because there was a full moon. 5. T

B. Reading Analysis (p. 199)

1. b **2.** b **3.** a. sign b. There is a comma and then the word *or* after the word *omen* which indicates that a synonym will follow. c. Lunar eclipses are bad omens.
4. a. Istanbul b. The information is in parentheses after *Byzantium*. **5.** a. 2 b. 2
6. a **7.** a. 1 b. 1 **8.** a. 2 b. 3 **9.** prediction **10.** a. 2 b. 1 **11.** a. a saying
b. There is a comma and then the word *or* after the word *maxim,* which indicates that a synonym will follow. c. immoral d. the use of *i.e.* e. the saying that each Chinese dynasty starts out when the previous dynasty becomes corrupt f. Signs in the sky will show that the emperor has become unworthy to rule. **12.** b **13.** a. 1 b. 3
14. a. soldiers of fortune b. There is an explanation at the bottom of the page. c. 2

C. Information Organization (p. 203)

Constantinople
Superstition:
Constantinople could never fall while the moon was becoming full.
Event and Date:
In 1451, sultan Mohammed II attacked Constantinople with 250,000 men. The 7,000 defenders did not give up.
Result of the Lunar Eclipse:
On May 22, 1453, the full moon went into an eclipse. When the sultan attacked the city again, the defenders lost their ability to protect their city. They lost the city to the sultan Mohammed II's army.
China
Superstition:
The Mandate of Heaven: Each Chinese dynasty starts out when the previous dynasty becomes corrupt. Signs in the sky will show that the emperor has become unworthy to rule.

Issues for Today, Book 3, Answer Key   35

Event and Date:
In 1851, the Taiping Rebellion took place in order to overthrow the Manchu Dynasty. The Manchus received help from a mercenary army led by Charles Gordon. Gordon was winning every battle against the rebels in their defense of the city of Soochow.

Result of the Lunar Eclipse:
Gordon decided to make a night attack on the east gate of the city. That night there was a lunar eclipse. His Chinese mercenaries interpreted the eclipse as an evil omen. They lost the battle and many of the mercenary soldiers were killed. It was Gordon's only loss.

D. Information Recall and Summary (p. 204)

1. They believed that their city could never fall while the moon was full.
2. The sultan Mohammed II attacked Constantinople in 1451.
3. a. The attacking army had more men.
   b. Yes, they were.
4. When the sultan attacked the city again, the defenders lost their ability to protect their city. They lost the city to sultan Mohammed II's army.
5. It stated that each new Chinese dynasty starts out when the previous dynasty becomes corrupt. Signs in the sky will show that the emperor has become unworthy to rule.
6. The Taiping Rebellion took place in order to overthrow the Manchu Dynasty.
7. Gordon decided to make a night attack on the east gate of the city. That night there was a lunar eclipse. His Chinese mercenaries interpreted the eclipse as an evil omen. They lost the battle, and many of the mercenary soldiers were killed.

Summary

History was changed because people in the past thought lunar eclipses were evil omens. A lunar eclipse resulted in the fall of Constantinople in 1453; in 1851, a lunar eclipse caused a British general his only loss during the Taiping Rebellion, resulting in many deaths.

E. Word Forms (p. 206)

Part 1

1. a. final b. finality 2. a. unpredictable b. unpredictability 3. a. abilities b. able
4. a. responsibilities b. responsible 5. a. capable b. capabilities

Part 2

1. a. advantages b. advantageous 2. a. superstitious b. Superstitions 3. a. mysterious b. mystery 4. a. rebellious b. rebellions 5. a. disastrous b. disaster

F. Dictionary Skills (p. 208)

1. (1) This happening was of great historical significance.
2. (3) An old prophecy predicted that Constantinople could never suffer a severe loss of power while the moon was becoming full.
3. (1) The Byzantine rulers governed over a large area for over a thousand years.
4. (4) Lunar eclipses have affected historical periods of time in many countries.

G. Vocabulary in Context (p. 209)

1. failed 2. disastrous 3. maxim 4. still 5. affects 6. also 7. attacked
8. prophecy 9. remains 10. mysterious

H. Topics for Discussion and Writing (p. 210)

Answers will vary.

I. Follow-Up Activities (p. 211)

Answers will vary.

J. Cloze Quiz (p. 212)

1. eclipses 2. For 3. take 4. again 5. succeed 6. attacked 7. advantages 8. only
9. capable 10. thick 11. repaired 12. Furthermore 13. time 14. however
15. prediction 16. Unfortunately 17. helpless 18. omen 19. ability 20. enemy

Chapter 12   Mars: Our Neighbor in Space

Prereading Preparation (p. 214)

1. Answers will vary but may include this information: Mars is called the Red Planet, it's the next planet over from Earth.
2. Answers will vary.

3. Answers will vary, but students may suggest sending a spaceship there to explore.
4–5. Answers will vary.

A. Fact-Finding Exercise (p. 217)

1. F. *Mars Observer* failed in 1993.   2. T   3. T   4. F. Scientists believe there was liquid water on Mars 4.5 billion years ago. *OR* Scientists believe there is ice on Mars now.
5. F. The two Viking landers performed four experiments.   6. T   7. T   8. T

B. Reading Analysis (p. 218)

1. c 2. c 3. a. 2 b. Because the sentence reads as follows: "*in addition* to mapping the planet, *Mars Observer* was going to study the Martian atmosphere and surface." The phrase *in addition* alerts the reader to look for a second task. 4. a. 2 b. *failed* and *success*
5. b 6. c 7. c 8. a. 2 b. Because water *was* abundant in contrast to ice (now).
9. a 10. a. 3 b. Because *NASA* is shorter, and the full name is in parentheses to explain it to the reader. 11. a 12. places, locations, areas 13. a 14. a. simple life forms b. 2 15. a. ancient remains of life b. Because *fossils* is followed by a comma and an explanation.

C. Information Organization (p. 221)

I.   *Mars Observer* Mission
   A. Date: August 1993
   B. Purpose: to move into orbit around Mars and send new information back to Earth
      1. map the planet
      2. study the Martian atmosphere and surface
   C. Outcome: the mission failed
II. Viking Lander Mission
   A. Date: 1976
   B. Purpose: to look for life on Mars
   C. Outcome: the mission was a success
III. Data About Mars and Earth
   A. Age of Mars and Earth: 4.5 billion years old
   B. Water on Mars and Earth: Water was abundant during the first billion years
   C. Conditions on Mars: warmer and had a thicker atmosphere of CO_2
   D. Life on Earth: began during its first billion years
      Life on Mars: may have begun during its first billion years
   E. Earth's atmosphere: Earth developed an atmosphere rich in oxygen, and an ozone layer
      Mars' atmosphere: Mars lost its thick atmosphere of CO_2, and became colder
IV. Three Theories About Life on Mars
   A. Life never developed.
   B. Life arose during the first billion years, but did not survive.
   C. Life arose, and simple organisms developed. When environmental conditions changed, life ended.
V.   The Viking Landers Experiments
   A. Three Experiments: tested for biological activity in the soil
   B. The Fourth Experiment: looked for evidence of life
   C. Results of all Four Experiments: negative
VI. Why Scientists Want to Investigate Mars Again
   A. An area in Antarctica resembles an area on Mars, and biologists found simple life forms there.
   B. They want to search for fossils.
VII. Questions That Scientists Want to Answer
   A. How is Earth different from Mars?
   B. How can we explain the development of life on Earth and not on Mars?
   C. Are we alone in the universe?

D. Information Recall and Summary (p. 223)

1. Mars and Earth are the same age. They both had abundant water.
2. Their atmospheres changed. Earth developed an atmosphere rich in oxygen, and an ozone layer. Mars lost its thick atmosphere of CO_2 and became colder.
3. a. Life never developed.
   b. Life arose during the first billion years but did not survive.
   c. Life arose, and simple organisms developed. When environmental conditions changed, life ended.

Issues for Today, Book 3, Answer Key

4. a. The Viking landers performed four experiments. Three experiments tested for biological activity in the soil. The fourth experiment looked for evidence of life.
   b. The results of all four experiments were negative.
5. An area in Antarctica resembles an area on Mars, and biologists found simple life forms there.
6. They want to discover how Earth is different from Mars; how we can explain the development of life on Earth and not on Mars; and whether we are alone in the universe.

Summary

The United States sent two missions to Mars. The most recent one failed, but the earlier one was successful. It performed several experiments on the surface of Mars to look for signs of past or present life.

E. Word Forms (p. 225)

Part 1

1. a. experimental b. experiments 2. a. environments b. environmental 3. a. developmental b. development 4. a. accident b. accidental 5. a. functional b. function

Part 2

1. a. intensified b. intense 2. a. simple b. will simplify 3. a. specific b. does not specify / doesn't specify 4. a. did not clarify / didn't clarify b. clear 5. a. pure b. will purify

F. Dictionary Skills (p. 227)

1. (4) Scientists lost communication with *Mars Observer* on August 24.
2. (4) The spacecraft landed on Mars in order to search for any evidence of life.
3. (1) They found life forms that were not complex.
4. (2) Scientists want to land a spacecraft in a location that shows more signs of a good result than the previous landing sites.

G. Vocabulary in Context (p. 228)

1. survive 2. investigate 3. abundant 4. theory 5. assumption 6. perform
7. intriguing 8. similar 9. arise 10. support

H. Topics for Discussion and Writing (p. 229)

Answers will vary.

I. Follow-Up Activity (p. 230)

Answers will vary.

J. Cloze Quiz (p. 231)

1. planet 2. Unfortunately 3. contrast 4. performed 5. possibility 6. assumption
7. similar 8. abundant 9. arose 10. protects 11. survived 12. intensified
13. theories 14. conditions 15. experiments 16. locations 17. support
18. investigation 19. fossils 20. intriguing

Unit 4 Review

K. Crossword Puzzle (p. 233)

Across Answers

2. omen 4. if 6. inquire 7. environment 11. to 12. custom 13. chamber
14. mercenary 17. not 19. worse 21. pharaoh 23. are 24. made
25. unfortunately 26. master 28. sat 31. experiment 34. had 35. definitely
37. theory

Down Answers

1. discover 2. overthrow 3. no 5. furthermore 8. very 9. microorganism 10. tomb
15. excavate 16. astronomer 18. up 20. superstition 22. her 27. simple
29. sealed 30. fail 32. easy 33. these 36. yes

Unit 4 Discussion (p. 235)

Answers will vary.

CNN Video Report: Water on Mars? (p. 236)

1. Answers will vary. 2. a. hydrogen b. 1–2 feet c. warmer d. abundant e. alone
3. Answers will vary.

Issues for Today
VIDEO SCRIPTS

Unit 1   Trends in Living

CNN Video Report: Nutrition Survey

Running time 02:14

Video Vocabulary

variety: different types of things
pesky: annoying, irritating
modifications: changes, alterations

Video Script

Reporter: Excuses, excuses. Americans are full of them when it comes to healthy eating habits.

Woman: No one knows what's healthy anymore. Go to the bookstore and look at all the books—you'll be totally confused.

Man 1: I feel I'll live longer if I don't know what's bad for me.

Reporter: A new survey by the American Dietetic Association finds eight out of ten people rate good nutrition as moderately to very important, although most of them don't do all they can to achieve it. It's not for lack of knowledge—most people know what they should be eating.

Man 2: A balanced diet's probably the best thing, a variety of food groups. Some meat, a limited amount. Vegetables, beef, um, assorted things, milk products.

Reporter: But knowing is one thing, doing is quite another.

Man 1: Being a parent . . . even though you don't have to finish your corn, you can make sure your kids finish their half.

Interviewer: Do as I say, not as I do?

Man 1: Exactly, exactly.

Reporter: And there are other problems, too, like keeping track of all those pesky fat grams. Half of the people surveyed said they were watching their fat intake. But just how much fat is too much?

Man 3: I have no idea. I know less is good.

Man 4: I don't have a clue, but all I do is eat salads.

Man 5: I don't know the percentage of it—I think it's about 20 grams, 25 grams a day, something like that.

Reporter: Give up? It's widely recommended that your diet contain no more than 30% fat.

Man 6: Well, them diets they be showing that it's healthy. Don't look like it's enough food for me. I mean, it takes a lot of food to keep me going.

Reporter: The number one reason for not eating right: 39% of those questioned say they don't want to give up foods they love. But dieticians say eating a low-fat, healthy diet doesn't mean giving up your favorite foods, just making some modifications. Like drinking low-fat milk and eating leaner cuts of meat. And if you trim enough fat here and there, it's okay to go ahead and splurge on that snack you've been dying for.

Reporter: But I also have it on high authority here that you just had an ice cream cone and not fat-free.

Man 3: See, I asked for fat-free and they just didn't understand that. But I've earned it, I've earned it.

Reporter: Anna Hoven, CNN, reporting.

Unit 2   Issues in Society

CNN Video Report: Grandparents as Parents

Running time 02:42

Video Vocabulary

addicts: people who are physically or mentally dependent on a substance such as a drug

Winnebago: brand name of a popular large recreational vehicle
flags: slows down, becomes weak, falters
strictness: the condition of requiring obedience and expecting rules to be followed
sanity: mental health
retirees: people who have retired from work

Video Script

Reporter: At first glance, Fay and Jim Strassburger look a little bit old to be Brandon and Sean's parents. That's because they're the children's grandparents. But they are their parents as well.

Jim Strassburger (Grandfather): How'd you do in school today?

Grandson: Good.

Reporter: This wasn't something the Strassburgers particularly wanted to do—become parents again. But they say the children's real parents were drug addicts, and if they didn't take over, the state would. It turned out to be an easy decision to make when the boys were first born, when they first picked them up.

Fay Strassburger (Grandmother): Once you hold them and you smell them and you feel them, I mean you're dead, you're dead in the water.

Reporter: Now the retired couple's Winnebago sits idly in the driveway and quiet moments are few and far to come by.

Jim Strassburger: This is the time when you stop and grab a few minutes to pick up on the news.

Reporter: Once again, quiet time is over and it's on to the homework. The Strassburgers find their energy flags a bit, but otherwise they're doing just fine and can even find the humor in the boys' complaints about their parenting style, complaints about their strictness.

Jim Strassburger: "Grandpa was right, you are . . ."(Laughter)

Fay Strassburger: "You are a selfish old lady . . ."

Jim Strassburger: That's Brandon! He's got a way with words.

Reporter: Yes, say the kids, sometimes Grandma and Grandpa are a little slow, but they don't really mind.

Grandson: I wait for them to hurry up.

Reporter: And hurry they do. It's not easy, but they say what saves their sanity is this support group called "Grandparents as Parents" and, this day, all the grandparents are talking about addicted children who want the little ones back.

And her daughter wants the little girl in grandma's arms. Grandma says she'll fight to keep her.

This woman isn't so lucky. The grandchild she helped raise is now back with his mother.

Grandmother 1: Now they won't let me see him, so I guess my next step is to go to court for visitation rights.

Grandfather: You just have to hang in there 'til you can . . .

Grandmother 2: You do just what you're doing, cry. You break your heart.

Reporter: Money can be a big problem, too. These retirees say they get little in the way of government aid compared to, say, foster families, so they're not terribly impressed with the government, especially not these days.

Grandmother 3: Here we're trying, we're trying . . . to do something and the government wants to open orphanages.

Reporter: At least talking together helps, most agree here. It helps them hang in there, like the Strassburgers hang in for that most difficult job, difficult and sometimes so easy.

Fay Strassburger: You know, with it all, I mean, you love them.

Ann McDermott, CNN, Los Angeles.

| Unit 3 | Justice and Crime |

CNN Video Report: Forensic Animation

Running time 02:13

Video Vocabulary

exonerate: to clear a person from guilt
driveshaft: the central mechanism that propels a vehicle
attorneys: legal counselors, lawyers
bias: a prejudice

Video Script

Reporter: When a U.S. Marine jet clipped an aerial tram cable above an Italian ski resort, killing 20 people in 1998, it was hard to imagine how it could have happened. But when the incident came before a military court, there was no need to imagine.

Jurors were able to put themselves in the pilot's seat.

Ginsberg (Computer Simulation Expert): Well, with the simulation that was shown there, yes.

Reporter: Arthur Ginsberg's company, Visual Forensics, prepared a computer simulation which helped exonerate the cockpit crew. It shows the pilot's view of the tram towers, which should have been marked on their map, but were not.

Ginsberg: You can't expect someone to really see something they don't expect to be there.

Reporter: In these TV-friendly times, people are accustomed to getting information through video, so it's no surprise judges and juries are comfortable with computer simulations, called forensic animation, in court.

Ginsberg: They're increasingly common because they're so powerful.

Reporter: And the animations are especially useful to explain complex issues in cases like this one, which alleged a mechanical defect in the driveshaft of a utility cart.

Ginsberg: How the vehicle then rolled and the person was ejected and eventually killed.

Reporter: Ginsberg has produced computer simulations for ten years. He and his staff take great pains to make sure their re-creations are true to the facts.

Carl Bahor (Computer Simulation Expert): We'll take photographs of that scene, of the vehicles, and we'll compare the simulation to those photographs.

Ginsberg: The computer simulations, if they're properly done, have a scientific foundation.

Reporter: And like any other evidence, it's subject to challenge by the attorneys. One thing you won't see—faces or graphic crash scenes.

Ginsberg: We don't go through the crash sequence and watching cars crumble, et cetera. What we want to do is make sure we present the facts and don't provide any emotional bias.

Reporter: Ginsberg says the re-creations typically cost ten to twenty thousand dollars, but they could end up saving time and money. He says it's common for lawsuits to be settled before trial once both sides get a chance to see what actually happened.

James Hattori, CNN, San Ramon, California.

Unit 4	Science and History

CNN Video Report: Water on Mars?

Running time: 02:10

Video Vocabulary

boon: something good, an important help

ecstatic: delighted, very happy

hydrogen: the lightest gaseous chemical element and one of two elements in water (2 molecules of hydrogen plus 1 molecule of oxygen = H_2O = water)

replenish: to replace something that was used, to resupply

Video Script

Reporter: Purple marks the spot, the evidence that there's lots of water on Mars. A potential boon for future space exploration.

Bill Feldman (Scientist): We knew that it was there, we just didn't know that it was going to be that much and so we were ecstatic.

Reporter: Substantial amounts of hydrogen were found at the Mars poles. This NASA image highlights those areas in blue and purple. Scientists suspect hydrogen in these quantities means water and lots of it. Actually, scientists think it's water-ice, mixed with dirt and rock, one to two feet underground. From on board the unmanned Mars Odyssey spacecraft, instruments that measure gamma rays and neutrons made the discovery. We've all seen earlier images of the Mars surface, which show val-

leys and canyons. They look like dry riverbeds and suggest evidence that this ice, trapped underground, could have once existed on its surface. Could Mars have had oceans like Earth?

Scientist's voice: Mars was perhaps much more like the Earth a long time ago, early in its history. The atmospheric pressure may have been higher, the temperature may have been warmer, and liquid water may have been stable on its surface.

Reporter: One astronomer says this is probably just the tip of the Martian iceberg, speculating icy layers could go as much as one mile deep. Are they sure it's water-ice?

Bill Feldman: In the north and south, there is so much of it there that it can be nothing else but water-ice.

Reporter: Today, Mars is a cold, dry, hostile environment with no atmosphere, no rain to replenish surface water, but the potential of so much underground water expands the scope for space exploration. Imagine using Mars as a stopover point for water and refueling. As for determining whether life ever existed on Mars . . .

Bill Feldman: It would be very, very exciting if we found life. Uh, you know, uh, the old question: "Are we alone?"

Reporter: To answer that, NASA says it would take sending a robot to the Red Planet, to scoop up and bring samples back to Earth to study. Even though NASA's talked about it, no such missions are planned. But, at least now, thanks to Odyssey, they're getting some good maps of where to look.

Ann Kellan, CNN, Atlanta.

Issues for Today
ASSESSMENT

Chapter 1 Review—A Cultural Difference: Being on Time

Focus: Information Recall

Read the questions first. Then read the passage on Student Book pages 3–4 again. Close your book and answer the questions without looking at the passage.

1. How did the American professor find out that Brazilian students have different ideas about being on time?

   _____

2. Did the students intend to be rude or impolite? Explain.

   _____

3. Give an example of an *informal* and a *formal* situation.

   a. *informal:* _____

   b. *formal:* _____

4. Did the class in Brazil end on time? Explain.

   _____

5. In the end, did the American professor or the Brazilian students adapt? Why?

   _____

Focus: Vocabulary Cloze

Read the passage below. Choose the best word for each blank from the box. Use each word once.

adapt	**apologize**	**behavior**	**fact**	**greeted**
informal	**prestige**	**punctual**	**rude**	**understand**

An American professor learned the hard way that people in different cultures can have very different ideas about being on time. In the United States, being (1) _____ for meetings and classes is very important. Being late is unacceptable (2) _____. It is considered very (3) _____. At the very least, you are expected to (4) _____ or say "I'm sorry." However, when the professor taught in Brazil, students acted very differently. Some students walked into his class more than an hour late. The students (5) _____ him, but they did not seem sorry to be late.

The professor explained the difference between formal and (6) _____ situations and asked the students what would be considered late in Brazilian culture. He wanted to (7) _____ more about the behavior of the Brazilian people. He learned that in Brazil, it is acceptable for a person to arrive or stay late. In (8) _____, Brazilians expect that successful people with high status or (9) _____ will arrive late. In time, the professor was able to (10) _____ his own behavior so that he would feel comfortable in his new surroundings.

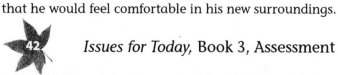

Chapter 2 Review—Changing Lifestyles and New Eating Habits

Focus: Information Recall

Read the questions first. Then read the passage on Student Book page 21 again. Close your book and answer the questions without looking at the passage.

1. Name three ways in which American lifestyles have changed.

   a. _____

   b. _____

   c. _____

2. Provide one reason why 60% of American homes have microwave ovens.

   _____

3. Is red meat an American favorite? Why or why not?

   _____

4. What kind of foods do people eat before playing sports? Give examples.

   _____

5. What foods do many Americans choose for romantic dinners?

   _____

Focus: Vocabulary Cloze

Read the passage below. Choose the best word for each blank from the box. Use each word once.

consume	employed	favorite	grow	habits
lifestyles	nutrition	rush	skip	survey

American eating (1) _____ have changed for many reasons. To begin with, there is a wider selection of food available than in the past. Not only do farmers (2) _____ a larger variety of fruit and vegetables, but many foods are imported from overseas. In addition, Americans are more informed about health and (3) _____, often resulting in healthier food choices. Finally, American (4) _____ have changed over the years, altering peoples' eating habits. For example, if both a husband and wife are (5) _____, there's often less time to buy and prepare food. As a result, many families (6) _____ their meals so that they can get to work in the morning or to activities after work. Sometimes, they even (7) _____ meals because they don't have enough time to eat.

A recent (8) _____ showed that Americans think you should eat different foods for different situations. Most adults (9) _____ foods rich in fiber for breakfast, while many prefer light meals, such as salads, before business meetings. Even though most people know that fast foods, sweets, and snacks are not good for you, they are still among most Americans' (10) _____ foods.

Issues for Today, Book 3, Assessment

Chapter 3 Review—Dreams: Making Them Work for Us

Focus: Information Recall

Read the questions first. Then read the passage on Student Book pages 38–39 again. Close your book and answer the questions without looking at the passage.

1. How long did Joseph continue to have the same bad dream?

    _____

2. Why does psychiatrist Milton Kramer think we need to change our bad dreams?

    _____

3. Name two things you can do that will help you to remember your dreams after you wake up.

    a. _____

    b. _____

4. According to Dr. Rosalind Cartwright, what do you need to identify about bad dreams?

    _____

5. What happened to Joseph's bad dreams? Explain.

    _____

Focus: Vocabulary Cloze

Read the passage below. Choose the best word for each blank from the box. Use each word once.

according	**discourage**	**frightened**	**gradually**	**grown**
harmful	**positive**	**practice**	**recall**	**tired**

It is not unusual for small children to be scared or (1) _____ by bad dreams. However, it is also not uncommon for adults to have terrible dreams. A (2) _____ man named Joseph had a series of nightmares. When he awoke each morning, he was so (3) _____ that he found it difficult to go to work. (4) _____ to psychiatrists, bad dreams can (5) _____ people, while good dreams can refresh them. Because dreams can have such a strong effect on us, it is useful to learn how to replace (6) _____ dreams with pleasant ones.

Researchers have suggested several ways to help us remember our dreams. They say we can (7) _____ our dreams more effectively if we try to recall the details as soon as we wake up. They also think it's possible to (8) _____ stop bad dreams by using dream therapy for a period of time. This (9) _____ can teach us to change terrible nightmares into (10) _____ dreams.

3 • ASSESSMENT

Chapter 4 Review—Language: Is It Always Spoken?

Focus: Information Recall

Read the questions first. Then read the passage on Student Book pages 61–62 again. Close your book and answer the questions without looking at the passage.

1. At what age do most babies start to make sounds?

_____

2. Why did Dr. Laura Petitto study both hearing and deaf infants?

_____

3. Name two things that were different about the deaf babies' hand motions.

   a. _____

   b. _____

4. According to linguists, what is special about human language ability?

_____

5. When babies have one deaf parent and one hearing one, how do they usually begin to communicate?

_____

Focus: Vocabulary Cloze

Read the passage below. Choose the best word for each blank from the box. Use each word once.

babies	deaf	innate	linguists	movements
observation	patterns	psychologists	speech	varied

Many doctors and linguists are interested in how infants learn to communicate. They know

that most (1) _____ start to make babbling sounds before they are capable of advanced

(2) _____. This is how hearing babies practice language. (3) _____ of both hearing and

deaf infants has revealed that all babies make different, (4) _____ motions with their hands. While

the hand (5) _____ of hearing infants are varied, the hand motions of (6) _____ babies

seem to show special (7) _____ that are repeated often.

(8) _____ who study human behavior and (9) _____ who specialize in human

language think that people are born with a special capacity to learn language. They call this an

(10) _____ ability. Even if people cannot hear or speak, they will learn to communicate with other

people using signs and body motions.

Chapter 5 Review—Loneliness: How Can We Overcome It?

Focus: Information Recall

Read the questions first. Then read the passage on Student Book pages 76–77 again. Close your book and answer the questions without looking at the passage.

1. What kind of loneliness do psychologists want to understand better?

   _____

2. Do people experiencing temporary loneliness need to visit a psychologist? Why or why not?

   _____

3. Name three kinds of loneliness and note how long they last.

   a. _____

   b. _____

   c. _____

4. Why can't chronically lonely people increase their social contacts?

   _____

5. How old are the loneliest people?

   _____

Focus: Vocabulary Cloze

Read the passage below. Choose the best word for each blank from the box. Use each word once.

chronic	**circumstances**	**instance**	**interested**	**normally**
overcome	**predict**	**serious**	**temporary**	**unfortunately**

Most people feel lonely sometimes, but not for long. (1) _____, people get over loneliness quickly. Psychologists don't worry about (2) _____ loneliness because it doesn't cause

(3) _____ problems. Under other conditions, however, loneliness can last much longer. For

(4) _____, situational loneliness can occur when someone goes through a divorce or a loved one dies. With time and support from friends and family, most people are able to (5) _____ this type of loneliness.

Psychologists are mostly (6) _____ in helping people who suffer from long-lasting or

(7) _____ loneliness. This type of loneliness is not caused by particular (8) _____.

(9) _____, people with long-term loneliness feel helpless and very unhappy. Also, doctors

(10) _____ that chronically lonely people are at greater risk of developing serious illnesses.

Name: _____ Date: _____

Chapter 6 Review—The Importance of Grandmothers

Focus: Information Recall

Read the questions first. Then read the passage on Student Book pages 91–92 again. Close your book and answer the questions without looking at the passage.

1. What kind of work do anthropologists do?

   _____

2. What other group of scientists are mentioned in the reading?

   _____

3. In some societies, who was more important—the father or the grandmother? Why?

   _____

4. In the study of people in Gambia, did the presence of the paternal or the maternal grandmother reduce the children's chances of dying?

   _____

5. In the historical study of Japanese children, did boys and girls have the same death rate? Explain.

   _____

Focus: Vocabulary Cloze

Read the passage below. Choose the best word for each blank from the box. Use each word once.

anthropologists	examined	households	influence	maternal
mortality	present	reduced	significant	survive

Recently, scientists held a conference to discuss whether grandmothers have an (1) _____ on whether their grandchildren (2) _____ childhood or not. (3) _____, people who study other people and cultures, presented their findings at this international conference. These social scientists collected and (4) _____ historical records of (5) _____, people who live together in one house. They tried to find out if having a grandmother (6) _____ in the household made a difference in the (7) _____ rate of the grandchildren.

In general, the researchers saw a clear pattern where the presence of the (8) _____ grandmother made a (9) _____ difference in survival. The important difference was that if this grandmother was present, the death rate was (10) _____.

Name: _____   Date: _____

Chapter 7 Review—Innocent Until Proven Guilty: The Criminal Court System

Focus: Information Recall

Read the questions first. Then read the passage on Student Book page 115 again. Close your book and answer the questions without looking at the passage.

1. What is the main purpose of the American court system?

    _____

2. If someone is accused of a crime, are they innocent or guilty? Explain.

    _____

3. Name two important Miranda rights that everyone has.

    a. _____

    b. _____

4. Why can some suspects go home without putting up bail?

    _____

5. In the American court system, who actually decides whether someone is guilty or innocent?

    _____

Focus: Vocabulary Cloze

Read the passage below. Choose the best word for each blank from the box. Use each word once.

appears	arrest	bail	crime	evidence
guilty	hear	innocent	jury	punishment

The American court system protects the rights of the people under the law. In this system, when a

(1) _____ takes place, police (2) _____ the person who they think has committed the illegal

act. However, the arrested person is not automatically (3) _____. In fact, it is just the opposite. The

arrested person is considered (4) _____ until a court proves that he or she is truly responsible for

the crime.

Many steps must take place for the court system to operate effectively. At the time of a person's

arrest, he must (5) _____ his Miranda rights. The suspect is then taken to the police station to be

booked. Following this, the person (6) _____ before a judge who decides whether to put the sus-

pect in jail, set (7) _____, or let him go free. Later, in a court hearing, a judge decides if the trial

should proceed. At the trial, a (8) _____ of 12 people listens to what people know about the crime.

Witnesses give (9) _____ as to what happened. Then the jury decides whether the accused person

is guilty or innocent of the crime. If the person is guilty, the judge tells him what the (10) _____

will be.

Issues for Today, Book 3, Assessment

48

Chapter 8 Review—The Reliability of Eyewitnesses

Focus: Information Recall

Read the questions first. Then read the passage on Student Book pages 132–133 again. Close your book and answer the questions without looking at the passage.

1. Why does Bernard Jackson have many bitter memories?

   _____

2. Name two factors that can influence the accuracy of eyewitness testimony.

   a. _____

   b. _____

3. Are police officers more reliable eyewitnesses than ordinary people? Explain.

   _____

4. In the American court system, how important is eyewitness testimony?

   _____

5. Who determines the accuracy of the witness's testimony?

   _____

Focus: Vocabulary Cloze

Read the passage below. Choose the best word for each blank from the box. Use each word once.

appearance **questions**	**eyewitness** **reliability**	**influence** **similar**	**lineup** **testimony**	**mistakes** **victim**

Someone who actually sees a crime occur is called an (1) _____. This could be anyone at the scene of a crime, but sometimes it is a (2) _____, a person hurt by the crime. Either way, an eyewitness is not always accurate.

Sometimes eyewitnesses can make (3) _____. Many different factors (4) _____ the reliability of eyewitnesses. For example, some people have better memories or eyesight than others. Some witnesses get confused when they see many photographs of people who look (5) _____. Large numbers of possible suspects standing in a (6) _____ can also affect the accuracy of eyewitnesses. People sometimes find it difficult to describe the (7) _____ of people of other races. The (8) _____ that police ask when they interview witnesses can also make their (9) _____ less reliable. Psychologists tested the (10) _____ of police officers as eyewitnesses, finding that they were not more reliable than ordinary people.

Chapter 9 Review—Solving Crime with Modern Technology

Focus: Information Recall

Read the questions first. Then read the passage on Student Book pages 152–153 again. Close your book and answer the questions without looking at the passage.

1. Name three types of modern technology used to solve crimes.

   a. _____

   b. _____

   c. _____

2. Why is it a problem that fingerprint files don't include prints for everyone?

   _____

3. What was special about Eric Berg's work with fingerprints?

   _____

4. How can police solve crimes from the past?

   _____

5. What can the laser light system do that couldn't be done before?

   _____

Focus: Vocabulary Cloze

Read the passage below. Choose the best word for each blank from the box. Use each word once.

apparent fluids	crimes identify	evidence match	expert reveals	fabric technology

    Police and law enforcement workers have always tried to find out who committed (1) _____.

Now they have new (2) _____ to help them (3) _____ criminals. Some of these new

techniques come from the field of genetics. DNA analysis allows police to match DNA from body

(4) _____ with the DNA of suspects. Every person's DNA is unique, so DNA analysis is very strong

(5) _____ in a court of law. On the other hand, sometimes DNA testing (6) _____ that an

(7) _____ suspect was not responsible for a crime. If this is the case, the innocent person is set free.

    Other new methods of crime detection depend on computers. In the past, clear fingerprints could

only be taken from hard surfaces such as mirrors and furniture. A crime (8) _____ in Washington

state used computer software that he developed to enhance a palm print taken from (9) _____.

The police were then able to (10) _____ it with prints from a suspect, solving a crime that had

been thought to be unsolvable.

3 • ASSESSMENT

Chapter 10 Review—Ancient Artifacts and Ancient Air

Focus: Information Recall

Read the questions first. Then read the passage on Student Book pages 177–178 again. Close your book and answer the questions without looking at the passage.

1. What was the *crypt* that the archaeologists discovered in Egypt in 1954?

   _____

2. Why did ancient Egyptians bury two boats with their dead kings?

   _____

3. What did the scientists hope to learn from the air in the second room?

   _____

4. Did archaeologists get useful information from the second chamber? Explain.

   _____

5. What did archaeologists do differently in the 1986 excavation?

   _____

Focus: Vocabulary Cloze

Read the passage below. Choose the best word for each blank from the box. Use each word once.

ancient	**chamber**	**crypt**	**custom**	**escaped**
excavation	**king**	**museum**	**predicted**	**sealed**

   In 1954, archaeologists near the Great Pyramid discovered an ancient (1) _____. The tomb was the burial place of an important pharaoh, a (2) _____ of ancient Egypt. Historians knew about the Egyptian (3) _____ of burying their kings with boats. Therefore, they (4) _____ that they would find two boats inside the tomb when they opened it. However, when archaeologists excavated the first chamber, only one boat was discovered. They hoped to find the other boat in the second chamber.

   Archaeologists were very surprised to learn that the air in the first room had been sealed so effectively that no air had (5) _____ for 4,600 years. It appeared the air had preserved the wooden boat. Their discovery made the scientists want to examine the quality of the air sealed within the second (6) _____ of the tomb. They wanted to be very careful to protect the (7) _____ air, so they took a lot of time to plan the (8) _____ of the other room. In fact, they waited for 32 years before beginning the excavation. During that time, the Egyptian government had built a (9) _____ on the site for the first boat. Unfortunately, the construction of this museum probably disturbed the second chamber. When scientists finally tested the second room's air, they discovered that the chamber was not (10) _____.

51

Chapter 11 Review—How Lunar Eclipses Have Changed History

Focus: Information Recall

Read the questions first. Then read the passage on Student Book pages 196–197 again. Close your book and answer the questions without looking at the passage.

1. Why were people in ancient times frightened of eclipses?

   _____

2. What was the old prophecy that Constantinople's troops had faith in?

   _____

3. Why was the Turkish army able to overpower Constantinople's troops?

   _____

4. Why was Charles Gordon's attack on Soochow unsuccessful?

   _____

5. In modern times, how do people know when a lunar eclipse will occur?

   _____

Focus: Vocabulary Cloze

Read the passage below. Choose the best word for each blank from the box. Use each word once.

ability	**attacked**	**eclipses**	**enemy**	**events**
helpless	**mercenary**	**omens**	**predict**	**unfortunately**

Strange as it may seem, (1) _____ have had a major effect on historical (2) _____. Before the scientific age, people believed that eclipses were (3) _____, indicating that something bad was about to happen. Even though some people had the ability to (4) _____ when an eclipse would happen, most people were taken by surprise. When the sun or moon disappeared, they were often left feeling (5) _____ and frightened.

(6) _____, sometimes eclipses happened when (7) _____ armies tried to take over cities. Sometimes they used (8) _____ soldiers who fought for money, not because they were fighting for their own people. If these armies (9) _____ at the same time a lunar eclipse occurred, troops often became afraid and lost their (10) _____ to fight back.

Chapter 12 Review—Mars: Our Neighbor in Space

Focus: Information Recall

Read the questions first. Then read the passage on Student Book pages 215–216 again. Close your book and answer the questions without looking at the passage.

1. What happened to the *Mars Observer* mission in 1993?

   _____

2. Name three things that *Mars Observer* was going to do.

   a. _____

   b. _____

   c. _____

3. What do scientists think is similar about Mars and Earth?

   _____

4. In what ways has Mars's atmosphere changed?

   _____

5. Why is southern Victoria Land in Antarctica important for studying Mars?

   _____

Focus: Vocabulary Cloze

Read the passage below. Choose the best word for each blank from the box. Use each word once.

abundant	**assumption**	**conditions**	**contrast**	**investigate**
locations	**performed**	**planet**	**possibility**	**theories**

Scientists have been intrigued with the (1) _____ of life on Mars for many years. In 1976, two American spacecraft, the *Viking* landers, landed on the (2) _____. These spacecraft (3) _____ four experiments, but scientists wanted to learn more. They hoped that the 1993 *Mars Observer* spacecraft would help them test their (4) _____ about Mars. Unfortunately, *Mars Observer* didn't provide information about Mars because the mission failed.

Scientists make an (5) _____ that water is necessary for any form of life. Since Mars and Earth developed under similar (6) _____ 4.5 billion years ago, they think that Mars may once have had (7) _____ amounts of water. Today, Mars is very cold and dry, except for two (8) _____ at the poles where there is ice. By (9) _____, Earth is much warmer and wetter. Scientists want to continue sending missions to Mars so that they can (10) _____ whether life ever existed on our close neighbor.

3 · ASSESSMENT

Concepts for Today
TEACHER NOTES

Chapter 1 **The Paradox of Happiness** Audio CD, Track 1

Psychologists have learned that happiness and unhappiness are two distinct feelings that increase and decrease independently of one another. Research indicates that a predisposition for unhappiness may be genetic, but happiness is something that individuals can control and develop. We can choose to increase the amount of happiness in our lives.

Suggestions for Prereading Activity

The questions on Student Book ("SB") page 2 about family background and environment set the stage for a major issue in the reading: to what extent is happiness genetically determined and what is the role of environment? Some students will recognize this as the famous nature-nurture argument in the social sciences. Explain to students that *environment* in the sense of prereading Question 5 means "surroundings" (experience with family and friends), not *environment* in an ecological sense.

According to *The Newbury House Dictionary*, a paradox is "a puzzling statement of two opposing truths or an impossible state of affairs." For example, some brides are both happy and sad on their wedding days, but for different reasons.

Culture Notes

The reading mentions two studies using twins. Identical twins are exactly the same genetically; whereas fraternal twins are genetically different. Studies involving twins provide a natural laboratory for studying the separate effects of genetics and environment. Identical twins are usually divided into two research groups: those that grew up together and stayed in contact, and those who were separated at birth such as babies who were adopted by different parents. Questions 2 and 3 in Critical Thinking Strategies on SB page 15 prompt students to think about studies using twins.

The research conclusion that happiness is self-determined is not a new idea. In fact, the ancient Greek philosopher Aristotle said, "Happiness depends on ourselves." About 2,200 years later, the American President Abraham Lincoln echoed the idea when he said "People are about as happy as they make up their minds to be." Lincoln's statement is especially interesting because he was a person prone to unhappiness.

Research has also shown a link between happiness and health. When we're happy, our brains produce endorphins, which strengthen our ability to fight disease, making us less likely to experience pain, and in general, making us feel good. By contrast, negative feelings stress us and produce hormones that are harmful to our bodies. Medical studies have shown that positive thinking is a powerful factor in maintaining good health.

It is important to recognize the difference between the type of unhappiness, which everyone experiences from time to time, and depression, a mental illness that requires treatment. Unhappiness is often situational, triggered by particular events such as the loss of a relationship. Depression is longer lasting and can lead to a feeling of helplessness. If the opportunity arises, point out that most college and university health services have staff who are skilled in dealing with depression.

Suggestions for Follow-Up Activities

Through the centuries, many famous people have made memorable remarks on happiness. Ask students to search the Internet or InfoTrac for happiness quotations. InfoTrac comes with the Student Book and provides students with an online research library. Divide the class into small groups and have each group compare and contrast ten quotations. Have students examine the quotations they selected for similarities and differences.

Explain to students that they are going to compare how they perceive their own happiness and unhappiness to other peoples' perceptions. This works best in pairs, allowing students to choose their partners. Each student writes a passage about their own happiness and unhappiness, as well as a description about their perception of the existence of these same emotions in their partner's life. Students then share their writing with their partner.

Chapter 2   **Close to Home: Technological Advances Erode Barrier Between Work and Home**   **Audio CD, Track 2**

Modern technology is blurring the boundaries between work and home. Many employees must be available during off-hours and hi-tech devices sometimes intrude upon family life and social activities. On the other hand, employees now tend to incorporate elements of domestic life into the workplace more than they did in the past. These changes can both positively and negatively affect personal and family life.

Suggestions for Prereading Activity

The prereading activity on SB page 20 focuses on examples of modern technology in the workplace. Let students know that often there are several names for the same device; cell phone, mobile, and GSM all relate to the same instrument. Also explain that sometimes technology becomes outmoded. For example, the *walkie-talkie* mentioned in the reading passage is a two-way radio. The earliest ones, at the time of World War II, were quite large. Transistor technology around 1950 made them much smaller. They are still used in police and fire departments and for other two-way communication.

Note that Question 2b asks for examples of jobs where workers must stay in contact at all times while Question 3 asks for reasons why workers must stay in contact. An *obstetrician*—a doctor who delivers babies—is an example for 2b. An obstetrician must be contactable because a woman might go into labor at any time of the day or night.

Culture Notes

As is common in authentic readings, this reading passage assumes some vocabulary items that may not be familiar to second language learners. Encourage your students to clarify the meaning of unfamiliar words. For example, an *armoire* (line 32) is a large cabinet usually used for storing clothing. In this case, it conceals the computer in the living room. In the past, it was common for people to use similar types of cabinets to hide television sets. You may also want to draw students' attention to the phrase *provide access*. In this reading it is used to mean "be able to reach" instead of a dictionary definition of "entrance."

Ensure students are familiar with the term *latch-key* children. Explain that these are children who look after themselves after school. The name comes from the fact that they have a house key and let themselves in when they return home. In the United States, child care is very expensive and often difficult to arrange for older children, especially those who are old enough to manage on their own for a short time.

The article omits reference to another common way in which technology blurs the distinction between home and work: *telecommuting.* This is when someone primarily works from home, keeping in contact with business colleagues and coworkers through communication technology.

Suggestions for Follow-Up Activities

Ask your students if they know people who are often on call outside of normal working hours. Do they know anyone who primarily works at home? Do any of these people set boundaries to help them lead a more balanced life? Conduct a class survey to determine how your students would feel about having a job where their family life and leisure activities can be interrupted by work demands.

The reading passage contains many idioms. Divide the class into two teams. Each team should see how many idioms they can identify in the reading and make a list of them. Then each team takes turns at providing the other team with an idiom that they have to explain. The team that provides the correct meaning of the most idioms wins.

Chapter 3　　**The Birth-Order Myth**　　**Audio CD, Track 3**

For many years, people thought that birth order within a family affected personality, intelligence, and achievement. Much of this research has now been discredited. Some studies show that parental attention may be important in promoting intelligence and achievement. In addition, research indicates that family size and spacing between children may play important roles in a child's development.

Suggestions for Prereading Activity

The prereading activity on SB page 39 presents an opportunity for students to use vocabulary that describes personality and intelligence. You may wish to direct students to the list of adjectives that are part of the survey on SB page 55. If the class discussion produces additional descriptive words, add them to the list in the survey.

Culture Notes

The Newbury House Dictionary gives two meanings for *myth:* "1. stories from ancient cultures about history, gods, and heroes;" and "2. an untrue or unproved story." The second meaning is intended by the title of the reading passage. In teaching critical thinking as a reading skill, it is essential to alert students to words like *myth,* which present a one-sided view. Such words are often used in popular periodicals to attract readers' attention because they are extreme. If this reading came from a scholarly journal, the title would be more moderate, perhaps "Importance of Birth-Order Reconsidered."

The statements in the article are less extreme than the title suggests, and in some cases, even equivocal. For example, the statement in line 31, "Many experts today suggest that birth order plays no role at all," leaves room for what other experts may assert. In line 38, the statement, "As for effects on personality, results are mixed," says that studies do not conclusively support one view or the other. An old proverb says, "One swallow does not make a summer," and it applies to controversies such as the effect of birth order. It means that a few studies do not definitively discredit a long-standing idea or other studies. They may, however, raise questions and suggest the need for further research. A better approach is to suggest that students explore the literature and then come to their own conclusions.

People have investigated possible connections between birth order and achievement for many years. In 1874, Francis Galton published a book about famous English scientists that explored important influences in their lives. Of the 99 scientists for whom he had birth-order information, he found that 48% were first-born sons (all the scientists were men). Other studies of achievement—such as U.S. presidents—have produced similar results.

Suggestions for Follow-Up Activities

The questions on SB pages 52, 53, and 54 require students to express and support their own opinions. If some students come from authoritative educational backgrounds, they may believe that either the textbook or the teacher will tell them "the truth." Encourage students to explore different perspectives and take risks in forming their own opinions. For some of the questions, it may be helpful to have small groups (a maximum of four students) work through the questions together out loud. Provide a comfortable, supportive atmosphere in which you encourage discussion and disagreement.

If students are interested in learning more about birth order, refer them to the Internet and InfoTrac resources for this chapter.

Unit 1 **CNN** Video Report

Have students watch the Unit 1 CNN video, *Hot Spots and Wireless Technology*. You might want to show the video for the first time after students have completed Chapter 2. The technology presented in the video, Wireless Fidelity, has the potential to further erode the barrier between work and home (the topic under discussion in Chapter 3). After students view the video, make sure they understand the term *hot spot*. Encourage students to think about this new technology by asking the following questions: Will hot spots replace home Internet connections? Where are you most likely to find hot spots now? How widely available is this technology?

In the video, a WiFi user says the new technology gives him access to a whole new way of working—an outdoor office. Ask students to consider the benefits and drawbacks of such an arrangement. Would your students prefer to study English outdoors? Why or why not?

After discussing the video, ask students to answer the Video Report questions on SB page 60.

Chapter 4

Why So Many More Americans Die in Fires

Audio CD, Track 4

The United States has one of the worst fire death records in the world because it spends more on fighting fires than preventing them. Americans rely heavily on technology to protect them from fires, often failing to apply stricter laws and social pressure. By contrast, in many European and Asian countries, tougher laws and better public safety education send clear messages about the importance of fire prevention.

Suggestions for Prereading Activity

As students look at the title and photograph on page 62, ask them about the source of the reading. Have they ever heard of *The New York Times?* If so, what do they know about this newspaper's reputation? What kind of reading do they expect this to be? Explain that it's an example of an expository reading, one that explains something.

Questions 4 and 5 may not make much sense to students until after they have read the passage, so if they are puzzled, return to these questions later. In the United States, the neighbors' reactions would depend entirely on the setting and circumstances. In situations where many people share an apartment building, neighbors are more likely to be concerned for their own safety. In suburban and rural areas, houses are often far enough apart that neighbors may not perceive the fire as a threat to their house.

Culture Notes

In the United States, 80% of fire fatalities occur in house fires, but the media tends to cover spectacular fires such as raging forest fires and fires in public places like hotels. Deadly house fires typically start as cooking fires in the kitchen or in a bedroom where someone has been smoking. Sometimes house fires start as electric fires, often the result of people overloading electric circuits or using broken equipment. Once fires get started, they develop very quickly and there is limited time to escape. Consequently, most victims of house fires are killed by carbon monoxide poisoning or by inhaling smoke.

Each year, during the national Fire Prevention Week, fire departments and the Red Cross tell people to review safety conditions in their homes. In particular, they urge families to have an escape plan that everyone knows about. They also encourage people to buy and learn to use fire extinguishers and smoke detectors.

In an office or a hotel, fire prevention and procedures are somewhat better organized. Companies usually have fire plans and hold fire drills. Hotels are required to post maps of floor plans and escape routes on the back of doors. These signs often give additional information such as warnings not to use elevators or open windows to balconies. They also make suggestions for preventing smoke inhalation. Guests should familiarize themselves when they first arrive, not wait until there is an emergency.

Wildfires have been a major problem in dry parts of the United States. These fires start from lightening strikes or are sometimes caused by humans. If a campfire is left unattended, the fire can quickly spread to nearby trees and soon an entire forest can be in flames. Firefighters are limited in what they can do to prevent forest fires from spreading to nearby housing areas.

Suggestions for Follow-Up Activities

Suggestion 4 on SB page 77 can be expanded to include a safety survey of both home and college. Divide students into teams of four and have them brainstorm on possible causes of fire in one of these locations. Then have them develop a checklist for fire safety. Finally, they should focus on one item from the checklist and create a poster. You may want to exhibit the posters in hallways or other common areas to increase general awareness of fire safety.

If it's possible, you could invite a firefighter to visit your class to present a talk on fire prevention. In advance of the visit, have the class prepare questions to ask the presenter. This encourages students to recycle information from the reading passage and provides "prelistening" preparation for the talk.

Chapter 5

Acupuncture: The New Old Medicine

Audio CD, Track 5

Many Americans turn to acupuncture when modern medicine fails to cure their illnesses. Acupuncture is an ancient Chinese medical treatment that uses needles to adjust the flow and balance of a basic energy force called qi in the body. The treatment seems to have good effects on a number of diseases and problems.

Suggestions for Prereading Activity

Ask students what they know about acupuncture. To help them understand how the treatment is performed, refer them to the photographs on SB pages 80 and 95.

Ask students about the source of the reading. Are they familiar with *Forbes?* Based on the title, what kind of reading do they expect this to be? Explain that it is an example of a narrative, a reading that tells a story. You may wish to point out that lines 1–26 are written in the first person singular.

Culture Notes

Several terms are used throughout Chapter 5 to describe different kinds of medical treatment: *traditional, modern, conventional,* and *alternative.* To clarify, *modern* medicine is the dominant type of treatment today. Based on scientific principles, it is taught in medical schools. Its practitioners—doctors of many types—go through a long period of training and are licensed to practice. It is also known as *conventional* medicine. According to the WHO (World Health Organization), *traditional* medicine is the "ways of protecting and restoring health that existed before the arrival of modern medicine." Traditional medicine would include acupuncture from China, ayurvedic medicine from India, Native American healing, and herbal medicines used in many cultures.

Today, it is not uncommon for "modern" doctors to recognize the value of some kinds of traditional medicine. When a mainstream doctor decides to use traditional medicine along with conventional practices, it is known as *complementary* medicine. In other words, the two kinds are used together as a balanced treatment. *Alternative* medicine is when someone decides to use traditional medicine instead of conventional treatment. The reading details people who were using acupuncture as alternative medicine.

The reading refers to several locations in New York City. Fifth Avenue is an affluent, upscale area with expensive shops, professional offices, and apartments. Doctors there would probably be specialists and charge high fees. Canal Street and Mott Street are in Chinatown, an area of the city settled years ago by Chinese immigrants. It still retains a strong Chinese identity and Chinese-

4 · TEACHER NOTES

Americans continue many traditional customs. Notice that the street sign in the photograph on SB page 91 has both Chinese characters and English names.

Suggestions for Follow-Up Activities

If your class is unfamiliar with jigsaw readings, explain the analogy with jigsaw puzzles. Everyone has some pieces to the puzzle, but you can't make sense of it until you see how all the pieces fit together. In preparation for the jigsaw reading on SB pages 96–99, you may want to preteach terms such as *pulse, vital organ, modality, adjunct,* and *chronic.*

Explain that you would like students to identify the kinds of traditional and alternative medicines that are available in their community. Students that live in the same area may wish to work in pairs or small groups. The following resources might provide some helpful starting points: the telephone book, newspaper advertisements, or the Internet.

Chapter 6   **Highs and Lows in Self-Esteem**   **Audio CD, Track 6**

A study of 350,000 people indicated that self-esteem varies across the human lifespan. Children typically have high self-esteem, but adolescence lowers it, especially for girls. Self-esteem rises in young adulthood and remains high through midlife as people develop a sense of competence and worth. In later life, after retirement, some people experience lower self-esteem due to losses in health, financial status, and their sense of usefulness.

Suggestions for Prereading Activity

The Newbury House Dictionary defines *self-esteem* as "a feeling of liking oneself, a sense of self-worth." This definition focuses on a positive interpretation of self-esteem. It is also possible to think of self-esteem in a negative context. For instance, the reading suggests that adolescents and some elderly people have low self-esteem. At this point, students might find it more helpful to adopt the following neutral interpretation of self-esteem: an assessment of how much one values oneself.

Culture Notes

Self-esteem is an important concept, but remains a difficult one to measure accurately. The reasons for this are many, but here are a few of the contributing factors: as noted above, the term itself is open to both positive and negative interpretations; most studies ask subjects to rate themselves so the data are very subjective; self-esteem is a component of both normal and abnormal personalities and interacts with any number of other variables; the overall concept of self-esteem means different things in different cultures; and finally, it is difficult to ascertain whether self-esteem is truly the way an individual regards himself or herself or whether it reflects the estimation of other people.

The reading discusses a few of the reasons why some older people may experience a drop in self-esteem. The author notes that not all elderly people experience this. A 2004 Canadian study with 17,626 participants indicates that loss of self-esteem seems to happen more often when older people have lower incomes than with more affluent people. In Western cultures, both self-identity and self-esteem are closely associated with one's occupational role and achievements, including the ability to earn enough to have a comfortable lifestyle.

Many people have unreasonably high expectations for a wonderful lifestyle after retirement, and the media often reinforces peoples' dreams of a carefree life with opportunities to do things that were deferred or postponed during the working years. However, the reality is that many retirees find that they have to reduce their expectations due to poor health or unexpected expenses. Common physical changes such as declining eyesight, hearing, mobility, or memory may result in lowered ability to be independent and capable. All of these factors can result in lower self-esteem.

Suggestions for Follow-Up Activities

There is a lot of interesting research on self-esteem and you may find that your students are keen to read more about this topic. If this is the case, suggest that students search for information on the Internet and InfoTrac. Due to the volume of information that exists on this topic, students will need to limit their search by combining the key words *self-esteem* with another topic. The following topic combinations would provide students with a good start: *self-esteem and childhood; self-esteem and adolescence; self-esteem and retirement;* and *self-esteem and gender.* Most search engines and InfoTrac will limit a search by using "and" between the two topics. For example, if you search *self-esteem and birth order,* you will get only articles that include both topics.

Unit 2 **CNN** Video Report

Have students watch the Unit 2 video, *Holiday House Fires.* Have students view this video after they have completed Chapter 4. Prepare students to view the video by engaging them in a "prewatching" discussion, similar to "prereading." Ask your class how their families decorate for holiday celebrations. Note that many cultures have light or candles as part of the festivities. For example, Hanukkah in Jewish culture, Diwali in Hindu culture, and Chinese New Year all feature candles. When using candles, do they practice special safety precautions?

    The video mentions checking the UL symbol to see if holiday lights are appropriate for both indoor and outdoor use. UL is the Underwriters Laboratory symbol found on many electrical appliances and devices. Have students ever noticed this symbol on electrical devices that they own?

    After discussing the ideas presented in video, have students answer the Video Report questions on SB page 127.

Unit 3	Government and Education

Chapter 7   **The Federal System of Government**   **Audio CD, Track 7**

American colonists tired of British colonial rule, so they declared themselves independent in 1776. The first 13 states became republics with elected governments and representative assemblies. In 1781, the Articles of Confederation established a national Congress, but it had few powers. By 1787, it was clear that the federal government needed to be reshaped in order to be stronger. Thus, the Constitution was written, creating three major branches of government controlled by a system of checks and balances. To this day, the Constitution assures freedom and representative government for Americans.

Suggestions for Prereading Activity

Students may not know the answer to some of the prereading questions on SB page 130 until they read the passage, so be prepared to discuss any ideas that students may have and then come back to them later. The second question refers to the first wave of settlement to the American colonies by people from the British Isles and northern Europe. The settlers came for a variety of reasons, including a desire for religious freedom, better economic opportunities, and available land.

The Newbury House Dictionary defines *constitution* as "the principles and rules, set forth in a written document, governing a country." For this chapter, it may prove useful to bring an almanac to class with you. Not only does an almanac provide a concise overview of the federal government and its components, it also provides an excellent opportunity for your students to explore another reference source. Encourage students to read the capsule statements about each nation that give its form of government, whether it has a constitution or not, and when it was established.

Culture Notes

For its entire existence, the United States has been characterized by tension between state and federal governments. After Independence but before the Constitution was written, individual states had almost complete power. At the time, Americans thought this was necessary because they felt that only states could guarantee individual freedom. Quite reluctantly, the people deemed it necessary to create a stronger federal government. When the Constitution was framed, one of the intentions was to limit the power of central government and allow the states to maintain control of most other areas.

The Constitution explicitly grants certain powers to the federal government. These exclusive federal powers include the right to enter into relations with foreign governments, levy taxes, coin money, spend for the public good, maintain a military force, and regulate interstate commerce. Many of these rights were matters of conflict when America was a British colony, particularly the levying of taxes and tariffs. The Constitution clearly states that all other powers belong to the state—except for those clearly prohibited by the Constitution.

In the years that followed the creation of the Constitution, the division of rights between the federal government and the individual states seemed clear enough. However, through the years, friction and problems arose as a result of differing state interests. For example, in the American South, much of the economy was based on plantation agriculture that used slaves. As some states began adopting laws that abolished slavery, some Southern states tried to nullify or veto the federal laws that were attempting to do the same within their territories. In 1861, several Southern states seceded from the national government because they disagreed with federal law. This resulted in the Civil War between the North and the South. After the war ended in 1865, the nation was reunited and, since then, no state has broken away.

In recent history, the role of the National Guard has received a great deal of media attention. The Constitution clearly states that the military comes under the control of the federal government. Despite this national control, members of the National Guard are recruited by and based in each of the individual states. The states use the National Guard to keep order and provide help with emergencies and local disasters. However, in times of war or when the nation is threatened, the federal government can mobilize the state-based National Guard. Many soldiers who were previously helping people in their home states could be serving overseas.

Suggestions for Follow-Up Activities

As mentioned throughout this chapter, the individual states have retained a great deal of their own identities, largely because they have successfully maintained an autonomous government. Explain that you would like students to explore the role self-government plays in maintaining a state's uniqueness. Have students interview students or faculty from other states and find out what they consider special or unique about their state, especially in terms of government. Students could share their findings in the form of a short presentation. If students need further information or clarification, suggest that they use the Internet or InfoTrac.

Chapter 8   **Too Soon Old, Too Late Wise**   **Audio CD, Track 8**

Professor Paul Weiss, a well-known philosopher, has had a long and successful academic career. However, at age 90, he was informed that he was being demoted to a part-time teacher of graduate students. Weiss and the U.S. Equal Employment Opportunity Commission believe this is age discrimination. The university thinks a younger scholar should replace him. Weiss, still a productive writer, disagrees and would like his old job back.

Suggestions for Prereading Activity

In addition to reading the passage's title and its source, ask students to look at the photographs on SB pages 156 and 162. What do they predict the article will say? What do they consider to be "old" and why do they think so? Keep in mind that there are cultural attitudes towards age that differ from American perspectives.

Questions 3, 4, and 5 on SB page 156 address the subject of mandatory retirement. For Question 5, ask what skills and abilities are important for certain jobs and whether these are affected by age. Discuss whether all people are affected in the same way.

Culture Notes

Professor Paul Weiss' situation is a case study that exemplifies the following related issues: the academic employment system, mandatory retirement, demographic structure, and systems of social welfare. In the United States, there is a distinction between public and private universities. Public universities fall under the control of the state and employment practices such as hiring, promotion, and retirement are similar to that of other state employees. Private universities have more autonomy in these matters. There has been a tradition in academia of awarding tenure (permanent employment) to college and university teachers once they pass a probationary period. Tenure is awarded on the basis of performance as a teacher and researcher, as well as one's publication record. Many professors know the saying "Publish or perish," meaning that if they fail to produce publications during the probationary period, they will not receive tenure. Although tenure means that the professor has a job for life at that institution, "life" depends on the institution's retirement policies. Some institutions really mean for life, as long as one can function and contribute to the academic community. In these institutions, professors called *emeritus* still participate in university affairs, even in their 80s and 90s.

One of the drawbacks to the tenure system is that during times of population growth, such as the baby boom that followed World War II, many talented and qualified young scholars cannot find academic employment because many positions are filled with older, tenured professors. This forms the basis for the idea expressed in the reading that Weiss should make way "for a younger man."

A century ago, most people did not live to the age of 65, but today the situation is very different. Life expectancy has increased enormously and, in general, people live longer. In the 1920s, some countries and companies started retirement or pension plans that would provide income after retirement. They also made mandatory retirement a law so you could not work after a certain age, typically 60 or 65. The United States Congress passed the Social Security Act in 1935. Until recently, you could draw full Social Security benefits from age 65, but this is gradually being raised to age 67. The dilemma is that money to fund Social Security comes from younger workers and with many "baby boomers" now about to draw pensions, there is concern that the system will run out of money, especially since many retirees will receive payments for decades.

Suggestions for Follow-Up Activities

Ask students to research jobs that have a mandatory retirement age. As a start, suggest that they investigate the requirements for airline pilots, firefighters, law enforcement officers, and the military. In each case, students should identify specific job requirements that might be affected by age. After completing this task, refer students back to Question 5 in the prereading section on SB page 156. Do they still agree with the thoughts they expressed at the beginning of this chapter?

Suggest that students use an encyclopedia to find out about life expectancy in the countries represented in your class. Why do people live longer in some societies than others? Ask students about retirement in their home country. Do most people look forward to retirement, or do they want to continue working for as long as they can?

Chapter 9   The Pursuit of Excellence   Audio CD, Track 9

Each year, over 400,000 foreign students come to study at American universities and colleges. In most other countries, higher education is for an elite few who qualify and enter an inflexible system where they specialize in a single field. By contrast, American institutions offer flexibility, choice, and a campus culture. Although U.S. colleges and universities are responsive to social change, their administrators must answer to many different constituencies who want to see good value for their investment.

Suggestions for Prereading Activity

Inquire about which students in your class have come from another country especially for their higher education. Why have they chosen to study in the United States? Some of your students may have first immigrated to the United States and are now seeking a college or university education. Ask these students if education played a role in their decision to move to the United States.

In responding to the questions about college requirements on SB page 171, students might find it helpful to describe the secondary educational system in their own country. There is considerable variation in the number of years of study entailed, the subjects studied, and examination systems. Discuss the cost of higher education. Who pays for higher education in other countries? Are there loans or scholarships?

Culture Notes

The reading details some basic contrasts between American and European higher education. One of the main differences is in the breadth of the academic program a student pursues. In the American system, the liberal arts model is widely used whereby an undergraduate student is required to take a distribution of general education courses in the major academic fields during the first two years. Only as an upper classman does the student start to concentrate in his or her major field. By contrast, the European student focuses on a specific area of study from the first year.

Another contrast between American and European higher education is the teaching style and degree of guidance by faculty. In most European countries, professors rarely meet with students on an individual basis. In fact, class attendance is optional. Britain is the exception; here, one-on-one tutorials are the main form of instruction. In the United States, professors usually meet with classes several times a week and attendance is expected. In smaller classes in America, discussions often replace or supplement lectures as a means of instruction. Many professors also have office hours, a time when students can speak privately about their studies.

In most European and Asian countries, much of the student's grade rests on high-stakes exams. These are given once a term or even once a year, and the results determine whether the student can continue in the program. In the United States, assessment is more frequent and the stakes are not so high. For admission to colleges and universities, though, American students must take standardized examinations such as the SAT or ACT. Foreign students coming to the United States usually have to achieve a good score on an English language proficiency exam, such as TOEFL, before they are admitted into an American degree program.

Suggestions for Follow-Up Activities

Refer students to the opening paragraph of the reading and ask them to identify the analogy. If students are not certain of your request, ask them what the American higher educational system is compared to. Why is it compared to a wounded beast? Can students find another analogy in the article? (Comparing guiding educational change with steering a supertanker, lines 75–77.) Ask students to create their own analogies.

Are there foreign student organizations on your campus? What is their function? If students in your class belong to one, perhaps they can share how these groups help them to adjust to American campus life and deal with issues such as homesickness, different customs, and any academic concerns or queries.

What do students wish they had known before they came to the United States? Your students can help prospective students by creating a brochure or Web page with useful information and helpful suggestions. The focus of their creation could be either academic and official (taking exams, getting visas) or practical (what to bring, what to expect).

Unit 3 CNN Video Report

Have students watch the Unit 3 video, *Vanishing Retirement*, after they have completed Chapter 8. While both the video and the reading in Chapter 8 deal with the issue of delayed retirement, each offers a unique perspective on the subject. Activate students' background knowledge before they view the video. Ask about the lives of older people they know, perhaps grandparents or other family members. Are they retired? If so, how do they manage financially? At what age did they retire? If the older people they know are still working, elicit why they are still in the workplace. Be sensitive to the possibility that some people might be reluctant to mention economic necessity.

Ask students why the Brenners are still working. Discuss how the financial market has contributed to their current situation.

After students have viewed the video a second time, ask them to focus on what Ted says: "And personally, you know, I've worked all my life. I don't want to do that." What does he mean by this comment? Perhaps students could compare the Brenners' feelings toward work to those of Professor Paul Weiss. Do they have anything in common?

After discussing the video, have students answer the Video Report questions on SB page 195.

| Unit 4 | Science and Technology |

Chapter 10   Antarctica: Whose Continent Is It Anyway?

Audio CD, Track 10

Before the first serious scientific study of Antarctica in 1957–58, the continent was considered to be a cold wasteland. Now, however, scientists know that Antarctica's ecosystem is vital to life on Earth for many reasons. International treaties have established that no country has control over Antarctica, and the Madrid Protocol states that its oil and mineral resources are protected until the year 2041. Different groups with conflicting interests may find it difficult to reach an agreement on the continent's future.

Suggestions for Prereading Activity

Before starting Chapter 10, brainstorm general facts about Antarctica with the class. To expand upon students' background knowledge, assign them to find five facts about Antarctica. After students have completed this activity, have pairs of students complete the chart on SB page 198. Then have students compare their charts with their classmates' charts. Encourage them to discuss the similarities and differences.

Culture Notes

Antarctica is a continent of superlatives: the coldest, the highest in average elevation (6,500 feet), the least inhabited, the iciest, the most isolated, the least land animals, the most recently explored—and the list goes on. Perhaps the class would like to make their own list of superlatives as they work through the chapter. Students' lists would make an interesting class display, and the creation of the lists would involve a review of grammar as well.

Medieval world maps sometimes showed a landmass in the Southern Hemisphere, but this was not based on actual knowledge or exploration. Years later, when Captain James Cook became the first to sail across the Antarctic Circle in 1771, he and his crew saw many icebergs. Although the ship didn't sail near Antarctica, Cook inferred that the icebergs must have come from a large body of land. A Russian expedition sailed closer to Antarctica in 1819, but still didn't actually see the continent. Many historians agree that this honor went to the British Navy officer Edward Bransfield in 1820. The first landing on Antarctica is often a matter of contention. An American captain by the name of John Davis claimed to have set foot on Antarctica in February, 1821. However, some historians argue that a Norwegian whaler was the first person to actually go ashore in 1895. That same year, participants in a Geographical Conference in London agreed that exploration of Antarctica was a high priority. Several scientific expeditions went to Antarctica during the next few years and some even wintered there.

Concepts for Today, Book 4, Teacher Notes

In the first years of the twentieth century, a number of explorers competed to be the first to the South Pole. Two well-known expeditions were led by British explorers Robert F. Scott and Ernest Shackleton. However, neither of these explorers reached the Pole on their first attempt. Both expeditions were troubled by shortages of food, bad weather, and illness among crew members. In addition to these perils, Shackleton's ship, *The Endurance,* became trapped in ice and was eventually crushed. His crew escaped by lifeboat and made their way to the South Shetland Islands. Desperate to find civilization, Shackleton and a few men finally made another voyage by lifeboat across the Antarctic Sea to South Georgia Island. Soon after, they returned to rescue the men who had remained on the South Shetland Islands. Their journey is one of the great adventure stories of all time.

In a later expedition, Robert Scott finally reached the South Pole in January, 1912, only to discover he was not the first. Norwegian Roald Amundsen had reached the Pole in December, 1911. Sadly, after all his efforts, Scott and his team of four died on the return voyage.

Despite the risks that Antarctica poses, people have continued to explore the continent, establishing research stations there by the 1940s. There are now more than 30 research stations on the continent. Antarctica's weather is so cold and extreme between the months of February and October that people in research stations there cannot be reached during this time. Ships cannot get through the ice pack and aeronautical fuel thickens and gels so that planes cannot fly. Twice in recent years American doctors working in Antarctic research stations have become seriously ill and have had to treat themselves until they could be evacuated when the weather permitted flying again. In both cases, computerized ultrasound scans were analyzed in the United States to diagnose the medical problems.

Suggestions for Follow-Up Activities

Students may be interested in finding out more about the explorers and expeditions mentioned above. They may also want to learn about the two doctors who developed illnesses when they were working in Antarctica, Dr. Jerri Neilsen and Dr. Ronald Shemenski. A basic Internet search for "Antarctica" on the Google search engine produces an enormous range of excellent resources. For more specific search words, refer students to the Internet and InfoTrac resources for this chapter.

The fifth Follow-Up suggestion on SB page 212 to write a journal article could also be completed from the perspective of a scientist working for a year in an Antarctic research station.

Chapter 11   **A Messenger from the Past**   **Audio CD, Track 11**

In 1991, hikers found the partially freeze-dried corpse of a Bronze Age man in Italy's Tyrolean Mountains near the Austrian border. Clothing, tools, and food found with the man provide insight into early Bronze Age societies that existed in Europe 4,000 years ago. Scientists are researching how they can thaw the body for testing purposes without destroying it.

Suggestions for Prereading Activity

The photograph on SB page 215 may not provide sufficient clues to activate background knowledge if your students have not heard about the discovery of the Ice Man. Therefore, also have students look at the graphics on SB page 217 and the time line on SB page 233. Elicit students' thoughts on what they think the reading will be about.

Draw attention to both the title and the name of the source, the magazine *Discover*. Does anyone in your class know this magazine? They may not, but perhaps they will make some inferences from television's Discovery Channel.

Culture Notes

The article from which the reading was taken was published shortly after the discovery of the Ice Man in 1991. At that time, scientists made several educated guesses about the time period the corpse was from, the culture he represented, and how he died high in the mountains. Several years elapsed before the debates about how to deal with the Ice Man were resolved so further investigation could proceed. Consequently, researchers have learned much more about the Ice Man. The exercises on SB pages 232 and 233 give students an opportunity to update information in the reading. More importantly, the exercises help students become aware that scientific knowledge is not static; it changes as new evidence is found and new forensic techniques are developed.

It is now known that the 45-year old Ice Man is from an earlier period in history than first thought. Radiocarbon dating shows that the corpse is from 5,300 years ago, not 4,000. Analysis of the man's stomach contents and particles of food near him indicate that the initial impression that he did not starve to death is correct: he ate a meal about eight hours before his death. Pollen analysis clearly proves that the meal included bread made from einkorn, a grain that is cultivated and not found growing in the wild. The significance of this find is that although the Ice Man is 5,300 years old, he lived in a Neolithic society where farmers deliberately planted and harvested domesticated grains. This information can be applied when students revise the table on SB page 233. Finding such early evidence of agriculture, together with the copper axe, indicates that the transition from the Middle Stone Age—when people made stone tools and collected wild plants—to the Neolithic period occurred much earlier than archaeologists thought before the discovery of the Ice Man.

The stomach analysis, the hunting tools, and accompanying animal bones all point to a diet that included meat, although scientists are still not sure what kind. However, the fact that the Ice Man was hunting animals may indicate that the man's society had not yet domesticated animals. Pollen analysis also shows that the Ice Man died in May or June and came from a warmer area to the south of where he died. Botanists say that the hop hornbeam pollen was detected, and this was from a tree that only blooms in those months. Lastly, life was not entirely comfortable for people living at this time. Scientists now know that the Ice Man had both fleas and whipworm. Moreover, chemical analysis of the Ice Man's hair shows unusually large amounts of arsenic. This may indicate that the Ice Man took part in the smelting process used to produce his copper axe.

The most startling evidence comes from DNA analysis and X-rays. Instead of a peaceful life in the mountains, the Ice Man experienced violence in the hours before he died. X-rays show that he died from an arrow wound in the back. The arrow is still in place. However, before he died, he was involved in a bloody fight with at least four other people. DNA analysis has discovered the DNA in blood from four separate individuals on the body of the Ice Man. Now, scientists are inclined to think that he was attacked while hunting in the mountains. He fought back and managed to escape his attackers with his tools, but died a few hours later. Scientists still think that it is possible that the injured man actually died from hypothermia (freezing to death).

Suggestions for Follow-Up Activities

While the Ice Man is a particularly well-preserved specimen from the past, he is not unique. In recent decades, frozen or mummified individuals have been found in several other parts of the world, most notably in the Peruvian Andes and Siberia. In 1998, the Public Broadcasting System's NOVA science documentary series presented a three-hour program, *Ice Mummies*, to compare several of these finds, including the Ice Man. See the Internet and InfoTrac resources for this chapter for more information. The NOVA Web site link provides some excellent classroom activities for this topic.

Chapter 12 **Is Time Travel Possible?** **Audio CD, Track 12**

A century ago, Albert Einstein stated in his famous Theory of Relativity that time is relative and that space is curved by gravity. Physicists have demonstrated that time slows down, or is stretched, with accelerated motion and closer proximity to the Earth's center of gravity. In principle, it ought to be possible to travel both forward and backward in time. In practice, no one has developed the technology to move at or beyond the speed of light.

Suggestions for Prereading Activity

Have the class look closely at the cartoon sequence on SB page 235. Can your students tell you who changes in the pictures? Can anyone explain what this means?

Ask if anyone in the class reads *USA Today*. How does this newspaper compare to other newspapers such as *The New York Times*? Which newspaper do they think is easier to read? Which one would be a better source for a research paper? Why?

Culture Notes

Time travel may seem like fantasy, but many scientists are interested in it as a real possibility. To gain a basic understanding of the concept, it is essential to realize that time is something relative, not fixed the way we usually think of it as being measured in minutes and hours. Time is also closely related to the concept of space or three-dimensionality. Some scientists put the two together when they refer to a single, interrelated "space-time continuum." This concept means that any event is affected by both time and space. Einstein's theory leads to the idea that time slows down with speed. The faster the speed, the more time slows until it is at the speed of light—186,282 miles a second—time would stand still. Based on this theory, many scientists believe that it may be possible to move matter fast enough that it is actually in the future compared to time on Earth. However, in order to travel to the past, it would be necessary for matter to move faster than the speed of light and many scientists are skeptical that this is possible.

How could such time travel happen? Two major ideas have been proposed. The first depends on technology to build a "time machine" in which enormous speeds could occur. The second idea would depend on some kind of natural shortcut that has not yet been discovered. When the astronomer and Pulitzer Prize winner Carl Sagan wrote a novel about time travel, he consulted with other scientists and theorized the device of a "wormhole" to move through black holes into space.

Even if time travel is possible, there are potential problems or paradoxes—two things that can't be true at the same time. For example, if you could travel back in time, you could go to a time before you even existed. A famous problem is the so-called grandparent paradox in which the time traveler kills a grandparent, which makes his or her own existence impossible. Some scientists interested in time travel speculate about "parallel universes," different versions of history that coexist with the versions we know. This is what the reading means when it talks about "alternative histories," using the assassination of Lincoln as an example.

Suggestions for Follow-Up Activities

Using the first Follow-Up suggestion on SB page 251, ask students to assume that parallel universes really do exist. Ask them to imagine it is possible that important past events turned out differently than we think they did. Ask students to work in pairs and discuss history-changing events. The pair should decide on one such event and write a short story in which the outcome was very different. For example, what if America had not won the War of Independence but remained a British colony?

If students are interested in learning more about time travel, refer them to the Internet and InfoTrac resources for this chapter.

Unit 4 CNN Video Report

Have students watch the Unit 4 video, *Antarctica's Future*, after they have completed Chapter 10, also on Antarctica. Before watching the video, ask students to use a K-W-L Chart to review what they learned from the reading and the activities in Chapter 10. After they have listed what they **K**now, have them think about the title of the video and write down what they **W**ant to learn from the video. After watching the clip, students should report what they **L**earned by filling in the third column. You may want to make several rows of topics such as environment, tourism, research, and mineral exploitation.

After viewing the video, ask students what Jacques Cousteau means when he says: "It is too risky to touch the Antarctic now." Discuss what happened after the Argentinean tanker accident. Did international treaties against oil and resource development have any effect on the environmental damage? What do your students think will happen to Antarctica in the future?

After discussing the video, have students answer the Video Report questions on SB page 257.

Concepts for Today
A N S W E R   K E Y

Chapter 1   The Paradox of Happiness

Prereading Preparation (p. 2)
1. a. Answers will vary, but *happy* can be defined as "cheerful, joyful, pleased." *Unhappy* can be defined as "sad, sorrowful, not satisfied."
2–5. Answers will vary.
6. A *paradox* can be defined as "a puzzling statement that states two opposing truths or an impossible state of affairs."

A. Fact-Finding Exercise (p. 5)
1. T   2. F. There is little relationship between the two.   3. F. Researchers have found that unhappiness is inherited.   4. T   5. F. It is possible to increase your happiness.   6. T

B. Reading Analysis (p. 6)
1. a. 1 b. 2 **2.** c **3.** unhappy **4.** a. 3 b. 1 c. 1 **5.** a. It is the capacity to enjoy life.   b. The sentence states that *happiness* is "defined as the capacity to enjoy life," and this definition is between dashes.   c. to emphasize how long some of the twins have been apart **6.** a **7.** a. going to a movie, talking with friends, playing cards   b. These activities follow a dash after the words *everyday pleasures* **8.** a. 2 b. 3

C. Word Forms (p. 8)
Part 1
1. a. appears b. appearance 2. a. avoids b. avoidance 3. a. existence b. exists
4. a. doesn't resemble / does not resemble b. resemblance 5. a. assistance b. don't assist / do not assist 6. a. performs b. performance
Part 2
1. a. indicates b. indication 2. a. participate b. participation 3. a. definition b. define 4. a. recognizes b. recognition 5. a. implies b. implication

D. Dictionary Skills (p. 10)
1. (2) acknowledgment   **2.** (5) intimate   **3.** (6) spend   **4.** (2) A person's natural qualities of mind and character

E. Information Organization (p. 12)
I.   What New Research Shows About Happiness and Unhappiness
    A. The tendency to feel unhappy may be in your genes
    B. We can create happiness for ourselves
    C. There is little relationship between happiness and unhappiness
II. Studies on the Role of Genetics in Happiness and Unhappiness
    A. University of Southern California
       1. subjects: 899 individuals (identical and fraternal twins, grandparents, parents, and young adult offspring)
       2. results: family members resembled each other more in their levels of unhappiness than in their levels of happiness
       3. conclusion: there is a genetic component to unhappiness

B. University of Minnesota
   1. subjects: twins, some raised together, some raised apart
   2. results:
      a. in terms of happiness, twins raised apart were less alike than twins raised together
      b. in terms of unhappiness, twins raised apart were similar
   3. conclusion: there is a genetic component to unhappiness
III. The Implications of the Studies on Happiness and Unhappiness
   A. Genes only predispose a person to unhappiness
   B. We can increase our happiness through our own actions
IV. Arizona State University Experiment on Happiness
   A. subjects: students as Arizona State University
   B. experiment:
      1. students were asked to list favorite activities
      2. half the students increased these activities, and half did not
   C. result: students who did more of the things they enjoyed were happier than the students who did not
   D. conclusion: the pleasure we get from life is largely ours to control

F. Information Organization Quiz and Summary (p. 13)

1. Researchers believe that there is little relationship between unhappiness and happiness, and that unhappiness is inherited but happiness is not.
2. Researchers at the University of Southern California studied 899 identical and fraternal twins, grandparents, parents, and young adult offspring with regard to happiness and unhappiness. They found that family members resembled each other more in their levels of unhappiness than in their levels of happiness.
3. Students at Arizona State University were asked to list favorite activities. Half the students did more of their favorite activities, and half did not. At the end of one month, the students who increased their favorite activities were happier than the students who didn't.
4. We can increase our happiness by doing more of the things that we enjoy and by taking control of our happiness.

Summary

According to the findings of many studies of twins and other family members, and of experiments on happiness and unhappiness, unhappiness seems to be inherited whereas happiness is not. Fortunately, it is possible to increase our own happiness by doing more of the activities we enjoy.

G. Critical Thinking Strategies (p. 15)

Answers will vary.

H. Follow-up Discussion and Writing Activities (p. 17)

Answers will vary.

I. Cloze Quiz (p. 19)

1. higher 2. level 3. emotions 4. researchers 5. relationship 6. recognition
7. unhappiness 8. close 9. happier 10. avoiding 11. miserable 12. less
13. advice 14. studies 15. genetic 16. run 17. found 18. appear 19. joy
20. largely

Chapter 2   Close to Home: Technological Advances Erode Barrier Between Work and Home

Prereading Preparation (p. 20)

1. Answers will vary but may suggest that the man is in a home office.
2. a. Answers will vary but may include cell phones, pagers, and laptop computers.
   b. Answers will vary but may include doctors, lawyers, and salespeople.
3–4. Answers will vary.

A. Fact-Finding Exercise (p. 24)

1. F. Cindy doesn't have to be at her office in order to answer the business phone.
2. F. It's no longer just business owners or professionals who need to be accessible; even

the average employee finds it difficult to get away from work sometimes. 3. T 4. T
5. F. Sixty million people bring their cell phones to work each day. *OR* Some children even fax homework and report cards to Mom or Dad to check at the office. 6. T 7. T

B. Reading Analysis (p. 25)
1. b **2.** a **3.** a. 2 b. You can't ever get away from the phone. **4.** a. 3 b. 3 **5.** a
6. b **7.** a. 2 b. Employees may eat, socialize, and even work out at the company. Parents may instant-message their children or connect with latch-key kids via telephone or personal cell phone. **8.** a. 2 b. 1 c. 3 **9.** a. 1 b. 1. Parents who instant-message their children to come down to dinner rather than shouting upstairs 2. Parents who read bedtime books to children over the telephone while on a business trip **10.** b
11. a. 1 b. 2

C. Word Forms (p. 28)
Part 1
1. a. expanded b. expansion 2. a. proliferated b. proliferation 3. a. depicted
b. depiction 4. a. Protection b. protected 5. a. didn't predict / did not predict
b. prediction
Part 2
1. a. inconvenienced (v.) b. inconvenience (n.) 2. a. feared (v.) b. fears (n.)
3. a. conducts (v.) b. conduct (n.) 4. a. changes (n.) b. haven't changed / have not changed (v.) 5. a. conflicts (n.) b. conflicted (v.)

D. Dictionary Skills (p. 30)
1. (1) able to be reached 2. (1) border 3. (1) praised 4. (2) break into

E. Information Organization (p. 32)
Problem: People are having a hard time getting away from work because of modern technology.
Examples of High-Tech Gadgets: Cell phones, pagers, two-way radios, and all-in-one radio and telephone sets
Effects: Cindy: It provides flexibility. She doesn't have to be at the office to answer the phone. She can never get away from the phone. It brings the business home.
Effects: Maggie Jackson: Mobile technology is turning homes into workplaces. Domestic life has moved from the home and neighborhood into the workplace. There is a lack of refuge in the home and a loss of private life. Loneliness and the distance of virtual relationships are drawbacks.
Possible Solutions: Companies should make efforts to protect the privacy of employees and limit the on-call time of employees.

F. Information Organization Quiz and Summary (p. 33)
1. High-tech gadgets make it difficult for people to get away from work.
2. High-tech gadgets include cell phones, computers, two-way radios, and all-in-one radio and telephone sets.
3. This technology allows for flexibility, access, and efficiency. The worker doesn't have to be at the office to answer the phone.
4. This technology can be inconvenient and cause interruption of family life and personal time. The lines between work and home are less defined. There is a lack of refuge in the home and a loss of private life.
5. Employers can make efforts to protect the privacy and limit the on-call time of employees.

Summary
In recent years, the boundaries between work and home have been blurred as a result of modern technology. Due to the proliferation of high-tech devices, the home is being turned into the workplace. These high-tech devices include cell phones, pagers, computers, and two-way radios. While this technology provides for flexibility and accessibility, it also creates a loss in privacy and a lack of refuge in the home. One solution to the problem created by modern technology is for companies to protect the privacy and limit the on-call time of the employees.

G. Critical Thinking Strategies (p. 35)
Answers will vary.

H. Follow-up Discussion and Writing Activities (p. 36)
Answers will vary.

I. Cloze Quiz (p. 37)
1. Take 2. conduct 3. conflict 4. affects 5. devices 6. access 7. interruption
8. phenomenon 9. technology 10. boundaries 11. unstoppable 12. employees
13. vacation 14. addition 15. workplace 16. connect 17. homework 18. advocates
19. companies 20. protect

Chapter 3   The Birth-Order Myth

Prereading Preparation (p. 39)
1–3. Answers will vary.

A. Fact-Finding Exercise (p. 42)
1. F. The firstborn child in the family is not different from the other children.   2. F.
Studies will probably find that birth order does not affect personality. 3. T 4. F.
Growing up in a small family does not have disadvantages. OR Growing up in a small
family has advantages. 5. T 6. T

B. Reading Analysis (p. 43)
1. a. 1 b. 2 **2.** b **3.** c **4.** a. 1 b. 3 c. 2 **5.** a. 1 b. 2 **6.** consider, think about
7. a. for emphasis b. 3 c. 2 d. At the end of the sentence, the comma and the phrase
for instance indicate that these are examples. **8.** a. the Scholastic Aptitude Test
b. There is a number after SAT that indicates more information is at the bottom of the
page. c. 2 d. 3 e. for emphasis **9.** a **10.** b **11.** c

C. Word Forms (p. 46)
Part 1
1. a. will encourage b. encouragement 2. a. achievements b. will not achieve
3. a. improvements b. will improve 4. a. stated b. statement 5. a. treat
b. treatments
Part 2
1. a. competent b. competence 2. a. intelligence b. intelligent 3. a. permanent
b. permanence 4. a. significant b. significance 5. a. difference b. different

D. Dictionary Skills (p. 48)
1. (1) fundamental 2. (2) say it is a fact 3. (3) sets; determines; decides 4. (2) help
the progress of

E. Information Organization (p. 49)
I.   The Myth and the Reality About Birth Order
    A. The Myth: birth order strongly affects personality, intelligence, and achievement
    B. The Reality: this myth is not true
II. The Findings of Studies on Birth Order and Personality and Intelligence
    A. The findings of Cecile Ernst and Jules Angst
        1. Birth-order differences in personality are nonexistent
        2. There is no evidence for a firstborn personality
    B. The findings of Judith Blake
        1. Birth order does not affect intelligence; she looked at birth patterns before 1938
           and compared them to SAT scores for that group of children, and she found no
           connection
III. Other Factors Affecting Personality and Intelligence
    A. Number of siblings
        1. It does affect intelligence; small families tend to be more supportive of the kind
           of verbal ability that helps people succeed in school

   B. Parents' expectations
     1. Parents who believe that firstborns are more capable or deserving may treat them differently, thus setting up a self-fulfilling prophecy
   C. Spacing between siblings
     1. Some psychologists believe there are more advantages to having kids far apart
     2. One study found that a firstborn was more likely to have high self-esteem if his or her sibling was less than two years younger
IV. Conflicting Research Regarding Family Size and Personality
   A. You're more likely to be outgoing, well adjusted, and independent if you grew up with few or no siblings
   B. Two studies found no differences on the basis of family size alone
   C. One study indicated that spacing had no effect on social competence

F. Information Organization Quiz and Summary (p. 50)

1. a. They believe that birth order affects personality, intelligence, and achievement.
   b. Birth order does not seem to affect personality, intelligence, or achievement.
2. Birth order differences in personality and intelligence do not seem to exist; there is no evidence for a firstborn personality.
3. a. Number of siblings: It seems that having few or no siblings has a positive effect on personality and intelligence.
   b. Parents' expectations: They may treat firstborns differently, setting up a self-fulfilling prophecy.
   c. Spacing between siblings: There are emotional advantages for children if they are spaced far apart.
4. The results of research about family size and birth were very different.

Summary

Hundreds of studies have been done on the effects of birth order on personality, intelligence, and achievement. Because many of the studies came up with conflicting results, it seems that the effect of birth order on these factors is a myth.

G. Critical Thinking Strategies (p. 52)

Answers will vary.

H. Follow-up Discussion and Writing Activities (p. 54)

Answers will vary.

I. Cloze Quiz (p. 56)

1. affects 2. intelligence 3. However 4. research 5. different 6. discredited
7. effects 8. personality 9. influences 10. permanent 11. birth 12. theory
13. time 14. assumption 15. studies 16. predictor 17. scientists 18. concluded
19. differences 20. evidence

Unit 1 Review

J. Crossword Puzzle (p. 57)

Across Answers

1. yes 7. offspring 10. have 13. evidence 15. assumption 16. squelch 17. emotions
18. that 20. devices 22. support

Down Answers

2. employee 3. was 4. largely 5. ran 6. commend 8. proliferation 9. drawback
11. rivalry 12. environment 14. resemble 19. hit 21. up

K. Unit 1 Discussion (p. 59)

Answers will vary.

CNN Video Report: Hot Spots and Wireless Technology (p. 60)

1. Answers will vary, but should state that it enables you to access information from wherever you are.
2. a. A *hot spot* is a place with an antenna enabling high-speed, wireless Internet access. Users need a receiver and a wireless card for their computers.

b. Answers will vary.

c. She can be outside and go to Starbucks. It is less depressing and lonely. There are very few disadvantages in her opinion.

d. Answers will vary.

e. Answers will vary.

3. Answers will vary.

Chapter 4   Why So Many More Americans Die in Fires

Prereading Preparation (p. 62)
1. Answers will vary, but may include accidents with matches, candles, or lit cigarettes.
2. Answers will vary, but may include being careful around fire and installing smoke alarms.
3–7. Answers will vary.

A. Fact-Finding Exercise (p. 65)
1. T 2. T 3. F. Children start very few of the fires that occur in the United States. *OR* Adults start most of the fires that occur in the United States. 4. T 5. T 6. F. Most homes in the United States have smoke detectors. 7. F. The high fire death rate in the United States is not the result of bad technology. *OR* The high fire death rate in the United States is the result of careless attitudes.

B. Reading Analysis (p. 66)
1. c **2.** a. a city b. a state **3.** b **4.** a **5.** a. It is very necessary. b. 2 **6.** This is not the attitude in other countries. **7.** a. 3 b. 2 c. **8.** b **9.** a. 2 b. 3 **10.** a. 1 b. 3 c. 3 **11.** a. 2 b. 3 c. 1

C. Word Forms (p. 69)
Part 1
1. a. important b. importance 2. a. negligence b. negligent 3. a. dependence b. dependent 4. a. indifference b. indifferent 5. a. excellent b. excellence
Part 2
1. a. fatal b. fatalities 2. a. public b. publicity 3. a. safe b. safety
4. a. responsibilities b. responsible 5. a. possible b. possibilities

D. Dictionary Skills (p. 71)
1. (1) carelessness 2. (1) make speeches to 3. (3) officials (Def. 4 is also acceptable.)
4. (3) influence; forces

E. Information Organization (p. 72)
People's attitude toward fires:
The United States
1. People are indifferent; they believe that fires are not really anyone's fault.
Europe
1. Public education and the law treat fires as either a personal failing or a crime.
Asia
1. Public education and the law treat fires as either a personal failing or a crime.

How countries deal with fires:
The United States
1. American fire departments are fast and well equipped.
2. The United States spends more money fighting fires than preventing them.
Europe
1. In the Netherlands, every room must have two fire exits.
2. In France, insurers cannot repay the full cost of damage.
3. In Switzerland, insurers pay only if an identical structure is built.

Asia

In Japan:

1. Penalties include life imprisonment.
2. Neighbors may ask you to move away.
3. Officials at fires embarrass the people responsible for the fire.

Public education:

The United States

1. Fire-safety lessons are aimed at children, who start very few fires.

Europe

1. In England, the London Fire Brigade spends $1 million a year on fire-safety commercials.

Asia

1. Korea holds neighborhood fire drills.
2. Hong Kong apartment buildings have fire marshals.
3. The Japanese learn to use fire extinguishers at work.

Technology for fire prevention:

The United States

1. There are smoke detectors in 85% of all homes.
2. Some building codes require sprinklers.
3. New heaters and irons shut themselves off.
4. New stoves will turn themselves off.

How attitudes towards fire are changing:

The United States

1. Some towns fine people if they have serious fires because they let smoke detectors go dead.
2. A landlord was charged with manslaughter because his building burned and people died as a result.

F. Information Organization Quiz and Summary (p. 73)

1. In the United States, people believe that fires aren't anyone's fault, but in other countries, fires are treated as a personal failing or a crime.
2. The United States does not rely on people. Instead, it relies on technology, for example, sprinkler systems and equipment that shuts itself off automatically.
3. It is different because in the United States, fire safety is aimed at children, but in Asia and Europe, it is aimed at adults.
4. Some towns are fining people who have serious fires because they let smoke detectors go dead. Additionally, a landlord was charged with manslaughter when tenants were killed.

Summary

In the United States, people believe that fires aren't anyone's fault, and rely on technology for fire prevention. In Europe and Asia, however, people treat fires as a crime. They educate adults in fire prevention and have strict laws.

G. Critical Thinking Strategies (p. 75)

Answer will vary.

H. Follow-up Discussion and Writing Activities (p. 76)

Answers will vary.

I. Cloze Quiz (p. 79)

1. ways 2. progress 3. destroy 4. kill 5. successes 6. worst 7. rates 8. experts
9. neither 10. technology 11. country 12. just 13. enough 14. preventing
15. fighting 16. lessons 17. entirely 18. fatal 19. attitude 20. fault

Chapter 5   Acupuncture: The New Old Medicine

Prereading Preparation (p. 80)

1. *Acupuncture* is a practice from Chinese medicine that treats diseases and pain by putting needles into the body.
2. Answers will vary, but may include these reasons: to stop smoking, to lose weight, to relieve aches and pains.
3–5. Answers will vary.

A. Fact-Finding Exercise (p. 83)

1. F. Dr. Gong is an acupuncturist. 2. T 3. F. Dr. Gong's office is on Mott Street.
4. F. Dr. Gong knows how to speak English. 5. T 6. F. Jack Tymann continues to visit an acupuncturist even though his back doesn't hurt anymore. *OR* He continues to visit an acupuncturist to prevent his back from hurting. 7. T

B. Reading Analysis (p. 84)

1. slipped into **2.** b **3.** c **4.** orthopedist **5.** a **6.** care; therapy; cure **7.** b **8.** a
9. a. 3 b. 1 c. 3 **10.** a. a life force b. the use of the word *called* **11.** b **12.** a. 3
b. 1 **13.** b **14.** c

C. Word Forms (p. 87)

Part 1

1. a. didn't explain / did not explain b. explanation 2. a. recommended
b. recommendations 3. a. stimulation b. stimulate 4. a. concluded b. conclusion
5. a. haven't decided / have not decided b. decisions

Part 2

1. a. extreme b. extremely 2. a. strangely b. strange 3. a. involuntary
b. involuntarily 4. a. adequate b. adequately 5. a. usually b. usual

D. Dictionary Skills (p. 89)

1. (3) arrived at the opinion 2. (2) hurried 3. (1) is unsuccessful 4. (2) a sudden

E. Information Organization (p. 90)

I.   The Author's Thoughts About His First Acupuncture Experience
   A. How the treatment felt
   1. no discomfort or pain
   2. a mild warming sensation
   B. Why he had come to Dr. Gong's office
     1. the pain in his left elbow
     2. no luck with Fifth Avenue neurologist or tests
II. A Description of Today's Acupuncturists
   A. as likely to be on Park Avenue as on Mott Street
   B. as likely to be Caucasian as Asian
   C. most are certified; many are M.D.s or dentists
III. A Description of Acupuncture
   A. Body has more than 800 acupuncture points
   B. A life force called qi (pronounced CHEE) circulates through the body
   C. Points on the skin are connected to specific organs
   D. Acupuncture points are stimulated to balance the circulation
   E. Acupuncture is at least 2,200 years old, but nobody really knows how it works
IV. Who Gets Acupuncture Treatments
   A. number of people: millions of Americans
   B. examples of people who have acupuncture treatments:
     1. Jack Tymann, for lower back pain
     2. Harwood Beville, for his shoulder
V.   Uses of Acupuncture
   A. to relieve anxiety, depression, back pain, smoking, high blood pressure, stress
   B. to cure drug addiction
VI. Effectiveness of Acupuncture
   A. effective in four to six weeks

F. Information Organization Quiz and Summary (p. 92)

1. He hadn't been cured, or even diagnosed, by the Fifth Avenue neurologist.
2. Acupuncture is a traditional form of medicine. A life force called *qi* circulates throughout the body. There are about 800 acupuncture points on the skin, which are connected to specific organs; these points are stimulated to balance the circulation of the life force, qi.
3. a. He had lower back pain. His treatment was successful.
   b. He had tennis shoulder. His treatment was successful.

4. Acupuncture is used to treat anxiety, depression, back pain, smoking, high blood pressure, stress, arthritis, and drug addiction.
5. Treatments usually take about four to six weeks.

Summary
Acupuncture is a traditional Asian form of medicine that has become popular in the United States. Many people, including M.D.s and dentists, have become certified acupuncturists, and many sufferers have turned to acupuncture because conventional medicine has not produced effective cures for them.

G. Critical Thinking Strategies (p. 94)
Answers will vary.

H. Follow-up Discussion and Writing Activities (p. 96)
Answers will vary.

I. Cloze Quiz (p. 103)
1. services 2. conventional 3. cure 4. typical 5. bothered 6. suggested 7. instead
8. education 9. skeptical 10. symptom 11. since 12. treatments 13. preventive
14. primary 15. president 16. acupuncture 17. visits 18. doctors 19. success
20. pain

Chapter 6   Highs and Lows in Self-Esteem

Prereading Preparation (p. 104)
1–3. Answers will vary.

A. Fact-Finding Exercise (p. 107)
1. T 2. F. A person's self-esteem plunges during adolescence. 3. F. Some people experience their lowest self-esteem during old age. 4. F. The people in the study were mostly Caucasian. 5. T 6. F. Our self-esteem is most delicate when we are adolescents.
7. F. Older people's self-esteem tends to drop when they get into their 70s, but not always.

B. Reading Analysis (p. 108)
1. c **2.** b **3.** drop **4.** b **5.** a **6.** b **7.** a. 1 b. 2 **8.** a. 1 b. 2 **9.** a **10.** a
11. b **12.** a. 1 b. 2 **13.** rise **14.** c **15.** a

C. Word Forms (p. 111)
Part 1
1. a. contributes b. contributions 2. a. will not participate / won't participate
b. participation 3. a. accumulation b. has accumulated / accumulates 4. a. never realized / did not realize / didn't realize b. realization 5. a. suggested b. suggestion
Part 2
1. a. dropped (v.) b. drop (n.) 2. a. gained (v.) b. gains (n.) 3. a. plunge (n.)
b. have plunged (v.) 4. a. survey (n.) b. did not survey / didn't survey (v.)
5. a. range (n.) b. range (v.)

D. Dictionary Skills
1. (2) effect; impression 2. (3) swollen; pumped-up 3. (2) system of measurement
4. (2) likely to be hurt

E. Information Organization (p. 115)
Age: Childhood (Up)
Reasons: Feelings about themselves are often based on relatively superficial information
High childhood confidence
Inflated sense of self-approval

Age: Adolescence (Down)
Reasons: Loss of childhood omnipotence
Society's emphasis on body image for girls

Age: Adult (Up)
Reasons: Gain a sense of competence and continuity
Development of ability to cope with change

Age: Senior (Down)
Reasons: Retirement
Loss of loved ones, health, financial status, or sense of competence

F. Information Organization Quiz and Summary (p. 116)
1. a. Childhood: Self-esteem rises
   b. Adolescence: Self-esteem plummets
   c. Adult: Self-esteem rises
   d. Senior: Self-esteem tends to drop
2. a. Children experience an inflated sense of self-approval based on relatively superficial information.
   b. Self-esteem of adolescents plummets due to loss of childhood omnipotence, changes in hormones, and self-doubt. Also, society's emphasis on body image for girls causes self-esteem to drop.
   c. Self-esteem rises as one gains a sense of competence and continuity in adulthood. Also, adults' self-esteem increases with development of ability to cope with change.
   d. Self-esteem of seniors tends to experience a drop in the 70s due to retirement and loss of loved ones, health, financial status, and/or sense of competence.

Summary
Throughout a person's lifetime, it is most likely that his or her self-esteem will follow a course similar to a roller coaster, filled with ups and downs. Beginning with childhood, people experience an inflated sense of self-approval based on relatively superficial information. With changes in hormones and an increased sense of self-doubt, adolescents experience a plunge in their level of self-esteem. As people grow into adulthood, they tend to gain a sense of competence and continuity, along with the ability to deal with change, which enable the self-esteem to rise. In their 70s, seniors tend to experience a drop in self-esteem due to retirement, a decrease in capabilities, or the loss of loved ones.

G. Critical Thinking Strategies (p. 117)
Answers will vary.

H. Follow-up Discussion and Writing Activities (p. 119)
Answers will vary.

I. Cloze Quiz (p. 121)
1. likens 2. inflated 3. plunges 4. edging 5. launched 6. adulthood
7. adolescence 8. disagrees 9. self-esteem 10. spearheaded 11. accumulation
12. transition 13. survey 14. social 15. passage 16. fare 17. dropped 18. blossom
19. bottomed out 20. upswing

Unit 2 Review

Crossword Puzzle (p. 124)
Across Answers
1. ailment 6. handful 7. conclude 9. read 12. wrong 13. adequate 15. arson
18. himself 19. liken 20. theirs 21. novel
Down Answers
1. address 2. transition 3. rode 4. fatalities 5. plummet 8. adolescence
10. launch 11. fail 14. useless 16. son 17. went

K. Unit 2 Discussion (p. 126)
Answers will vary.

CNN Video Report: Holiday House Fires (p. 127)
1. There are more fires in December because of the use of lights for holiday decoration. The fires are caused by negligence.

2. 1. c
2. e
3. a
4. b
5. d
3. They can blow out candles before leaving a room. They can turn off lights before leaving the house or going to bed. They can keep candle wicks trimmed to ¼ inch. Answers to second half of question will vary.

Unit 3   Government and Education

Chapter 7   The Federal System of Government

Prereading Preparation (p. 130)
1. The people of the United States fought Britain for independence in the Revolutionary War.
2. a. The first Europeans to become Americans were English.
   b. They came in search of religious freedom.
3. a. The United States is a democracy.
   b. Answers will vary.
4. A *constitution* is defined as "the principles and rules, set forth in a written document, governing a country." Answers will vary, but may suggest that governments have constitutions to describe their laws and beliefs.
5. Answers will vary.

A. Fact-Finding Exercise (p. 134)
1. F. The United States became independent in 1776.   2. T   3. T   4. F. The U.S. Constitution described three branches of the government: the legislative, the judicial, and the executive.   5. T   6. F. A bill can still become a law if the Congress passes it again by a two-thirds majority vote.

B. Reading Analysis (p. 136)
1. a   **2.** a. independence from British domination   b. the Continental Congress
3. a. 2   b. 1   c. 1   **4.** c   **5.** a. 3   b. 1   c. 2   d. 3   **6.** b   **7.** It was not given control to pass tax laws, to have the sole authority to coin money for use by the states, or to regulate trade between the states.   **8.** a. 2   b. The system of government under the Articles of Confederation was not working out.   **9.** c   **10.** a. 3   b. 1   c. the checks and balances system   **11.** b   **12.** a. A *bill* is what a law is called before it is signed by the president.   b. There is a reference to the line at the bottom of the page that gives the definition of a bill.   c. footnote   **13.** a. to refuse to sign into law   b. 3   c. 1   **14.** a. He was the principal writer of the Declaration of Independence and the third president of the United States.   b. in a footnote at the bottom of the page

C. Word Forms (p. 140)
Part 1
1. a. will establish   b. establishment   2. a. didn't agree / did not agree   b. agreement
3. a. replacement   b. replaced   4. a. didn't pay / did not pay   b. payment
5. a. enforcement   b. don't enforce / do not enforce
Part 2
1. a. reluctant   b. reluctance   2. a. vigilant   b. vigilance   3. a. resistant
b. resistance   4. a. distance   b. distant

D. Dictionary Skills (p. 142)
1. (4) principle   2. (2) legislative bodies   3. (2b) nullify   4. (3) restraint; limit

4 • ANSWER KEY

E. Information Organization (p. 144)

I. The Origin of the Federal System of Government
   A. In 1775, the war against the British began; there was no central American government established by law
   B. The Continental Congress existed, but had no legal power
   C. Legal governments in the states were established to replace colonial rule
   D. In 1781 the Articles of Confederation were adopted, but the government had very restricted authority

II. The Constitution of the United States
   A. Its purpose: to insure freedom for the citizens of the United States for all time
   B. The feelings of the writers of the Constitution:
      1. They did not want a king
      2. They did not want a strong central government
      3. They wanted to keep the states as they were
      4. They wanted a government that would make laws, carry out those laws, and provide justice under the law

III. The "Checks and Balances" System of the Constitution
   A. The purpose of this system: to guard the rights and interests of the people by establishing three major branches of government
      1. The legislature branch, or Congress: makes laws
      2. The executive branch: carries out laws
      3. The judiciary branch: watches over the rights of the people
   B. The powers not given to the government belong to the states
   C. The powers of each branch are checked and balanced by the powers of the other two branches

IV. How Laws Are Made
   A. The legislature, or Congress, drafts a law
   B. The bill is passed by the Senate and the House of Representatives
   C. The chief executive, the president, either approves the bill or vetoes it
      1. If the president approves the bill, it becomes a law
      2. If the president vetoes the bill, Congress can pass it anyway by a two-thirds majority vote
   D. If someone challenges the law, the judicial branch determines whether the law is constitutional or not

F. Information Organization Quiz and Summary (p. 145)

1. a. It had a confederation of states.
   b. No, it wasn't successful. The Congress had little power and no money, and couldn't borrow money.
2. They didn't want a king, they didn't want a central government that was too strong, and they didn't want the states to lose their individuality and freedom.
3. a. Its purpose is to prevent any one person or group from becoming too powerful and using that power for personal profit rather than for the people.
   b. The system works by making each part of the government dependent on the other two parts in order to function.
4. Laws are made by being drafted in Congress as bills. A bill must be passed by both houses of Congress. Then a copy is sent to the president for his approval. If he signs it, it becomes a law. If he refuses to sign it, it goes back to Congress. If the bill is passed again by a two-thirds majority vote, the bill becomes a law regardless of the president's vote.

Summary

The United States became independent in the eighteenth century after a revolution against British domination. After the first democratic form of government—a confederation—was unsuccessful, people drafted a new form of government based on a system of checks and balances. This system, which was intended to protect the rights of the people, is the system still in use in the United States today.

G. Critical Thinking Strategies (p. 147)

Answers will vary.

H. Follow-up Discussion and Writing Activities (p. 149)
Answers will vary.

I. Cloze Quiz (p. 155)
1. easy 2. men 3. pioneers 4. democratic 5. really 6. king 7. too 8. afraid
9. freedoms 10. states 11. dilemma 12. hand 13. strong 14. undesirable
15. endanger 16. other 17. government 18. solution 19. found 20. Constitution

Chapter 8 Too Soon Old, Too Late Wise

Prereading Preparation (p. 156)
1–5. Answers will vary.

A. Fact-Finding Exercise (p. 159)
1. T 2. T 3. F. Prof. Paul Weiss wants to continue teaching. 4. F. Prof. Weiss wants to go to court to settle his problem with the university. 5. F. Prof. Weiss was a faculty member at Yale College. 6. T

B. Reading Analysis (p. 160)
1. c **2.** c **3.** a **4.** b **5.** c **6.** the Equal Employment Opportunity Commission **7.** a
8. b **9.** a. They are well-known philosophers who worked until they were quite old.
b. The previous sentence refers to philosophers getting wiser as they get older. It is logical that the next sentence gives examples of such people. **10.** a **11.** c **12.** b **13.** a. 2
b. students who came to Alfred Whitehead's rooms at Harvard **14.** a. the administrators at Catholic University b. for emphasis **15.** a. 2 b. a poor memory

C. Word Forms (p. 163)
Part 1
1. a. equal b. equality 2. a. infirmity b. infirm 3. a. publicity b. public
4. a. senility b. senile 5. a. anxiety b. anxious
Part 2
1. a. defied b. defiance 2. a. don't disturb / do not disturb b. disturbance
3. a. insistence b. insist 4. a. didn't refer / did not refer b. references
5. a. insurance b. will insure / insures

D. Dictionary Skills (p. 165)
1. (3) extremely unpleasant 2. (3) stated emphatically 3. (4a) lawsuit; action in law (legal action) 4. (3) not thinking clearly; not expressing his thoughts clearly

E. Information Organization (p. 166)
Professor Paul Weiss: 90 years old; world-class philosopher; emeritus professor; author of many books
Event: Catholic University allowed Professor Weiss to teach in his apartment after he'd had an operation.
Catholic University's Position: This permission was unprecedented.
Professor Weiss's Position: It is not unprecedented.
Examples: (1) Wittgenstein had students come to his rooms at Cambridge; (2) Alfred North Whitehead had students come to his rooms at Harvard.
Event: Catholic University demoted him to teaching graduate students part-time.
University's Position: The university had "shifting priorities."
Professor Weiss's Position: He wants his job back and is willing to go to court.
EEOC decision: The university discriminated against Prof. Weiss because of his age.

F. Information Organization Quiz and Summary (p. 167)
1. Prof. Weiss is 90 years old; he is a philosopher, author, and professor of philosophy.
2. a. Catholic University permitted him to teach in his apartment.
   b. The university said this permission was unprecedented.
   c. He said that this permission was not unprecedented and gave two examples.
3. a. The university demoted Prof. Weiss to teaching graduate students part-time.
   b. The university said it demoted him because of "shifting priorities."

c. Prof. Weiss wants his job back, and he is willing to go to court.

4. The EEOC said that the university must reach a settlement with Prof. Weiss within a year, or the EEOC will sue for age discrimination.

Summary

At Catholic University, Professor Weiss, a philosopher, was demoted from his full-time teaching position because he is 90 years old. The Equal Employment Opportunity Commission has intervened; Catholic University must reach a settlement with Prof. Weiss within a year or face a lawsuit. Prof. Weiss does not want to stop teaching.

G. Critical Thinking Strategies (p. 168)

Answers will vary.

H. Follow-up Discussion and Writing Activities (p. 169)

Answers will vary.

I. Cloze Quiz (p. 170)

1. pilots 2. age 3. infirmity 4. profession 5. supposed 6. worked 7. until
8. determined 9. even 10. wait 11. insists 12. care 13. allowed 14. after
15. operation 16. Such 17. unprecedented 18. students 19. modest 20. compares

Chapter 9   The Pursuit of Excellence

Prereading Preparation (p. 171)

1. Answers will vary.
2. Answers will vary but may include passing the TOEFL. For an American student to attend college, usually a high school diploma or GED certificate is required. Many students have the opportunity to go to college.

3–5. Answers will vary.

A. Fact-Finding Exercise (p. 175)

1. F. Asia has the largest number of students studying in the United States. 2. T 3. F. They attend for educational reasons as well as for other reasons. 4. T 5. F. It is very likely that students will be in direct contact with their teachers. 6. T

B. Reading Analysis (p. 176)

1. b **2.** c **3.** a **4.** privileged **5.** a. 3 b. 1 **6.** a. high school exams b The sentences that follow explain that they are foreign high school exams. **7.** a. 1 b. 3
8. a. 1 b. 2 **9.** b **10.** c **11.** a. 2 b. 3 c. 1 d. 2 **12.** a. options, menu b. 2
13. a. 3 b. 2 **14.** b **15.** b

C. Word Forms (p. 180)

Part 1

1. a. individual b. individuality 2. a. creativity b. creative 3. a. diversity
b. diverse 4. a. national b. nationalities 5. a. flexibility b. flexible

Part 2

1. a. independence b. independent 2. a. difference b. different 3. a. dominant
b. dominance 4. a. excellence b. excellent 5. a. importance b. important

D. Dictionary Skills (p. 182)

1. (2) approximately 2. (3b) compare favorably with 3. (1b) customary action
4. (1) show clearly

E. Information Organization (p. 183)

Percent of high school graduates who attend college:

The United States: 60%

Japan: 37%

Europe: Germany—30%; France—28%; Britain—20%

Differences between universities:

The United States

1. People can go back to college.
2. Students can move from department to department and from school to school.

3. The community is part of a student's life.
Japan
1. It is very difficult to transfer credits from one school to another.
Europe
1. In France, students are expected at age 16 to select both a university and a specific course of study.
Differences in types of colleges:
The United States
1. There are research universities, state institutions, private liberal-arts schools, community colleges, religious institutions, and military academies
Europe
1. There is one system.
Funding for education:
The United States
1. Students pay for their education.
Japan
1. Education is government funded.
Europe
1. Education is mostly state funded.

F. Information Organization Quiz and Summary (p. 184)

1. a. 60% of U.S. high school graduates enter college.
   b. 30% of German, 28% of French, 20% of British, and 37% of Japanese graduates enter college.
2. American colleges offer education to rich and poor families, to people of any age; students can move from department to department and from school to school; students are involved in community life. In France, students are expected to select a university and a specific course of study at 16; Japanese students usually cannot transfer credits from one school to another; the United States has different types of schools; in Europe, there is only one system.
3. In the United States, students pay their own tuition; the colleges compete for students, faculty, and research grants. This competition stimulates creativity. Most foreign universities have state funding; they have less opportunity to develop distinctive personalities and define their own missions.

Summary

Although many American professors and administrators feel that there are serious problems with American universities, thousands of foreign students come to the United States to study. The American university system offers them many opportunities and advantages that they do not get in their own or other countries.

G. Critical Thinking Strategies (p. 185)

Answers will vary.

H. Follow-up Discussion and Writing Activities (p. 187)

Answers will vary.

I. Cloze Quiz (p. 190)

1. provide 2. colleges 3. envy 4. troubles 5. flooded 6. countries 7. students
8. followed 9. foreigners 10. undergraduate 11. equal 12. flexibility 13. expected
14. practice 15. impossible 16. initially 17. attracted 18. community 19. emphasis
20. campuses

Unit 3 Review

J. Crossword Puzzle (p. 192)

Across Answers
3. call 5. majority 9. demonstrate 11. can 13. demoted 14. all 15. legislative
18. priorities 19. public 20. did 22. democracy 23. optional
Down Answers
1. balances 2. dilemma 4. last 6. unprecedented 7. vague 8. excellence 10. end
12. no 16. practice 17. vigilant 21. have

K. Unit 3 Discussion (p. 194)

Answers will vary.

CNN Video Report: Vanishing Retirement (p. 195)

1. Answers will vary. 2. a. T b F c. F d. T e. T 3. A nest egg is a good investment or retirement plan. Answers to the other parts of this question will vary.

Unit 4 — Science and Technology

Chapter 10 — Antarctica: Whose Continent Is It Anyway?

Prereading Preparation (p. 198)

1. Antarctica is the continent that covers the South Pole.
2–4. Answers will vary.

A. Fact-Finding Exercise (p. 201)

1. F. Most scientists agree that Antarctica should be used for research. 2. T 3. F. Most of Antarctica is covered by ice. 4. F. Antarctica is a useful continent. 5. T 6. T 7. F. Most tourists feel that Antarctica should be dedicated to scientific research and to tourism. 8. F. The Madrid Protocol prohibits countries from exploring Antarctica for natural resources.

B. Reading Analysis (p. 203)

1. a cruise ship **2.** the authors' **3.** b **4.** a. 3 b. the chance to visit the most remote and unusual place on Earth **5.** c **6.** Antarctica **7.** d **8.** a **9.** b **10.** International Geophysical Year **11.** a. 1 b. 2 **12.** c **13.** a **14.** a **15.** areas **16.** when the treaty was negotiated and went through **17.** nations that haven't agreed to the treaty **18.** a. 2 b. 3 **19.** c

C. Word Forms (p. 206)

Part 1
1. a. employment b. didn't employ / did not employ 2. a. established
b. establishment 3. a. government b. will govern 4. a. will manage
b. management 5. a. equips b. equipment

Part 2
1. a. reflection b. reflected / reflects 2. a. has reduced / is reducing b. reduction
3. a. are depleting / have depleted b. depletion 4. a. exploit b. exploitation
5. a. negotiations b. negotiated

D. Dictionary Skills (p. 208)

1. (2) far removed in space 2. (3) maintain; assert 3. (3a) barred (the continent) from serious consideration 4. (3) incorporate (it) within their domain

E. Information Organization (p. 209)

I. People with Conflicting Interests in Antarctica
   A. scientists
      reason: They treasure the advantages for research
   B. tourists
      reason: They prize the chance to visit Earth's last frontier
   C. environmentalists
      reason: They feel that increases in research and tourism will jeopardize Antarctica
   D. oil and mineral seekers
      reason: They contend the world will be deprived of natural resources if Antarctica is not exploited.

Concepts for Today, Book 4, Answer Key

II. The Madrid Protocol
    A. date: October, 1991
    B. original number of participating nations: 39
    C. purpose: bans oil and gas exploitation for 50 years
III. A Description of Antarctica
    A. Only 2.4% of its 5.4 million-square-mile land mass is ice-free
    B. 70% of the world's fresh water is trapped in its ice
    C. Winds blow at more than 200 mph
    D. Temperatures drop to $-128.6°F$
    E. There are no villages, towns, or plants
IV. Antarctica Is Vital to Life on Earth
    A. It reflects sunlight back into space, preventing Earth from overheating
    B. Cold water from icebergs produce currents, clouds, and complex weather patterns
    C. Antarctic seas are an important link in the food chain
    D. Southern Ocean is home to unique animals
V. The Antarctic Treaty's Purpose
    A. Establish Antarctica as a continent for science and peace
    B. Temporarily set aside all claims of sovereignty
    C. Open to all: People need neither passport nor visas.

F. Information Organization Quiz and Summary (p. 210)

1. There are conflicting interests because scientists, tourists, environmentalists, and oil and mineral seekers have different, conflicting plans for Antarctica.
2. It is a treaty signed by 31 nations. The nations agree to ban oil and gas exploration in Antarctica for the next 50 years.
3. It is almost completely covered with ice, it is extremely cold and windy, has no villages or even plants, and contains 70% of the world's fresh water.
4. Yes, it is necessary. Antarctica keeps Earth from overheating, produces weather patterns, is an important link in the food chain, and is home to unique animals.
5. Its purpose is to protect Antarctica from exploitation and from claims of ownership, while keeping it open for peaceful and scientific purposes.

Summary

Although no one lives on Antarctica and no nation claims ownership of it, many groups of people have conflicting interests in studying and exploiting it. Treaties have been signed by many nations to protect Antarctica—a cold, icy, remote continent.

G. Critical Thinking Strategies (p. 211)

Answers will vary.

H. Follow-up Discussion and Writing Activities (p. 212)

Answers will vary.

I. Cloze Quiz (p. 214)

1. scientists 2. continent 3. research 4. useless 5. explorations 6. countries
7. Argentina 8. However 9. question 10. Antarctica 11. agreement 12. effect
13. number 14. all 15. established 16. science 17. temporarily 18. claims
19. long 20. remains

Chapter 11   A Messenger from the Past

Prereading Preparation (p. 215)

1–3. Answers will vary.

A. Fact-Finding Exercise (p. 218)

1. T 2. F. The Ice Man was discovered in Europe by hikers. 3. T 4. T 5. F. Scientists haven't examined the Ice Man yet to get genetic information. 6. F. More bodies of mountain climbers who died 50 years ago were discovered.

B. Reading Analysis (p. 219)

1. c **2.** the Ice Man's body **3.** b **4.** a. a stone knife, a wooden backpack, a bow and a quiver, a small bag containing a flint lighter and kindling, and an arrow repair kit in a leather pouch b. 2 **5.** c **6.** c **7.** b **8.** a. 2 b. 3 **9.** a **10.** b **11.** a. 2 b. 3 **12.** a **13.** the discovery of an ancient body

C. Word Forms (p. 222)

Part 1

1. a. insulation b. insulated 2. a. demonstrations b. demonstrate 3. a. will explore / are going to explore b. exploration 4. a. preservation b. don't preserve / do not preserve 5. a. destruction b. destroyed

Part 2

1. a. alert (n.) b. alerted (v.) 2. a. didn't repair / did not repair (v.) b. repair (n.) 3. a. will return (v.) b. returns (n.) 4. a. release (v.) b. releases (n.) 5. a. damage (n.) b. didn't damage / did not damage (v.)

D. Dictionary Skills (p. 225)

1. (1a) traces 2. (1) routine 3. (1a) firmly established / (1c) permanent 4. (1b) severe weather conditions

E. Information Organization (p. 227)

The Ice Man:

His Body

He was tattooed on his back and behind his knee.

His Clothing

Remnants of leather garments; boots stuffed with straw

His Equipment

A bronze ax; an all-purpose knife; a wooden backpack; a bow and a quiver; flint lighter and kindling; an arrow repair kit

Purpose of Expedition

Maybe hunting; maybe searching for metal ore

His Society

Small, stable villages; language ancestral to current European languages; a farming culture

Possible Cause of His Death:

Starvation?

No; remnants of animal skin and bones and the remainder of a pile of berries were found near him, so he probably did not starve to death.

Injury?

Maybe; an autopsy will be performed on the Ice Man's body; it may show evidence of injury.

Freezing Weather?

Maybe; the trench gave the Ice Man shelter; he had a grass mat to keep him warm; however, he may have been in the trench so long that he died of the cold anyway.

F. Information Organization Quiz and Summary (p. 228)

1. a. He was wearing remnants of leather garments and boots stuffed with straw.
   b. He had tattoos on his back and behind his knee.
2. a. He had everyday gear with him: a bronze ax, an all-purpose stone knife, a wooden backpack, a small bag containing a flint lighter and kindling, and an arrow repair kit in a leather pouch.
   b. He might have been hunting, or searching for metal ore.
3. He lived in a farming culture in a society that was built around small, stable villages and spoke a language ancestral to current European languages.
4. Where he was found, there were remnants of animal skin and bones and the remainder of a pile of berries; the trench provided him with shelter, and he had a mat to keep him warm. Death by starvation can be ruled out, but an injury or freezing to death are possibilities.

Summary

In September, the well-preserved, freeze-dried body of a 4,000-year-old man was discovered. His body and the everyday gear he had with him may provide important information about his biology and his society. Furthermore, since the glacier he was found in is melting, more Ice Men may be found.

G. Critical Thinking Strategies (p. 229)
Answers will vary.

H. Follow-up Discussion and Writing Activities (p. 231)
Answers will vary.

I. Cloze Quiz (p. 234)
1. Unlike 2. civilizations 3. authority 4. society 5. probably 6. ancestral
7. Furthermore 8. culture 9. hunting 10. contained 11. exploration 12. revealed
13. remainder 14. Clearly 15. starve 16. die 17. illness 18. circumstances
19. evidence 20. details

Chapter 12   Is Time Travel Possible?

Prereading Preparation (p. 235)
1. *Time travel* refers to the concept of journeying to a past or future time.
2–5. Answers will vary.

A. Fact-Finding Exercise (p. 240)
1. F. If you could move at the speed of light, your time would stand still. OR If you could move faster than the speed of light, your time would move backward. 2. F. Scientists have not discovered a form of matter that moves as fast as light. 3. T 4. T 5. F. The closer you are to the Earth's core, the slower you will age. 6. T

B. Reading Analysis (p. 241)
1. a. 186,282 miles per second b. 3 **2.** Accelerated motion causes a traveler's time to be stretched. **3.** a. 1 b. 2 c. particles of matter that move faster than light
4. b **5.** a **6.** c **7.** b **8.** a. the Twin Paradox b. There is a footnote at the bottom of the page that gives the name of this hypothetical situation. c. 1 **9.** c **10.** Space does not actually curve; this is a way of explaining the theory. **11.** It's an example of creating an alternative history. **12.** b **13.** going from Earth to the Spiral Nebula, then back to Earth **14.** a. a search b. A quest involves looking for something, as in line 86, and results in finding something, as in line 88.

C. Word Forms (p. 244)
Part 1
1. a. experimental b. have experimented / experimented 2. a. causes b. causal
3. a. survival b. survived 4. a. arrival b. arrives
Part 2
1. a. avoids b. avoidance 2. a. resistance b. resist 3. a. doesn't accept / does not accept / will not accept / won't accept b. acceptance 4. a. insists b. insistence
5. a. exists b. existence

D. Dictionary Skills (p. 246)
1. (2b) material substance 2. (3) extend (time) in length 3. (3a) came to a decision by reasoning 4. (1a) ponder; reflect

E. Information Organization (p. 248)
Time speeds up:
Gravity
The farther you are from the earth's center of gravity
Time slows down:
Speed
Moving faster than the speed of light

The closer you are to the Earth's center of gravity
Experimental evidence:
Speed
In 1972, scientists who took four atomic clocks on an airplane trip around the world discovered that the moving clocks moved slightly slower than atomic clocks that had remained on the ground.
Gravity
An atomic clock in Washington D.C., near sea level, was moved to Denver, which is one mile high. The results demonstrated that people in Denver age more rapidly than people in Washington.
Hypothetical example:
Speed
If you travel back and forth to the nearest star at one half the speed of light, you'll be gone for 18 Earth years. Your hypothetical twin will have aged 18 years, but you will have aged only 16 years.
Gravity
If you live near the beach and work deep under the sea, and avoid living in the mountains or working in a high building, you will slow your aging process by a few billionths of a second.

F. Information Organization Quiz and Summary (p. 249)

1. If you move at the speed of light, time stops; if you move faster than the speed of light, time slows down.
2. In 1972, scientists took four atomic clocks in airplanes around the world. They discovered that the moving clocks moved slower than atomic clocks on the ground.
3. An atomic clock in Washington, D.C., near sea level, was moved to Denver, one mile high. The results demonstrated that people in Denver age more rapidly than people in Washington.
4. Time reversal means that you could go back in time and do something that changes the present, even preventing your own birth, for example.

Summary
Some scientific experiments have demonstrated that Einstein's Special Theory of Relativity is correct. If we can discover matter that moves faster than the speed of light, then time travel may be possible in the future.

G. Critical Thinking Strategies (p. 250)
Answers will vary.

H. Follow-up Discussion and Writing Activities (p. 251)
Answers will vary.

I. Cloze Quiz (p. 253)
1. Contrary 2. waits 3. time 4. slows 5. faster 6. survive 7. space 8. return 9. future 10. speed 11. still 12. than 13. move 14. yet 15. light 16. experiments 17. motion 18. predicted 19. concept 20. part

Unit 4 Review

J. Crossword Puzzle (p. 254)
Across Answers
3. equal 4. put 5. ax 6. corpse 8. wrote 10. nsulation 13. negotiate 18. came 19. evidence 20. matter
Down Answers
1. quest 2. furthermore 5. Antarctica 7. ordinary 9. stretch 11. speculate 12. existence 14. equipment 15. exploit 16. remote 17. site

CNN Video Report: Antarctica's Future (p. 257)

1. Answers will vary.
2. a. Antarctica is very cold, the temperature goes down to 120 degrees below zero. Wind speeds go up to 200 miles per hour.
   b. The Antarctic Treaty of 1961 has prohibited exploration for oil and minerals up until now.
   c. Answers will vary.
   d. The oil tanker spill killed thousands of penguins and fish.
   e. The Wellington Convention would amend the 1961 Antarctic Treaty. It does not allow exploration for oil and minerals, but it provides a plan that would require unanimous agreement before any development.
3. Answers will vary.

Concepts for Today
VIDEO SCRIPTS

<table>
<tr><td>**Unit 1**</td><td>Living in Society</td></tr>
</table>

CNN Video Report: Hot Spots and Wireless Technology
Running time 01:48

Video Vocabulary
sport: to show something in an obvious way
hindered: slowed the progress of something, impeded
antenna: a rod, wire, or dish used to receive or send electronic signals
sprouting: starting to grow

Video Script
Reporter: Lynn Walker's *hot,* so is he. She's not. No, we're not talking about looks. Lynn and the spiky-haired guy are *hot* because they're wirelessly connected to the Internet. This New York park is a hot spot, so is this street corner in Southern California. They sport antennas enabling high-speed access. The technology is called WiFi, short for Wireless Fidelity.

Lydia Loizides (Wireless Expert): What the Internet did was it opened doors to an entire world of information that was not hindered by geography. And, what wireless does is it unchains you from cords and all of a sudden allows you to access that information from wherever you are.

Reporter: WiFi uses radio waves. Antennas link a laptop as far as 300 feet away to a base station. You have to outfit your notebook PC with receiver, a card selling for about 50 bucks. You can get free access at many community-based hot spots.

Male WiFi user: This is kind of like an outdoor office I've been using. Sure, it's great.

Lynn Walker: I work at home a lot. It was getting kind of lonely and depressing, so I bought a laptop and . . . so that I could come out into the Starbucks and into the parks.

Reporter: T-Mobile provides access at Starbucks and Borders bookstores for $30 a month. No company offers complete nationwide coverage, but the number of hot spots in the United States has more than quadrupled in the past year to around 3,500.

WiFi antennas are sprouting up everywhere. From parks to airports, hotels, and convention centers. As networks expand and hardware prices drop, the number of WiFi users has mushroomed to roughly 18 million people.

Fred Katayama, CNN Financial News, New York.

<table>
<tr><td>**Unit 2**</td><td>Safety and Health</td></tr>
</table>

CNN Video Report: Holiday House Fires
Running time 01:33

Video Vocabulary
engulfed: enclosed and swallowed up, overwhelmed
potentially: possible, capable of something
frays: small bits of material that have become thin from rubbing against something
festive: joyful, with feasting and good spirits

Video Script
Reporter: In less than a minute, this living room is engulfed in flames because of a potentially deadly combination: a Christmas tree and holiday lights.

Fire Expert: There are about 400 fires involving Christmas trees.

Reporter: To reduce fire risks, start with a fresh tree. Shake it or run your fingers over the needles. If they fall off, the tree is already too dry. And know the difference between indoor and outdoor lights. Experts say don't trust the packaging. You need to look more closely.

Lights Expert: If it's a green UL mark—that's the UL in the circle—that means the light strings have been tested only for indoor use. If it's a red UL mark, that means additional tests have been given to the light strings and it's suitable for indoor and for outdoor use.

Reporter: Also, check the plugs and the conditions of the light strings. If there are any frays, throw them out and start over.

More than one third of candles are purchased around the Christmas holiday. With the rise in candle use as holiday decorations, house fires nearly double in the month of December. But by simply extinguishing the flame before leaving the room, you can significantly reduce your chance of a fire.

Candle Expert: Make sure that you keep the wick trimmed to a quarter inch. Make sure that you remove all the labels from the candle. Make sure you don't keep the flame anywhere where children or pets can get near it.

Reporter: While adding lights may increase festive charm, turning them off before leaving the house or going to bed will keep holiday cheer from going up in smoke.

In Washington, I'm Julie Vallese.

Unit 3	Government and Education

CNN Video Report: Vanishing Retirement
Running time 02:43

Video Vocabulary
401(k) plan: a savings plan offered by some companies in which an untaxed portion of an employee's salary is invested and held until retirement
nest egg: a sum of money saved for a specific purpose, such as retirement
blessing in disguise: a hidden, unexpected benefit
trillion: a thousand billions, written as $1,000,000,000,000

Video Script
Michael Brenner: I have an 8:00 coaching call from home.

Roberta Brenner: I have a 10:00 . . . 9:30 coaching call.

Michael Brenner: We could do it from 7:00 to 8:00.

Roberta Brenner: That would be great.

Michael Brenner: O.K. Let's do it from 7:00 to 8:00.

Roberta Brenner: O.K.

Michael Brenner: Yeah, because that . . . actually I'd be happy to get to work early.

Reporter: Michael Brenner is 68. His wife, Roberta, is 58. They're still working, even though they had planned to retire by now.

Michael Brenner: The amount of assets we had three years ago would have been sufficient that we didn't have to work at all. But all of a sudden it dropped below the threshold, and we really needed to work.

Reporter: Michael Brenner is in good company. The National Council on Aging finds 43% of people over 65 are working full- or part-time. In large part, that's because they can't afford to quit. And according to an Employee Benefit Research Institute study, one quarter of all workers 45 or older plan to delay their retirement date, mostly for financial reasons.

Alicia Munnell of the Center for Retirement Research at Boston College says in her new book that Americans are coming up short.

Alicia Munnell (Retirement Expert): If you look at the amount of money people have in their 401-type accounts, of people just approaching retirement, the typical amount is not very much. It's a little bit more than $50,000. So, to the extent that people think that they're going to get a substantial retirement income out of that, they're . . . they're going to be severely disappointed.

Reporter: Even the man who invented the 401(k) back in the 80s is still working, at 62.

Ted Brenna: One of the reasons that I haven't retired myself is that I realize that it takes a very large nest egg to be able to spend 20 to 30 years in retirement. And personally, you know, I've worked all my life. I don't want to do that.

Reporter: The Brenners have made going back to work work for them. They now work together in Roberta's executive search and coaching business, which she started at age 53. The Brenners say returning to work has its rewards beyond paying the bills. Sometimes we look at each other and say, "We're too old to be working this hard." And other times we come home at the end of the day, or I work at home often, and say, "It was a great day, really rewarding." So, it has been a blessing in disguise.

Reporter: Blessing in disguise or new way of life? Working well into retirement age is becoming more common in this country. It explains what's happened to some of the Americans who lost three trillion dollars in the market decline.

Jan Hopkins, CNN New York.

CNN Video Report: Antarctica's Future

Running time 03:26

Video Vocabulary

foreboding: an omen or prediction; especially of coming evil
pristine: pure, especially in nature, unspoiled
plummeting: plunging, going downward rapidly and far
ban: a stop, a block
inaccessible: impossible or difficult to reach

Video Script

Reporter: Barren and beautiful, there is at once a sense of awe and of foreboding, gazing at the pristine bays and glittering glaciers of Antarctica. A placid scene such as this can be wiped away in minutes by 200-mile-an-hour winds and temperatures plummeting to 120 degrees below zero. Undisputedly, it is the harshest continent on Earth. And some say, it is also the richest—in oil and minerals. There has been an unofficial ban on any exploration for deposits, but the oil crisis of the 70s increased fears that some may try. That, in turn, has fueled a growing debate on how best to handle the threat.

Jacques Cousteau: The positive part is to have the nations declare and agree to declare Antarctica a natural reserve . . . land of science.

Government Expert: We support a mechanism to ensure that, if interest emerges in mineral activity there, that interest does not become a source of conflict or dispute.

Reporter: The issue is gaining more attention amid preparations for renegotiation of the 1961 Antarctic Treaty. The thirty-three countries involved are torn between declaring the continent a reserve and making it off limits for all oil and mineral exploration, or amending the treaty with a plan called the Wellington Convention. Six years in the making, Wellington would require unanimous agreement before any such developments could be allowed.

Government Expert: There is a view that somehow a convention about activities means that the activities will take place. The agreement itself does not call for activities. It provides a system for deciding whether they could be acceptable or not.

Reporter: Given the fragile Antarctic environment and the continent's influence on global weather patterns, many believe exploration should not even be an issue.

Jacques Cousteau: When we look at the danger that could come—famine, droughts, inundations, floods, whatever—we think that the game is too dangerous. It is too risky to touch the Antarctic now.

Reporter: Those wanting to create an Antarctic reserve argue precautions are not always enough. They point to this Argentine tanker, which went aground and sank near the United States' Palmer research station last January, spilling 170,000 gallons of oil. A year later, the *Bahía Paraiso* is still leaking. Thousands of penguins and fish have died. It will be years before the full extent of the damage is known.

Environmental Expert: If you damage something, it will have a long recovery time and that's a great problem of polar regions, especially Antarctica, so you should be very careful with everything you do here.

Reporter: For now, Antarctica's climate and inaccessibility make mineral exploration much too costly. But, if that should change, those lobbying for the Wellington Convention argue declaring Antarctica a world reserve would not be enough to protect the continent from exploitation. Despite the differences, both sides agree on one thing. No matter what safety mechanism is in place, any major oil or mineral discovery could create competition that would destroy not only the Antarctic Treaty, but Antarctica itself.

Catherine Crier, CNN, reporting.

Concepts for Today
A S S E S S M E N T

Chapter 1 Review—The Paradox of Happiness

Focus: Information Recall

Read the questions first. Then read the passage on Student Book pages 3–4 again. Close your book and answer the questions without looking at the passage.

1. Are happiness and unhappiness two sides of the same feeling? Explain.

   _____

2. If you reduce factors that make you unhappy, will your happiness increase? Explain.

   _____

3. How does the reading passage define *happiness*?

   _____

4. Are *identical* or *fraternal* twins more likely to display a similar level of unhappiness? Why?

   _____

5. What did the psychologists from Arizona State University learn from the students who increased their favorite activities?

   _____

Focus: Vocabulary Cloze

Read the passage below. Choose the best word for each blank from the box. Use each word once.

appear	emotions	genetic	identical	joy
miserable	relationship	researchers	studies	unhappiness

It seems like a paradox that you can be happy and unhappy at the same time, but

(1) _____ have learned that it is true. Psychologists have discovered that these (2) _____ to

be two separate (3) _____. Decreasing the amount of (4) _____, or sadness, does not auto-

matically increase the amount of (5) _____ in your life. If you want to be less (6) _____,

you can change the things that make you unhappy. If you increase time spent on things that you find fun

and pleasurable, you may be happier.

In several (7) _____ of twins, scientists found that unhappiness seems to have a

(8) _____ connection. (9) _____ twins with exactly the same genes were especially similar

in their level of unhappiness. The research shows that there is little (10) _____ between family

heritage and an individual's capacity for joy.

Concepts for Today, Book 4, Assessment

Name: _____ Date: _____

Chapter 2 Review—Close to Home: Technological Advances Erode Barrier Between Work and Home

Focus: Information Recall

Read the questions first. Then read the passage on Student Book pages 21–23 again. Close your book and answer the questions without looking at the passage.

1. Why did Cindy take a walkie-talkie to her children's sports events?

   _____

2. Name an advantage and a disadvantage for workers who can be reached at home.

   a. *advantage:* _____

   b. *disadvantage:* _____

3. According to Maggie Jackson, what percentage of workers must be accessible to their jobs at home?

   _____

4. How do working parents stay in touch with their children? Give an example.

   _____

5. What advice did someone give during a past time of technological change?

   _____

Focus: Vocabulary Cloze

Read the passage below. Choose the best word for each blank from the box. Use each word once.

affect	boundaries	conduct	conflict	devices
employees	interruptions	technology	vacation	workplace

In the past, the (1) _____ between work and home were a lot clearer. When (2) _____ left the (3) _____ at the end of the day, their time was free until they arrived back at the office the next day. Today, communications (4) _____ has changed where, when, and how people work. With modern (5) _____ such as cell phones, PDAs, video conferencing, and wireless computers, many workers can (6) _____ business anywhere. Unfortunately, this also means that employers can access workers when they are at home, or even during a family (7) _____. This ability to contact people away from the workplace has created (8) _____ in many lives. Endless (9) _____ of family life and leisure activities can eventually (10) _____ how people feel about their work. Some people would like to go fishing or attend a concert without their cell phone ringing!

Concepts for Today, Book 4, Assessment

Chapter 3 Review—The Birth-Order Myth

Focus: Information Recall

Read the questions first. Then read the passage on Student Book pages 40–41 again. Close your book and answer the questions without looking at the passage.

1. According to an older psychological theory, by what age was your personality determined?

   _____

2. What did the Swiss scientists find about a "firstborn personality"?

   _____

3. What is a "self-fulfilling prophecy"? Give an example.

   _____

4. What is there about family size that is important for academic success?

   _____

5. How do parents sometimes treat brothers and sisters who are very close in age?

   _____

Focus: Vocabulary Cloze

Read the passage below. Choose the best word for each blank from the box. Use each word once.

affect	assumption	birth	effects	influences
intelligent	personality	research	studies	theory

For over a hundred years, people believed that (1) _____ order—your place in your family—
(2) _____ your intelligence and personality. In particular, they thought that the firstborn child
would be more (3) _____ than younger brothers or sisters. Recent (4) _____ shows that
there are many other factors that (5) _____ a person's development. Some (6) _____
suggest that family size can have important (7) _____ as well.

Psychologists used to have a (8) _____ that a child's (9) _____ was fixed at an early
age. Now some social psychologists say that this (10) _____ is incorrect. Most now believe that a
person's personality continues to develop as they have different life experiences.

Chapter 4 Review—Why So Many More Americans Die in Fires

Focus: Information Recall

Read the questions first. Then read the passage on Student Book pages 63–64 again. Close your book and answer the questions without looking at the passage.

1. What year did the fires happen in Chicago and Peshtigo?

   _____

2. Why has Japan had so many fires that damaged over 10,000 buildings?

   _____

3. When a fire occurs in Japan, how do the neighbors react?

   _____

4. Give two examples of good public education on fire safety in other countries.

   a. *Place:* _____ *Example:* _____

   b. *Place:* _____ *Example:* _____

5. Where do U.S. fire departments spend most of their education dollars?

   _____

Focus: Vocabulary Cloze

Read the passage below. Choose the best word for each blank from the box. Use each word once.

destroy	experts	fatalities	fault	kill
neither	prevent	progress	responsibility	worst

In the 1800s, several terrible fires killed thousands of people and burnt a large part of Chicago. Compared to these fires with many (1) _____, the United States has made (2) _____ in fighting fires. Today, fires still (3) _____ people and (4) _____ property, but they don't compare with the (5) _____ fires in the nation's history.

However, safety (6) _____ worry that Americans aren't doing enough to (7) _____ fires from happening. They say that Americans have an attitude that fires aren't their (8) _____. In other words, they don't take (9) _____ for fires. Other countries have tougher laws and better public education about fire safety. The United States has (10) _____ of these and continues to spend more on fighting fires than on preventing them.

Chapter 5 Review—Acupuncture: The New Old Medicine

Focus: Information Recall

Read the questions first. Then read the passage on Student Book pages 81–82 again. Close your book and answer the questions without looking at the passage.

1. What was the author's medical problem? What part of his body hurt?

   _____

2. What did the neurologist have the patient do as part of his treatment?

   _____

3. According to acupuncturists, what is *qi?*

   _____

4. Jack Tymann tried acupuncture as an alternative to _____ _____

5. Who gave Harwood Beville the idea of going to an acupuncturist?

   _____

Focus: Vocabulary Cloze

Read the passage below. Choose the best word for each blank from the box. Use each word once.

balanced instead	cure preventive	energy skeptical	healthier symptoms	inserting traditional

When conventional medicine fails to (1) _____ an illness, some people visit an acupuncturist. Acupuncture is a (2) _____ system of medicine based on *qi*, a form of (3) _____ that circulates through the body. Acupuncturists believe that in order for a body to be healthy, the circulation of *qi* must be (4) _____ in a healthy body. When there is an imbalance, treatment is performed by (5) _____ needles into special points on the skin. These points are connected to internal organs and body structures.

Although some Americans are (6) _____ about whether acupuncture really works, many people who have tried the procedure say it has eased their (7) _____ and relieved their pain. Some doctors use acupuncture along with other treatments, but many patients use it (8) _____ of conventional medicine. Still other people use acupuncture as a (9) _____ measure so they don't get sick. They believe that regular treatments will help them to lead (10) _____ lives.

4 · ASSESSMENT

Chapter 6 Review—Highs and Lows in Self-Esteem

Focus: Information Recall

Read the questions first. Then read the passage on Student Book pages 105–106 again. Close your book and answer the questions without looking at the passage.

1. According to the study under focus in the reading, during what parts of life is self-esteem generally high?

   _____

2. Do Jeff and Aly agree about self-esteem in adolescence? Explain.

   _____

3. What is similar about adolescence and old age?

   _____

4. What was a situational factor when Eileen was 17? How did this affect her self-esteem?

   _____

5. What does being in jeopardy mean?

   _____

Focus: Vocabulary Cloze

Read the passage below. Choose the best word for each blank from the box. Use each word once.

accumulation	adolescence	adulthood	inflated	plunge
social	survey	transition	upswing	vulnerable

   A recent (1) _____ of 350,000 people shows that self-esteem varies throughout life. Children often have (2) _____ opinions of themselves during late childhood, but when they enter (3) _____, most will experience a (4) _____ in self-esteem. This drop is usually greater for girls than boys, largely because of (5) _____ factors that contribute to girls' heightened awareness of body image.

   The (6) _____ to young adulthood is marked by an (7) _____ in self-esteem. This higher level of self-esteem often continues throughout (8) _____, a direct reflection of a growing sense of confidence and competence. With the passage to old age, people again become (9) _____ to low self-esteem because of an (10) _____ of losses. However, some people with good health, many interests, and strong relationships continue to enjoy high self-esteem throughout the challenges and changes of retirement and beyond.

Chapter 7 Review—The Federal System of Government

Focus: Information Recall

Read the questions first. Then read the passage on Student Book pages 131–133 again. Close your book and answer the questions without looking at the passage.

1. What did the Continental Congress believe in?

   _____

2. What did the Articles of Confederation create in 1781?

   _____

3. When and where was the Constitution of the United States written?

   _____

4. What was the dilemma the Constitutional convention faced?

   _____

5. What branch of government makes laws in the United States?

   _____

Focus: Vocabulary Cloze

Read the passage below. Choose the best word for each blank from the box. Use each word once.

assembly	balances	Constitution	dilemma	enforce
establish	federal	freedom	solution	states

After the War of Independence, the new American (1) _____ needed to (2) _____ their own system of government. At that time, each of the new states had a governor and an (3) _____ that represented the people. The first national government was formed under the Articles of Confederation in 1781. The main purpose then, as always, was to guarantee (4) _____ for all citizens. However, the new country faced a (5) _____ because the central government did not have the power to (6) _____ laws throughout the nation.

Six years later in 1787, representatives worked out the (7) _____ of the United States as a (8) _____ to the dilemma. Under the new form of (9) _____ government, three independent branches were formed to make laws, to carry out those laws, and to secure the rights of the people. Under a system of checks and (10) _____, these three branches were given equal power. With only a few amendments, this same system still exists as the foundation of the U.S. government.

Chapter 8 Review—Too Soon Old, Too Late Wise

Focus: Information Recall

Read the questions first. Then read the passage on Student Book pages 157–158 again. Close your book and answer the questions without looking at the passage.

1. At the time of the article, where did Professor Weiss teach?

   _____

2. At what university was Dr. Weiss an emeritus Sterling Professor?

   _____

3. According to a report by the U.S. EEOC, why was Dr. Weiss's teaching load reduced?

   _____

4. Name three famous philosophers who taught past the usual retirement age.

   a. *philosopher's name:* _____ *taught until age:* _____

   b. *philosopher's name:* _____ *taught until age:* _____

   c. *philosopher's name:* _____ *taught until age:* _____

5. What health problems has Professor Weiss had?

   _____

Focus: Vocabulary Cloze

Read the passage below. Choose the best word for each blank from the box. Use each word once.

allowed	determined	demoted	infirmities	insisted
liability	modest	philosophers	profession	unprecedented

   Some people think of philosophers as scholars who are happy to work quietly in their offices and have (1) _____ self-esteem. Professor Paul Weiss doesn't fit that description. At 90 years old, he was furious when his university (2) _____ him to teach part-time. Dr. Weiss publicly (3) _____ that he was still capable of teaching students and continues to contribute to his (4) _____ through writing.

   That is not how the university saw the situation. They said that Professor Weiss had physical (5) _____ that interfered with his teaching. The university administration said they had made an (6) _____ arrangement when it (7) _____ Weiss to teach in his apartment when he had health problems. Weiss pointed out that there were several cases of famous (8) _____ teaching from home. The professor says his problems are not a (9) _____ for the university. Weiss is (10) _____ to stay active in his field.

Chapter 9 Review—The Pursuit of Excellence

Focus: Information Recall

Read the questions first. Then read the passage on Student Book pages 172–174 again. Close your book and answer the questions without looking at the passage.

1. What does the author compare the American higher educational system to?

   _____

2. How do some American institutions show they value European secondary education?

   _____

3. According to Marvin Bressler, the American right to an education is based on a student's _____,

   not necessarily their ability to pay.

4. In Europe and Japan, what are two things that Ministries of Education do for universities?

   a. _____

   b. _____

5. Is regular attendance important in British universities? Explain.

   _____

Focus: Vocabulary Cloze

Read the passage below. Choose the best word for each blank from the box. Use each word once.

attract	campus	choices	community	countries
different	flexibility	foreign	students	graduate

Every year, U.S. colleges and universities (1) _____ large numbers of (2) _____ students from many different countries. These overseas students come to American colleges for a variety of reasons. For one thing, they like the (3) _____ of the American educational system. They also like the (4) _____ that are made available to them at American institutions. If they wish, they are able to change their major, and they can even transfer to a (5) _____ program altogether. Smaller colleges have advantages for many students. In a small academic (6) _____, foreign students can get to know their professors and classmates. They can meet people from many different (7) _____ and come to understand them. Foreign students can participate in (8) _____ life and learn a lot about American culture. Most importantly, (9) _____ can receive an excellent undergraduate education and become well prepared for (10) _____ programs.

Name: _____ Date: _____

Chapter 10 Review—Antarctica: Whose Continent Is It Anyway?

Focus: Information Recall

Read the questions first. Then read the passage on Student Book pages 199–200 again. Close your book and answer the questions without looking at the passage.

1. Why did the authors visit Antarctica?

   _____

2. Environmentalists fear that an increase in _____ and _____ will pollute

   the continent and jeopardize its fabulous creatures.

3. According to the Madrid Protocol, what is prohibited for 50 years?

   _____

4. Name four ways in which Antarctica is important to life on Earth.

   a. _____

   b. _____

   c. _____

   d. _____

5. What did the Antarctic Treaty do?

   _____

Focus: Vocabulary Cloze

Read the passage below. Choose the best word for each blank from the box. Use each word once.

continents	countries	contend	established	explorers
exploited	remote	resources	scientists	temporarily

Antarctica's location is very distant from the other six (1) _____. Perhaps the fact that it is

so (2) _____ resulted in its being ignored for so long. Early in the twentieth century, teams from

European (3) _____ raced each other to be the first (4) _____ to reach the South Pole. It

wasn't until the International Geophysical Year in 1957–58 that (5) _____ first realized how valu-

able Antarctica was. By then, several countries had (6) _____ research stations on the continent.

Now, groups with different interests disagree about how Antarctica should be (7) _____,

and indeed, whether it should be exploited at all. Environmentalists (8) _____ that the continent

should be kept unspoiled. Others say the world needs the valuable oil and mineral (9) _____ that

lie under the ice. (10) _____, the Madrid Protocol not only prevents many countries from claiming

ownership of the region, but it also protects the region's valuable natural resources.

104 *Concepts for Today,* Book 4, Assessment

Name: _____ Date: _____

Chapter 11 Review—A Messenger from the Past

Focus: Information Recall

Read the questions first. Then read the passage on Student Book pages 216–217 again. Close your book and answer the questions without looking at the passage.

1. Where did the German hikers find the Ice Man?

   _____

2. What did the Ice Man have on his back and behind his knee?

   _____

3. Name three of the items that were found with the Ice Man.

   a. _____

   b. _____

   c. _____

4. According to Ian Kinnes, why was the discovery of the Ice Man so exciting?

   _____

5. What do scientists believe about the climate of the Tyrol region now?

   _____

Focus: Vocabulary Cloze

Read the passage below. Choose the best word for each blank from the box. Use each word once.

circumstances	civilization	destroying	details	evidence
gear	insulation	preserved	remnants	starve

   In 1991, German hikers were very surprised when they found a dead man high in the Italian

Tyrol mountains. Although the corpse was well (1) _____, it was evident that this person had lived

long ago. The Ice Man was wearing (2) _____ of leather clothing and he carried hunting

(3) _____. (4) _____ of animal bones and berries showed that he had food, so he didn't

(5) _____ to death. The braided grass mat under him probably provided some (6) _____

from the cold.

   Scientists wanted to know more about the (7) _____ of the Ice Man's death as well as

(8) _____ about how he lived thousands of years ago. They think he probably lived in an agricul-

tural village, not in a great (9) _____ like Mesopotamia with cities and central authority. Before

evolutionary biologists could reveal more details about this mysterious person from our ancient past,

experts needed to figure out how to thaw the body without (10) _____ it.

Chapter 12 Review—Is Time Travel Possible?

Focus: Information Recall

Read the questions first. Then read the passage on Student Book pages 236–239 again. Close your book and answer the questions without looking at the passage.

1. What would happen to time if you could move at the speed of light?

   _____

2. When did Albert Einstein introduce the concept of relative time?

   _____

3. Name two ways of measuring time and time's relativity other than using a clock.

   a. _____

   b. _____

4. If you travel at half the speed of light to the nearest star and return to Earth, who will be older, you or your twin who stayed on Earth?

   _____

5. Would you age faster on Mt. Everest or at sea-level? Why?

   _____

4 • ASSESSMENT

Focus: Vocabulary Cloze

Read the passage below. Choose the best word for each blank from the box. Use each word once.

| backwards | concept | contrary | experiments | light |
| predicted | slower | speed | stretch | speculate |

(1) _____ to the idea that time is fixed and passes at a constant (2) _____, scientists know that you can (3) _____ time. Based on Einstein's (4) _____ of relativity, physicists understand that as you move faster towards the speed of (5) _____, time actually becomes (6) _____. If it were possible to go faster than light, you would actually travel (7) _____ in time. (8) _____ with atomic clocks have demonstrated that what Einstein (9) _____ is true. Some scientists (10) _____ that if we could find a source of energy that allowed us to travel beyond the speed of light, we may just be able to travel to the future.

Topics for Today
TEACHER NOTES

Unit 1	Society: School and Family

Chapter 1   **Hop, Skip . . . and Software?**   **Audio CD 1, Track 1**

There is a wide range of educational philosophies about the use of computers in elementary schools. This diversity is reflected in the varying degrees of access that elementary students have to computers, and in the ways that computers are integrated into the curriculum. Most educators agree that in order to ensure the successful application of technology in the classroom, teachers must be trained to use computers effectively.

Suggestions for Prereading Activity

Ask students to look at the photographs on Student Book ("SB") pages 2 and 6. Elicit information from your students by asking questions: How are the students in the photographs using computers? How old are they? Where do they think the teacher is? Also, ask students about the source of the article, the newspaper *Christian Science Monitor*. What kind of publication is this? You may also wish to find out when and where your students first used a computer.

Culture Notes

The examples cited in the reading portray several different perspectives on the use of computers in childhood. Note that much of the debate concerns elementary school children, particularly those at the younger end of the spectrum. Some of these perspectives are based on theories of social, emotional, and cognitive development. Theorists, such as Jean Piaget and Erik Erikson, purport that children go through a sequence of stages where certain types of learning are especially important. Educators who oppose the use of computers during early childhood are concerned that technology might displace crucial experiences and human interaction that would interfere with healthy development.

    A related concern is how computers are actually used in the learning process. Do students interact individually with a computer (as in the photograph on SB page 2) or do several students work together, interacting with the technology and with each other (as in the photograph on SB page 6)? Are computers a means to explore higher order thinking skills such as integration and application, or are they simply mechanical teacher replacements for drill and practice? Generational familiarity is still a factor in how effectively teachers integrate technology into their classrooms. Teachers who are not comfortable with computers themselves may need extra training or coaching so that they are able to maximize the benefits of technology.

Suggestions for Another Perspective

Ask students to look at the photograph on SB page 16. What is the boy doing? Where is he? Could he access the Internet there? How? What advantages does his computer have over desktop computers usually found in schools? In the title, what does *rural* mean? What is a word that means the opposite of *rural?*

Program to Bring Computers to Rural Schools

Audio CD1, Track 2

A pilot program will provide laptop computers to students in five states and Washington, D.C. The touch-operated computers, meant to replace textbooks and library books, weigh less than two pounds and do not have hard drives. The computers use wireless technology and have filtered Internet access. In places like the mountains of rural Arkansas, educators not only hope the computers will link students with the wider world, but provide solutions to school consolidation problems.

Culture Notes

The two readings both explore how the access to computer technology varies considerably throughout the United States. Greater access often exists in suburban schools with less access in urban and rural schools. In some of the rural school districts, educators are hopeful that computers will have a positive impact on both individual students and the state public education system. In the past, rural students have been disadvantaged by their remote locations. Computers make it possible to link schools and even enable districts to share teachers through videoconferencing.

According to the founder of the company coordinating the pilot project, one goal is to replace textbooks and library books with electronic versions. While this may cut costs for print materials, some studies indicate that this is not an advantage unless the materials are interactive. As noted in the previous reading, the key to effective use of computers is not just the presence of the technology; it depends on careful, thoughtful integration with the whole teaching and learning process.

Suggestions for Follow-Up Activities

As this is the first follow-up activity in *Topics for Today*, students should complete a Self-Evaluation of Reading Strategies. The forms that assist students in this process are located in the last chapter of each unit. The form for Unit 1, Chapter 1 is on SB page 67. The first time students use the form, it might be useful to go through it as a class so you can clarify the strategies.

The first article contrasts using computers for "drill and practice" and using them for "simulations and applications" (see the ETS study, lines 38–43). If students use CALL (Computer Assisted Language Learning) software, is it more like one of these than the other? Do students feel that you could learn a language just by using a computer? Ask them to explain.

If students are interested in learning more about technology in the classroom, refer them to the Internet and InfoTrac resources for this chapter. InfoTrac comes with the Student Book and provides students with an online research library.

See http://www.heinle.com for student and instructor activities and materials to accompany this student book. Crossword puzzles, flash cards, and worksheets are just some of the resource you'll find at this site. The answer keys for chapter assessments found in this book will be found in the Instructor Resources location for each book.

Chapter 2

My Husband, the Outsider

Mixed marriages between people of different cultural backgrounds can create confusion for the couple's families. Traditional families need to overcome stereotypes and accept the new spouse as a person on their own merits. These adjustments can be difficult for some people and acceptance can take time.

Suggestions for Prereading Activity

Before students answer the following questions, have them look at the photograph on SB page 23. How are these two people alike and how are they different? What are some other examples of mixed marriages? Religion, ethnic background, race, and social class are a few differences you could discuss. What's an *outsider?* Ask your students if they have ever experienced what it feels like to be an outsider.

Prereading Question 2 on SB page 24 asks students to respond to what being an American means by writing in their journal. Please note that in using *Topics for Today,* all students should regularly keep a journal. The journal is intended to be a place to write personal reflections or reactions to a topic. You may choose to read the students' journals and respond to them (but not grade them), making them a dialogue journal in which a student and you privately communicate about ideas. On the other hand, you may opt to make journal writing a solo exercise, a private opportunity for students to process and express their ideas about the readings and activities.

Culture Notes

Mixed marriages in the United States are both more common and more accepted than they were a generation ago. This is probably a result of several factors, including greater opportunities to meet and know people from various backgrounds, more media exposure to a wide variety of cultures and lifestyles, and more positive attitudes toward diversity. However, Americans are only a generation away from a society that generally supported racial segregation and legal restrictions on mixed marriages. *Miscegenation* a term used to describe marriage or cohabitation between a white person and a member of another race, was often used to express a very negative view of racial mixing.

Use the term *first-generation* to describe Marian Hyun's situation. *First-generation* means the first children of immigrants to be born in the new country. Discuss how Marian's background and experiences in America are different from her parents' upbringing in Korea.

You might want to use movies to reinforce the idea that a variety of differences (religion, race, social class) can form the basis of mixed marriages. Possible films range from the classic *Guess Who's Coming to Dinner* to the more recent *My Big Fat Greek Wedding.*

Suggestions for Another Perspective

Ask students to look at the photograph on SB page 38. What's happening in the photograph? Where are the people? What language do you think they are speaking? Look at the second reading's title, subtitle, and the author's name. What do you predict the article will be about?

5 · TEACHER NOTES

Unwelcome In Chinatown Audio CD1, Track 4

An American-born Chinese (ABC) woman describes how it feels to be snubbed when she visits Chinatown. Although the author looks Chinese, she was raised in America and doesn't speak Cantonese. She claims that Chinese speakers in Chinatown discriminate against her and other ABCs because they don't know the language.

Culture Notes

Both readings are by first-generation Americans who didn't learn their parents' native language because they wanted to assimilate or fit in with American culture. First-generation people are often pulled in two directions. At home, they are exposed to many aspects of their cultural heritage, but outside the home they want to be accepted by their peers. Some first-generation children become "cultural brokers" for their parents and grandparents when the older family members don't adjust to American society. In some ethnic neighborhoods or enclaves, it is possible for some people to manage as though they had never left the "old country." Many people often speak the same native language, there are social groups composed of people from the same background, and a wide range of traditional goods and foods from their native country are available. Therefore, sometimes there is very little incentive to adjust to the new society.

Suggestions for Follow-Up Activities

Remind students to complete the Self-Evaluation of Reading Strategies on SB page 67. Then conduct the survey on SB page 41 and compile the results from all class members. Compare the results to the first survey (on SB page 24).

Make a list of books or films that deal with mixed marriages and/or the experiences of young people adjusting to life in America. Compile this list in print form or electronically and distribute it to the class. If students have read the books or seen the films, have them write a brief review. Display students' reviews in your classroom.

Chapter 3   Beyond Rivalry   Audio CD, Track 5

During childhood, brothers and sisters may be rivals, but in later life, siblings typically become emotionally closer and they share a more positive relationship. Psychologists report that as support networks dwindle with age, elderly people typically find strength in their relationships with siblings and the memories that they share since childhood. Among siblings, sisters are the most likely to maintain family bonds.

Suggestions for Prereading Activity

Have students look at the photographs on SB pages 49 and 54 before answering questions. How do the sisters in these pictures relate to each other? The girls in the first picture are younger than the other set of sisters. Does age affect their relationship? You may want to explain that *rivalry* means competition and the word often collocates with *sibling* to denote the particularly strong competition that exists between brothers and sisters, especially when they are children.

The in-class sibling survey on SB page 50 recycles the term *birth order,* which featured in *Concepts for Today,* Chapter 3. The items in parentheses suggest that the norm is a three-child family. For purposes of collecting data, an only child is considered the eldest child and in families of four or more, all children who are not the eldest nor the youngest are "middle children."

Culture Notes

The concept of sibling rivalry goes back to the Biblical story of Cain and Abel and also features as fratricide (murdering one's own sibling) in many myths as well as in historical accounts. As part of the nineteenth century Viennese school of psychoanalysis that included Sigmund Freud, Alfred Adler was the first to coin the term *sibling rivalry*. Adler believed that a sense of inferiority was the basic motivating force in human life and much of this stemmed from childhood rivalry within the family. Adler strongly believed in the effects of birth order on personality.

Modern individuals are born into what sociologists term their *family of origin* in which they mature. As adults, they marry and form their *family of procreation* by having children of their own. The term *nuclear family* is used to describe a family of two parents and their children. This term contrasts with *extended family* which is a larger unit encompassing three or more generations. In the United States, nuclear families typically live separately from other family members. In many cases, adults may live far away from their parents and their siblings. It is not uncommon for adult siblings to see each other infrequently. This is a sharp contrast to cultures where the extended family is the norm and some siblings live together, along with their spouses and children, on a permanent basis.

Suggestions for Another Perspective

Ask students to look at the photograph on SB page 64. What is the relationship of the three young men? In general, is the relationship between brothers different from the relationship between sisters? How?

Middle Children and Their Position in the Family   **Audio CD1, Track 6**

Middle children in a family are easily overlooked because of their structural position between older and younger siblings. Middle children frequently respond by placing greater emphasis on peer groups than family ties and are often the first to leave home and live far away. This does not imply that they don't get along with their family. On the contrary, their position within the family often results in good mediation or negotiation skills and the ability to compromise.

Culture Notes

Recent research on middle children finds them more likely to become rebels against the status quo than their older or younger siblings. The exact type of attention and care middle children receive depends a lot on birth spacing in a family and how occupied the mother and father are with older or younger siblings. In other words, if there are a number of years between adjacent siblings, the middle sibling may be treated similar to a first or last child. Therefore, the family dynamics depend on the number of children, the spacing of children, the presence or absence of children with special needs, and the amount of attention parents can give to individual children in the family.

Suggestions for Follow-Up Activities

Remind students to complete the Self-Evaluation of Reading Strategies on SB page 67. After students have completed their self-evaluations, ask them to identify strategies they haven't used up to this point and remind them to use these strategies in the next unit.

Ask if any students in your class have taken part in a family reunion or have worked on a genealogy (family history). If so, who are the people in their families who usually spearhead such projects? Who usually participates? Are these family members in regular contact with one another?

Have students in the class sort themselves into four groups: only children, eldest children, middle children, and youngest children. Working within their groups, have them identify the advantages and disadvantages of their position within the family. For example, middle children might complain that they always get hand-me-down clothes and toys from their older siblings, but they don't experience the pressure to perform that the eldest child does.

Unit 1 CNN Video Report

Have students watch the video *High-Tech Job Shortage*. Since the video is about technology skills, have students view the clip after completing Chapter 1. While the readings focus on technology in the classroom, the video focuses on developing computer skills in preparation for the workforce. Before viewing the video, ask students about the computer skills they would need to find a job in the IT field. It may be useful to bring representative job advertisements to class. Could students meet the requirements with everyday computer experience and knowledge? Are computer skills also helpful in jobs outside the high-tech industry? Ask students if they received computer training when they were in school. After viewing the video, have students reflect on the views they formed in response to Chapter 1. Should technology be introduced in early education? How would doing a simulation with eBay, as in the video, help prepare school children for real-world jobs later in life?

After discussing the video, have students answer the Video Report questions on SB page 74.

Unit 2	Influences on Our Lives: Nature versus Nurture

Chapter 4   **Who Lives Longer?**   Audio CD, Track 7

Scientists believe there are two types of factors that influence longevity: genetic factors fixed from birth and changeable factors over which we have control. Recent research has identified seven changeable factors, but by far the most important is eating less food. In addition, a number of psychosocial factors (social integration, autonomy, stress and job satisfaction, environment, and socioeconomic status) have shown an effect on lifespan.

Suggestions for Prereading Activity

Have students look at the photographs on SB pages 76 and 88 before answering the following questions. How would they describe the people in these pictures? How old are they? What is their attitude? How do they feel about each other? What do you think their hobbies are?

Based on their own cultural experience, ask students how long people generally live in their home country. How about people they know? In general, what sort of lifestyle do these people lead? Do students think living for a long time is good or bad? Why?

Culture Notes

The search for a long life and the "fountain of youth" have featured in cultures for much of human history. In both Chinese and Japanese cultures, there are gods of longevity. In Western culture, Aristotle wrote a famous essay *On Longevity and Shortness of Life* in 350 B.C. In 1512 A.D., Ponce de León became the first of many people to visit Florida seeking the fountain of youth. In addition, much of the present-day cosmetic industry is devoted to disguising signs of aging by restoring a youthful appearance.

Starting in the mid-twentieth century, scientists explored different facets of aging. The scientific study of aging, *gerontology,* produced a special branch of medicine dealing with elderly people, *geriatrics.* Researchers developed several theories to explain the process of aging. One area of research focuses on why cell division seems to proceed normally until a certain point at which cells stop dividing. Another theory looks at the immune system to understand why it becomes weakened in elderly individuals whose production of antibodies slows down. A third area of research involves changes in the endocrine system where glands alter their hormone production as humans age. A fourth major area for geriatric research is the Human Genome Project, which aims to map DNA sequences in hopes that genetic bases for specific diseases can be identified. Some hereditary diseases have been identified, but other diseases that widely affect elderly populations have not as yet. Geneticists hope that the study of DNA will also show them other factors that influence the aging process.

Suggestions for Another Perspective

Ask students to look at the title of the reading on SB page 88. What is the meaning of the title "More Senior Citizens, Fewer Kids"? Remind students that in Chapter 3's self-evaluation, they identified reading strategies that they hadn't yet used. Encourage students to try a new strategy with this reading.

More Senior Citizens, Fewer Kids
Audio CD1, Track 8

Taiwan is experiencing a demographic shift from the situation it found itself in just three decades ago. Since the 1980s, birthrates have dropped and longevity has risen, and as a result, a greater proportion of the current population is elderly. Implications for Taiwanese society are that social needs will change: fewer young working people will be supporting more senior citizens, and the cost of health care will rise. Another consequence of a smaller workforce is that economic growth is likely to slow. Government officials are considering returning to a moderate pronatal position to slow these trends.

Culture Notes

Taiwan's experience is more generally called *demographic transition* in social science literature. As countries develop and better health care is available, death rates and then birthrates fall, and the rate of natural increase stabilizes or slightly declines. This has happened in developed countries throughout the world and has major implications for the nature of society.

Suggestions for Follow-Up Activities

Remind students to complete the Self-Evaluation of Reading Strategies on SB page 137. Again, remind students to note the strategies they have not used. Encourage them to practice new strategies with each reading passage.

As noted under the first reading's Culture Notes, much of the cosmetic industry is obsessed with marketing products that claim to diminish signs of aging. While cosmetic advertising is evident in many magazines, advertisements for anti-aging products are more evident in certain magazines. Have students work in pairs and collect cosmetic ads from four different magazines; their sampling should include magazines aimed at women, as well as those aimed at men. Have students compare all the ads by what they claim to do. What magazines feature the most anti-aging cosmetic ads? What does this reveal about society's perspective on aging? Ask students to discuss their findings in small groups.

| Chapter 5 | **The Mindset of Health** | **Audio CD, Track 9** | |

Most people regard their minds and bodies as separate entities, but recent research has shown that our mindset can influence how our bodies react to illness and disease. The author advocates that we control our health by adopting mindful attitudes instead of mindlessness.

Suggestions for Prereading Activity

Question 1 on SB page 97 asks students to examine the photographs on pages 97 and 104 and make inferences about the doctors and patients photographed. Teach students to pay particular attention to physical settings, facial expressions, nonverbal communication, and the nature of the relationships between doctor and patient. Who seems authoritative, as though he is giving a definitive opinion to the patient? Who seems sympathetic, as though he is open to questions and supportive of the patient? Which patient feels depressed by what the doctor said? How can you tell? Which patient is ready to ask a question?

Prior to having students complete Question 4 on SB page 98, you may wish to ask if visits to a doctor or hospital in other countries are the same as in the United States. For example, is it customary for patients to ask questions about their treatment or request a second opinion?

Culture Notes

Doctor-patient communication has become a major issue in the United States. While the following statements are based on socioeconomic forces that have created general trends, it is important to realize that there are always exceptions to such generalizations.

In the past, it was assumed that the doctor was an authority whose opinions were valued and not to be questioned. The patient was grateful for medical treatment and largely passive in the interaction. As a receiver of medical information, the patient had no responsibility for independently learning about his or her own medical condition. As an indication of their professional training and power, doctors frequently used medical *jargon*—specialized scientific words for describing a condition. Patients seldom understood what they heard, but they were reluctant to ask questions. In medical school, doctors did not receive training in interpersonal communications. Some patients felt that they were not treated as a whole person with an ailment; they became whatever part of the body was diseased. For example, it was not uncommon for doctors to refer to a patient as "the appendectomy in 13A."

Now, in a society where patients see themselves as consumers of medical care, many people want to play a more active role when they interact with their physicians. As patients, they know that they have specific rights and the responsibility to learn about their own conditions. In fact, by federal law, doctors must inform patients of their medical rights. Patients are encouraged to understand the benefits and drawbacks of different treatments and medications. If they feel that a second opinion from another doctor is in order, many patients will request one if their physician hasn't already suggested one. Some of these changes have come about gradually as the population has become more educated, and as medical information and care have become much more readily available. However, other factors are at play as well. Doctors have become defendants in malpractice lawsuits and generally pay huge amounts in insurance against such legal actions. Many Americans have medical coverage through HMOs—health maintenance organizations—which require second opinions or advance permission from the company for all but emergency medical procedures. The cost of medical care and prescription drugs has skyrocketed, so as consumers, patients are more inclined to consider alternative treatments. In addition, a sizeable number of people can't afford either medical insurance or medical care.

Suggestions for Another Perspective

Ask students to look at the photograph on SB page 111. What does it suggest about the type of care in this hospital? Who is talking with the patient? Is the patient in a private room or a busy ward?

How to Behave in a Hospital   Audio CD1, Track 10

From the perspective of the medical staff, the best patient is quiet, undemanding, thankful, and uncritical. The author contends that few hospitals and doctors give patients the respect they deserve. Rather, a patient is treated as an outsider, even when it's their own treatment being discussed.

Culture Notes

The "Blue Cross" comment is indicative of the "bottom line" attitude of many insurers and HMOs who want to reduce the length of hospital stays to cut costs.

The Culture Notes from the first reading can also be applied to this reading.

Suggestions for Follow-Up Activities

Remind students to complete the Self-Evaluation of Reading Strategies on SB page 137.

In preparing the doctor-patient role play described in Question 3 on SB page 114, students could consult family health guides. These guides are available in most libraries as well as online. They feature flowcharts which show which symptoms are considered serious and when you should seek immediate medical help. Using the health guides provides practice with common vocabulary used to describe illnesses. For examples of specialized medical language, you could have students look up the same disease or illness in a *Merck Manual* (a standard physician's reference guide) and a family medical guide. *Merck Manuals* are also readily available in libraries.

Are child prodigies born or made? Children who show exceptional talent before age 10 share several characteristics. They typically have a single-minded drive to learn and excel in particular areas. They also have an unusual ability to concentrate. Neuroscientists say this is because their brains function differently from those of average children. These factors may be inborn, but prodigies thrive when their parents recognize their gifts and encourage them.

Suggestions for Prereading Activity

The prereading for Chapter 6 is different from other chapters because it presents the beginning of the first reading passage. This provides an authentic reading experience because students will often encounter an abstract or other reading before the main passage in their academic work. In searching the Internet, students will typically read the first portion of an article that appears as part of the search results. They will decide whether to read the full article based on their reading of the preliminary citation.

The Newbury House Dictionary defines *prodigy* as "genius, someone of great ability." However, it doesn't mention that a prodigy displays adult-level abilities while still a young child.

Ask your students about the source of this article (*Time,* Asian edition). Draw students' attention to the fact that some news media have different editions targeted to geographical regions. How might this alter the article?

Culture Notes

In the United States, many school systems have special educational programs for gifted and talented students. Definitions of gifted and talented vary, but typically, these would be the top ten percent of all students. Students at the high end of the spectrum learn more quickly and are better able to grasp abstract concepts and complex ideas. They also show creative approaches to problem solving. In 1988, the U.S. Congress established a special act to support programs for gifted and talented students, but limited federal funding has been available at the state and local levels.

Prodigies are in a category by themselves. Their gifts are so pronounced that their needs cannot usually be met within the regular educational system. They are very rare and form the top category of gifted and talented students. Prodigies share certain characteristics, regardless of the field their special talents are displayed. First, they are *precocious,* meaning that their talents are apparent at a very early age. Second, they are *independent* and often highly *intuitive.* As noted in the reading, Son always knew what chess moves to make. No one had to teach him certain procedures. Additionally, prodigies are *driven to master their field,* what Ellen Winner describes as a "rage to learn." They become obsessed with the subject in which they excel. Their ability to focus and ignore distractions was obvious even before MRI scans confirmed that their brains function in a way that heightens concentration.

Suggestions for Another Perspective

Ask students to look at the photograph on SB page 133. How old is this person? What kind of classroom is she in? What does the title suggest that the article will be about?

Reading at 8 Months?
That Was Just the Start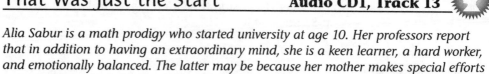

Alia Sabur is a math prodigy who started university at age 10. Her professors report that in addition to having an extraordinary mind, she is a keen learner, a hard worker, and emotionally balanced. The latter may be because her mother makes special efforts to ensure that Alia socializes with children her own age.

Culture Notes

The reading passages in Chapter 6 note that Abigail Sin and Alia Sabur are outstanding in both mathematics and music. This is not an unusual co-occurrence. There is an abundance of literature that shows that both fields—as well as chess—require similar kinds of neural processing and that skills in one area seem to influence the other. An excellent example of this is Harvard math Professor Noam D. Elkies, who excels in all three areas. However, not all brilliant students are equally gifted in multiple fields. Researchers are now studying why some prodigies display giftedness in just one area.

Unfortunately, prodigies often miss out on social interaction with their own age group. Gifted children usually prefer to pursue their chosen area alone. Most gifted children interact with adults or much older students. This is especially true if the child has skipped grades in school or entered university at a very young age. A consequence of missing childhood social experiences is delayed emotional maturation. Special educators try to provide opportunities for social interaction and counseling to encourage social development. Many parents also try to provide their gifted children with age-appropriate social experiences.

Suggestions for Follow-Up Activities

In completing the Self-Evaluation of Reading Strategies on SB page 137, students should note which strategies have become automatic. If there are some strategies that are still underused, students should focus on applying these in the reading passages that follow.

Ask students if they know of any present-day child prodigies. Is there anyone who is gifted and talented in their families?

Ask students to imagine that they are the parent of a toddler. The child is precocious in many ways and perhaps started reading when they were a baby. The child is particularly interested in numbers and music. How would they deal with this? Ask students to work in small groups and develop some ways to make the most of their "child's" gifts. Have students prepare for this activity by researching the Internet and InfoTrac (see Internet Resources/InfoTrac, Unit 2, Chapter 6).

Unit 2 CNN Video Report

Have students watch the video *Michael Kearney, Child Prodigy*. Since the video features a child prodigy, students will enjoy viewing this video after completing Chapter 6. After viewing the video, encourage students to share their thoughts. How does Michael feel about his "fast-track," accelerated academic program? Do you think he ever wished he was like average children? In what way was he still a little boy?

How do Michael's parents feel about the choice they made to send Michael to college instead of kindergarten? Do his parents agree about this? What does

5 · TEACHER NOTES

the father mean when he says: "I don't advocate raising children like this; I think you do it because you have to."?

After discussing the video, have students answer the Video Report questions on SB page 143.

Chapter 7

Matters of life and Death (an excerpt)

Assisted Suicide: Multiple Perspectives

Audio CD2, Track 1

Dr. Francis Moore, a highly respected doctor from Harvard Medical School, discusses when to help a patient die. He compares two cases and notes that the decision to end a patient's life requires extensive medical experience and strong personal judgment.

Suggestions for Prereading Activity

On SB page 146, students are asked to list people who might have different viewpoints on assisted suicide. Then students predict responses to questions used in an interview with Dr. Timothy Quill, publicly known to have prescribed a lethal dose of sleeping pills for a patient dying of leukemia. Next, students read Dr. Quill's responses to the questions. They then compare what they predicted with his actual answers.

Before students start the Prereading Preparation, you may wish to briefly introduce the ethical issues that are featured in Unit 3. The topics contained in this unit may be controversial for many people because of their religious and personal beliefs. Remind your class that all students' views are to be respected.

Culture Notes

As Dr. Moore notes in the first reading, assisted suicide is nothing new. Many doctors have admitted to quietly prescribing lethal amounts of morphine for terminally ill patients under certain circumstances. *Euthanasia,* sometimes called "mercy killing," is meant to end a patient's pain and suffering when there is no hope of recovery. In the 1930s, euthanasia societies were formed in the United States and Britain, but they did not attract very much attention. The issue of euthanasia has come to the fore because of highly publicized cases of people in a persistent vegetative state. When someone is in this condition, they are in a comatose state with involuntary movement carried out by machine.

At other times, euthanasia has attracted media attention and public response when physicians have made their involvement in ending life public. For example, the activities and trial of Dr. Jack Kevorkian polarized public opinion. Kevorkian invented "suicide machines," which aided the demise of terminally ill patients. Technically, the patients inflicted their own deaths, but they were assisted by Dr. Kevorkian.

At this point, only one American state, Oregon, and two countries, the Netherlands and Belgium, legally allow euthanasia. *Voluntary euthanasia* is the term used when doctors administer a lethal injection at the patient's request. When patients take a fatal dose of medication by mouth, it is termed *physician-assisted suicide. Passive euthanasia* is not supplying mechanical life support systems to people who need them.

Suggestions for Another Perspective

Ask students to look at the photograph on SB page 160. What might the medical personnel be discussing?

Should Doctors Be Allowed to Help Terminally Ill Patients Commit Suicide?

Audio CD2, Track 2

Derek Humphry, founder of the Hemlock Society, argues that irreversibly, terminally ill individuals should be allowed to choose to die. Daniel Callahan takes the opposing view, arguing that assisted suicide violates medical traditions and the confidential role of a physician.

Culture Notes

The controversial topic of euthanasia/assisted suicide is extremely complex and fraught with moral, ethical, medical, and legal questions. Opponents of these measures fear that individuals will die for the wrong reasons. Proponents say this will not be the case if certain safeguards are made law.

The Culture Notes from the first reading can also be applied to the this reading.

Suggestions for Follow-Up Activities

Remind students to complete the Self-Evaluation of Reading Strategies on SB page 206.

Question 1 on SB page 164 mentions "living wills," otherwise known as "advance directives." This is a legal document that instructs doctors to withhold certain life support systems if the person becomes terminally ill. To assist students with answering the question, obtain copies of these forms from any hospital or community health center and have students discuss them in small groups. Should young people have advance directives?

Are you or your students aware of any current situations in the news that involve end-of-life decisions? If so, discuss them in small groups and explore the range of possible outcomes. If not, ask students to research a past situation. In the United States, there have been three young women whose conditions have attracted attention: Karen Ann Quinlin, Nancy Cruzan, and Terri Schiavo. In each case, one party argued that there was no chance of recovery and regaining quality of life. These arguments were countered by those who see life itself as worth preserving, even if it is mechanically sustained. To reflect on their research, ask students to write a short response in their journal.

Chapter 8 **Sales of Kidneys Prompt New Laws and Debate**

Audio CD2, Track 3

Trading Flesh Around the Globe

The demand throughout the world for transplant organs far exceeds the supply. This has lead to the creation of a thriving black market in which some impoverished people choose to sell certain body parts, typically their kidneys.

Suggestions for Prereading Activity

Ask students to look at the photograph on SB page 167 and the diagram on SB page 169. What are the people doing in the photograph? What organs can a person live without? Not live without?

The prereading preparation asks students to read a *Time* magazine article about the trade in human flesh. After reading the article, students conduct a survey about whether they would consider selling one of their organs. Students who respond positively are asked to provide a rationale. Students could also complete this survey from the perspective of someone who leads a poverty stricken life. Would such circumstances change their opinions?

Culture Notes

Only a few transplant organs and other body components can be taken from live donors. These typically include one of a person's two kidneys or corneas, a patch of skin, or a lobe from the lung. It is also possible to take bone marrow and stem cells from live donors, and mothers can agree to donate their baby's umbilical cord at birth. All other organs—heart, liver, pancreas—are taken from recently deceased donors. In most cases, these are healthy individuals who have died suddenly. Sometime before their death, they completed an organ donor card and let their family know about their desire to donate organs in the event of an untimely death.

Medical transplants have become feasible only in the last 50 years. Over 20,000 transplants occur each year in the United States, but nearly four times that number of people are on waiting lists for suitable donations. Unfortunately, thousands of these people die because their diseases become fatally acute before an appropriate transplant organ becomes available. The U.S. Congress passed a law to regulate transplants in 1984 and there is a unified national registry for donors and potential recipients. Patients who need transplants go through a thorough evaluation before their names are added to the national registry. Given the scarcity of available organs, it is important that the donor and recipient are matched as closely as possible to increase the chances of a successful transplant. Potential recipients are also screened for the urgency of their condition.

Suggestions for Another Perspective

Ask students to look at the photograph on SB page 172. What is the message? Is this a real situation? Someday, is it possible that receiving an organ transplant will solely depend on how much money you have to purchase the replacement organ? Discuss the danger of this situation.

Sales of Kidneys Prompt New Laws and Debate  **Audio CD2, Track 4**

In response to the growing black market in human organs, many countries are working to tighten laws that prohibit the sale of body parts. At the same time, these same countries are struggling with how to encourage organ donation. Some individuals have proposed that a controlled payment system may provide an appropriate and beneficial "gift" to the donor.

Culture Notes

Many states ask people who are applying for driver's licenses if they want to become organ donors in the event of their death. These states provide the information on the driver's license. Another approach is to complete a donor's card. These cards are downloadable from several sites on the Internet.

A study in the *Journal of the American Medical Association* investigated the long-term effects of kidney sales in a large city in southern India. Follow-up studies of kidney donors indicated that although most people sold kidneys to pay off debts, 75% of them still remained in debt, and 85% of the commercial donors suffered ill health as a result of the surgery. The research concludes that the sale of organs exploits instead of benefits people. The report also states that the sale of organs is unfair to recipients because those who can afford to pay the most get the organs, and perhaps these are not the people who need them most.

Suggestions for Follow-Up Activities

Remind students to complete the Self-Evaluation of Reading Strategies on SB page 206.

There are numerous good sources for organ donor cards. Have students visit the U.S. government and the Red Cross Web sites to look at donor cards and read about the procedure for becoming a potential donor.

Some people believe that their religion prohibits organ donation or reception. In actual fact, very few religions hold this belief about organ donation. Most religions view organ donation as an act of charity. The Red Cross Web site contains position statements by many religious organizations.

Chapter 9

The Gift of Life: When One Body Can Save Another

Audio CD2, Track 5

Modern medicine has made it possible to remove organ parts or tissues from living donors to transplant into critically ill patients. Sometimes unable to find a compatible donor, a family will conceive another child for the purpose of saving an older child's life. Such cases have raised a number of ethical issues.

Suggestions for Prereading Activity

Ask students to look at the chapter title and photograph on SB page 188. What might this chapter be about? Do students notice a family resemblance between the two girls? After they read the first reading, they should return to the photograph of Anissa Ayala and her little sister Marissa (it was taken about six years after their operations).

The prereading activity on SB pages 188 and 189 present two transplant scenarios. The first concerns a doctor's decision about the best recipient for a donor liver. The second raises the ethical issue of using organs and tissues from anencephalic babies. The questions explore students' personal opinions about the scenarios. After students have discussed their answers with a partner, discuss the two scenarios as a class.

Culture Notes

The topics in these readings all raise ethical and moral issues. Many of these topics were introduced in Chapter 8. The first prereading passage raises the issue of determining which patient should receive an available organ. The criteria used to determine the best recipient basically covers the following two factors: compatibility of blood and genetic structures, and the severity of the recipient's condition. Typically, those individuals closer to death are prioritized over healthier patients, although healthier patients stand a greater chance of successful implantation.

The second prereading passage introduces the moral dilemma of using an anencephalic infant's organs and tissues. Babies with anencephaly, a neural tube defect that occurs early in pregnancy, are born without most of their brains. They are blind, deaf, unconscious, and certain to die in a short time if they are not stillborn. There is no treatment for the condition, so the babies are given "comfort care." Although they have only rudimentary brains, other organs are normal. However, because of the absence of the brain, it is difficult to apply the usual criteria of "brain death" in time to save the organs from damage. In a well-publicized case, a mother pregnant with an anencephalic child sought potential recipients for the organs of her unborn child. Since organs from healthy infant donors are in very short supply, this seemed a way to help another baby live. The controversial case resulted in sLeveral hospitals and the American Academy of Pediatrics forming policy statements about the use of anencephalic babies as organ and tissue donors.

The Ayala family case raises issues about another controversial area, the use of stem cells. Stem cells are taken either from embryonic material or from bone marrow. Embryonic stem cells are undifferentiated cells that have the possibility of developing into a variety of organs and tissues. Bone marrow stem cells can produce both red and white blood cells. Bone marrow transplants require especially closely matched cells, preferably from a very close relative. Rejection can occur when the white cells of the donor attack the recipient of the transplant, something called *graft-versus-host disease*. To reduce the chances of this, the recipient undergoes radiation to destroy the existing cells before the transplant. In a new procedure, the immune cells or T-cells are removed. This is sometimes done with a patient's own bone marrow before the individual has radiation treatment. The stem cells are cleansed and returned to the patient's bloodstream after the radiation treatment is finished. The 1990 Nobel Prize in medicine was given to pioneers of these techniques.

Suggestions for Another Perspective

Ask students to look at the photograph on SB page 203. Based on the photograph and the title of this reading, what has happened to this family? What is the "breath of life"?

Two Parents Offer Their Daughter the Breath of Life—to No Avail   **Audio CD2, Track 6**

When a young girl's lungs failed after falling ill with pneumonia, her parents underwent traumatic surgeries in order to give their daughter a chance at life. Sadly, the lung transplants were not a success and their daughter died. Some contend that modern medicine has taken the limits of parental sacrifice to a new, and perhaps unreasonable, level.

Culture Notes

Lung-lobe transplants from living donors were first performed in 1990. Used mostly for cystic fibrosis patients, the preferred procedure is to use two lobes—one lobe from each of the two donors. The two lobes replace all five of the diseased lobes. Since it is a more recent procedure, the survival rate for lung transplants is somewhat lower than kidney transplants.

Since accurate matching is such a critical aspect of all transplants, family donors are more suitable than unrelated donors. However, there is always some risk to the donor, and the procedure certainly isn't always a success for the recipient.

Suggestions for Follow-Up Activities

Remind students to complete the Self-Evaluation of Reading Strategies on SB page 206.

In order to make ethical issues more relevant, students might find it helpful to read or watch personal accounts of a transplant experience. In pairs, students could research a specific type of transplant or an ethical issue. Ask students to report their findings to the class. The Ayala family's experience was made into a commercial film entitled *For the Love of My Child.* Copies of the film are available on the Internet.

Unit 3   **CNN**   Video Report

Have students watch the video *Baby Donor.* Since the video features an interview with Mary Ayala (Marissa and Anissa's mother, Chapter 9 reading), students should view the video after completing Chapter 9. After watching the video, discuss the clip in the context of what students already know about the Ayala family. How soon after the operation do students think this video was made? What are the relationships of the people in the video? How do they feel about each other? What do you think they will tell Marissa when she grows up? Has watching this video made students think about the ethical issues that were discussed in Chapter 9? Has it changed their ethical position in any way?

After discussing the video, have students answer the Video Report questions on SB page 213.

Unit 4:	The Environment

Chapter 10   **Playing with Fire**   **Audio CD2, Track 7**

Every year fires are lit in the Amazon rain forest to make way for farming and cattle ranching. However, if this tradition continues, it has the potential to disturb Earth's entire ecosystem. Amazonian rain forests contain a large proportion of the world's biological diversity and genetic heritage. The moisture and nutrient cycles in the Amazon have an enormous impact on global climate.

Suggestions for Prereading Activity

Ask students to look at the photograph and diagrams on SB pages 215, 216, and 220. What is this chapter about? Are any of your students from the countries where the world's major rain forests are located? If so, what can they tell you about them?

The prereading questions on SB page 216 ask about the double meaning of the phrase "playing with fire." *Literal* and *figurative* are opposite terms. *Literal* means that you keep the exact meaning of the words as they are. *Figurative* means that you intend to create a mental picture by using words in a certain way, similar to a metaphor. Students may not know that the figurative meaning of the phrase is that you are doing something extremely dangerous that could turn into a disaster.

Culture Notes

The world's great rain forests are all found in developing areas where two types of economic exploitation are evident. Some people, especially indigenous people or settlers without access to other techniques, use fire to clear the forest for farming. Others, typically large multinational corporations, cut and remove timber commercially on a large scale. The use of fire for clearing land has had a worldwide practice among horticultural groups since the beginnings of agriculture in the Neolithic Era. Anthropologists refer to it as *slash-and-burn* meaning the trees are cut down and the land is burned. The ash from the fires provides nutrients to the soil, and acts as a type of fertilizer. In theory, new growth of plants is stimulated. However, sometimes the bare land does not retain water and erosion occurs. The rich forest habitat for plants and animals is destroyed. In addition, carbon dioxide from the fires goes into the atmosphere, adding to CO_2 buildup. Carbon dioxide in the atmosphere can trap heat and excessive amounts of it may lead to global warming. To this point, the absorption of CO_2 by rain forests has moderated this effect. However, if people destroy rain forests through burning, they increase the chances of contributing to the "Greenhouse Effect."

As the first reading notes, rain forests serve as storehouse for large numbers of plants and animals that are found nowhere else on Earth. Scientists are just beginning to identify and understand many of the plants, but there is widespread concern that the plants may be destroyed before we realize how valuable they are.

Suggestions for Another Perspective

Ask students to look at the photograph on SB page 230. Who is the person pictured in the photograph? What is he doing? Have students imagine that they are farmers participating in the queimadas tradition—how would they feel about what they are doing?

Taking Two Steps Back   **Audio CD2, Track 8**

Queimadas, a tradition as old as agriculture itself, is endangering the very existence of the Amazon. For several months each year, local farmers light thousands of fires to clear the forest, resulting in the destruction of vast areas of rain forest.

Culture Notes

The Amazon Rain Forest is the largest rain forest in the world, covering more than a million square miles surrounding the Amazon River. Two other large areas of rain forest are in Southeast Asia and Africa. All rain forests face problems as a result of economic exploitation, but these are most severe in the Amazon and Asian rain forests. In Asia, forests have been destroyed for valuable woods such as teak, used for furniture and shipbuilding. Developers also destroy rain forests to obtain crude oil and natural gas.

Research reported in the journal *Nature* in 1999 indicates that the Amazonian rain forest is disappearing even faster than scientists previously believed. Previously, satellite photographs measured deforestation. However, the new study was carried out on the ground in Brazil by interviewing loggers and landowners, and then taking low-altitude aerial photographs of more than 1,000 locations. The results showed that the rain forest is disappearing at twice the rate estimated by the satellite photographs.

Suggestions for Follow-Up Activities

Remind students to complete the Self-Evaluation of Reading Strategies on SB page 282. Ask students to reflect on how well the strategies worked.

Have students prepare for Questions 3 and 4 on SB page 234 by researching the Internet and InfoTrac (see Internet Resources/InfoTrac, Unit 4, Chapter 10).

Ask students to find out what ecological groups exist in your community and on your campus. Ask students to find out what issues or causes these groups are concerned with. What programs do they have to help the environment? What can students do to support them?

See http://www.heinle.com for student and instructor activities and materials to accompany this student book. Crossword puzzles, flash cards, and worksheets are just some of the resource you'll find at this site. The answer keys for chapter assessments found in this book will be found in the Instructor Resources location for each book.

Chapter 11   Wilder Places for Wild Things

Audio CD2, Track 10

Most modern zoos try to recreate natural habitats for animals so that they experience similar sights, sounds, activities, and privacy to what they would experience in the wild. In response, many zoo animals are breeding for the first time and are exhibiting a range of normal behaviors that weren't seen when they lived in cages in traditional zoos. Zoo managers want to increase public awareness and appreciation of wild animals.

Suggestions for Prereading Activity

On SB page 239, students are asked to compare traditional and modern zoos. However, some students may lack a range of experience with zoos. Use the pictures of the caged panda on SB page 239 and the open habitat on SB page 243 to cue students about the differences. For students with zoo experience, ask if they have ever seen baby animals in zoos. Where did they come from? Why do they sometimes receive very special treatment?

Note the byline for the authors. What does it mean when someone writes an article *with* other authors? What special information could contributors from these four cities provide?

Culture Notes

Zoos as collections of animals have been around for thousands of years. Historical writings and drawings show that the pharaohs of ancient Egypt kept displays of monkeys and giraffes from south of the Sahara Desert. During the Roman Empire, fierce and dangerous animals were collected to be used in public fights between people and animals. Royalty of long ago collected exotic or strange animals from the places they conquered. The collections served partly for scientific purposes, but mostly for entertainment. European royalty had *menageries,* collections of animals from newly discovered areas. And even travelers brought back unusual animals which were kept in cages, often in botanical or plant gardens.

Caged animals were the norm in the first public zoos. It was considered sufficient to offer the public a chance to observe animals from distant parts of the world, and very little, if any, consideration was given to how the animals were treated or kept while in captivity. During the eighteenth and nineteenth centuries, the supply of animals was considered unlimited, so if some caged animals died, they could simply be replaced by others. During this same time and continuing into the twentieth century, wealthy people went on safaris in Africa and India with the goal of shooting animals and bringing the skins and heads home to display.

The first zoos in North America date to the 1860s in Philadelphia, Chicago, and New York. By 1900, some zookeepers started to think about keeping animals in more naturalistic surroundings, although cement cages and iron bars remained the norm for much of the century. Naturalistic zoos are a relatively recent trend. The San Diego Zoo and its Wild Animal Park were among the first zoos to emphasize natural environments for animals.

Modern zoos have several important missions. One of their goals is to create natural conditions so that animals will reproduce in captivity. Another goal is to educate the public about the importance of maintaining habitats for wild animals. The natural setting helps zoos achieve this goal by showing animals in a realistic context. The third goal is to maintain healthy zoo specimens with genetic diversity so that biologists can hopefully replenish endangered wild populations.

Suggestions for Another Perspective

Ask students to look at the photograph and title on SB page 252. What animal is this? What is a *predator*? What is *prey*? Is hunting an inborn instinct?

Predators on the Prowl   **Audio CD2, Track 10**

Americans have mixed opinions about wild animals. Not long ago, many wild animals, such as cougars, were threatened with endangerment, so laws banned hunting them. In many cases, these laws and certain habitat changes created favorable conditions for population increase. At the same time, development of human living areas encroached on the animals' habitats. Now, some wild animals and humans share the same territory, sometimes with disastrous results.

Culture Notes

In a number of areas in the United States, sightings of predators and other formerly rare wild animals have become common. Public opinion about whether this is good or bad is divided. Some people enjoy seeing wild animals and encourage the animals by feeding. However, the animals are still wild predators and occasionally attack humans, sometimes with fatal results. Wildlife specialists have started public education campaigns to promote safe co-existence. In National Parks such as Yellowstone, rangers also try to train wild animals like bears to avoid places frequented by humans. In some states, hunting seasons for previously protected animals have resumed to reduce population sizes.

Suggestions for Follow-Up Activities

Remind students to complete the Self-Evaluation of Reading Strategies on SB page 282. Have students mastered all of the strategies?

If there is a zoo nearby, encourage your students to visit, either as a group or on their own. Ask them to take notes about the animals and the conditions in which they are kept. Suggest that they look to see if there is any attempt to simulate the animals' natural environment. They could also find out if the zoo has captive breeding programs. In class, students could work in small groups to create a poster about the zoo. Encourage students to include any photos that they took.

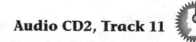

The focus on Nevada's Yucca Mountain as the potential burial place for nuclear waste has created a great deal of controversy. Scientists have presented competing evidence for the safety or risk of the site with regard to upwelling ground water or tectonic events such as earthquakes and volcanic eruptions. The design of the facility is another contentious topic. Federal officials are trying to find an alternative site for the repository by offering a variety of incentives.

Suggestions for Prereading Activity

The prereading activity directs students to complete the exercise on SB page 283. Explain that they should use background knowledge and the nuclear power plant diagram to label the steps in the process. Ask students to work in pairs, paying close attention to the letters for the sequence. In deciding on the order of statements, students may want to draw a line from the last part of one statement to the first part of the next. When students have completed the labeling of the diagram, have them compare their results with others in the class. If they disagree, ask them to explain their reasoning.

Next, students should read *Introduction: A Nuclear Graveyard* on SB page 261. Have pairs of students use the text to complete the flowchart on SB page 262. When they have completed this task, ask students to identify the main concerns about storing nuclear waste.

Culture Notes

Nuclear wastes remain radioactive for thousands of years, so the controversy about their storage is based partially on immediate concerns and partially on projections of what conditions will be like for ten thousand years. The following are important considerations in both cases: the wastes must be completely sealed in durable containers; the containers must remain dry so that they don't rust or corrode; the site must be remote with limited and secure access; and the storage site should be in a stable area.

Another concern about nuclear waste is how it will be safely transported from nuclear power plants all over the United States to a central storage facility. Again, concerns are based on accidents that have occurred in the transport of low-level nuclear wastes. The Department of Energy plans to transport the waste by truck and train through 43 states. Many people are extremely concerned about the risk this poses to citizens throughout the country.

In the end, the disposal and long-term storage of nuclear wastes is a NIMBY issue—Not In My Back Yard. Despite the fact that many people benefit from nuclear power plants in their everyday lives, no one wants to risk having the place where they live contaminated by radioactive waste. Yet, because there are no true "wastelands," the problem is a difficult one to resolve.

Suggestions for Another Perspective

Ask students to look at the map on SB page 278. What are the concentric rings on the map? What large cities lie within 200 miles of the Yucca Mountain site? Why is this a concern?

5 · TEACHER NOTES

Many of Nevada's citizens are angered by the process that led the federal government to select Yucca Mountain as a nuclear waste storage site, claiming political maneuvering. Nevadans are skeptical of the DOE's environmental record although DOE officials say stronger standards are now in place. People also argue that Nevada has no economic need for the site.

Culture Notes

Nevada's citizens are not happy with the political process by which the Yucca Mountain repository was selected. One of their concerns is the poor safety record of the Department of Energy. One of the other sites that had been under consideration in Hanford, Washington, experienced leakage of liquid radioactive wastes in 1973. Citizens have been concerned that the liquid would seep into groundwater and eventually contaminate the Columbia River. At the time of the accident, the Atomic Energy Commission assured people that their concerns were groundless, that the radioactivity would fall before the water reached the river. Accidents like this one, Three Mile Island, and Chernobyl raise concern about whether safety assurances can be trusted.

Suggestions for Follow-Up Activities

Remind students to complete the Self-Evaluation of Reading Strategies on SB page 282. Encourage students to discuss the strategies they found particularly useful.

Ask students about nuclear power plants and nuclear waste disposal in their countries. Is the disposal of nuclear waste a concern for places that don't have nuclear facilities? Should there be an international agency that deals with all nuclear waste?

Refer students to the InfoTrac and Internet key words and Web sites listed under Internet Resources/InfoTrac, Unit 4, Chapter 12. Ask students to locate either a government or citizen information group that they can write to for further information about the proposed storage site at Yucca Mountain.

Unit 4 CNN Video Report

Have students watch the video *Ivan the Gorilla*. Since this video is about a gorilla's new home at Zoo Atlanta, students will enjoy watching this clip after completing Chapter 11. Ask students why Zoo Atlanta believes Ivan will be happier in his new surroundings. How is his new home better than his last? Will Ivan adjust to the zoo's "natural" habitat?

Ask what students know about gorillas in the wild. Have they seen the film *Gorillas in the Mist* about the life and work of the late Dian Fossey? The mountain gorillas she studied are threatened with extinction because of the loss of their forest habitat and illegal hunting. The loss of habitat is a natural tie-in with deforestation in rain forests in Chapter 10.

After discussing the video, have students answer the Video Report questions on SB page 289.

Topics for Today
ANSWER KEY

Chapter 1   **Hop, Skip . . . and Software?**

Prereading Preparation (p. 2)
1. Answers will vary: *software* is defined in the *Newbury House Dictionary* as "in a computer a set of instructions that lets a person perform certain tasks, such as word processing, adding numbers, or reading information on the Internet; software is not part of the machine itself." The term *hardware* refers to the machine itself.
2–3. Answers will vary.

A. Reading Overview: Main Idea, Details, and Summary (p. 7)
Main Idea:
The writer contrasts two schools in the same area that have different standpoints on technology and computer use in the classroom. The article includes arguments for and against computer use in the classroom.

Details:
Name of School or Organization: Charlottesville Waldorf School
Name of Spokesperson: Jody Spanglet, Nancy Regan, and Kim McCormick
What is this person or group's opinion about the use of computers in the classroom?: This group opposes having computers in the classroom. They believe actual experience is vital for young children. "It is important for students to interact with one another, with teachers, and with the world—to explore ideas, participate in the creative process, and develop their knowledge, skills, abilities, and inner qualities."

Name of School or Organization: B.F. Yancey Elementary School
Name of Spokesperson: Paula White
What is this person or group's opinion about the use of computers in the classroom?: This group supports having computers in the classroom. Students at Yancey interact with teachers as well as with computers. Even kindergartners are using computers in the classroom, but the teacher is the one entering the information.

Name of School or Organization: The Alliance for Childhood
Name of Spokesperson: N/A
What is this person or group's opinion about the use of computers in the classroom?: This group opposes having computers in the classroom. Concerns range from health issues to the need for stronger bonds between children and adults and more hands-on, active play in learning.

Name of School or Organization: Columbia University's Teachers College
Name of Spokesperson: Gene Maeroff
What is this person or group's opinion about the use of computers in the classroom?: This person supports having computers in the classroom. "Computers can enhance education. But those possibilities become greater as kids get older, particularly at the secondary level, and absolutely at the college or postgraduate level."

Name of School or Organization: Educational Testing Service
Name of Spokesperson: N/A
What is this person or group's opinion about the use of computers in the classroom?: This group supports having computers in the classroom, when used correctly. They found that middle school students with well-trained teachers who used computers for "simulations and applications" in math class outperformed students on standardized tests who had not used them for that purpose. Meanwhile, eighth graders whose teachers used computers primarily for "drill and practice" performed even worse.

Name of School or Organization: The University of Michigan's Center for Highly Interactive Computing in Education
Name of Spokesperson: Elliot Soloway
What is this person or group's opinion about the use of computers in the classroom?: This group has not expressed an opinion about the use of computers in the classroom, but has studied actual classroom computer use. They surveyed 4,000 schools last year and found that 65 percent of students in public schools, including high schools, spend less than 15 minutes a week using computers to access the Internet.

Name of School or Organization: Department of Technology for the Albemarle County Schools
Name of Spokesperson: Becky Fisher
What is this person or group's opinion about the use of computers in the classroom?: This group supports having computers in the classroom. "Adding technology to the mix only makes a great teacher even better." The issue is not whether technology is appropriate for students. . . . Rather, it is whether our teachers are supported in a way to maximize the benefits of technology."

Name of School or Organization: Maine Learning Technology Initiative
Name of Spokesperson: Bette Manchester
What is this person or group's opinion about the use of computers in the classroom?: This group supports having computers in the classroom. The success of the program depends heavily on leadership among teachers in the state, as well as the complete integration of laptops into every school's curriculum.

Summary
There is a current debate about whether to introduce computers to elementary school children. Some educators believe that children need more hands-on, active play in learning, while others believe that the use of computers at a young age can stimulate a strong desire to learn.

B. Statement Evaluation (p. 9)
1. F 2. F 3. T 4. T 5. I 6. F 7. T

C. Reading Analysis (p. 10)
1. a. Charlottesville Waldorf School b. 2 c. 3 d. 1 **2.** There are no computers at the Charlottesville Waldorf School. In contrast, computers are considered a rich resource and are used everywhere at the B.F. Yancey Elementary School. **3.** a. **4.** a. 3 b. the Alliance for Childhood c. 2 d. educators and technology enthusiasts who believe that the use of computers at an early age can open a child's mind and kindle a great desire for learning e. 1 f. parents and guardians g. 3 **5.** b **6.** b **7.** a. 2 b. 2 c. She wants her children to get to know the world on a firsthand basis. **8.** a. 3 b. 1 **9.** b

D. Dictionary Skills (p. 13)
1. 3a: to take up especially readily or gladly; this expresses the abstract quality of *embrace* as opposed to physical meaning, as in hugging
2. 2c: a way or means of access; this communicates the context of the sentence
3. 2a: a continuous sequence or range
4. 1b: an uneasy state of blended interest, uncertainty, and apprehension

E. Critical Thinking Strategies (p. 15)
Answers will vary.

F. Questions for "Program to Bring Laptop Computers to Rural Schools" (p. 18)

1. Free Pad is a pilot program to put technology in rural schools. The computers will replace textbooks and library books used by kindergarten through 12th graders in the county's eight school districts.
2. Students are at a disadvantage because they do not have a link to the rest of the world. Before going to larger cities, students from rural Arkansas are at a disadvantage both socially and globally, compared to their peers.
3. The program will provide a link to the outside world. With videoconferencing, the program will allow school districts to share teachers in subjects such as upper-level math and science.

G. Follow-up Activities (p. 19)

Answers will vary.

H. Topics for Discussion and Writing (p. 20)

Answers will vary.

I. Cloze Quiz (p. 21)

1. exception 2. technology 3. debate 4. introduced 5. spectrum 6. moratorium
7. range 8. bonds 9. educators 10. age 11. kindle 12. middle 13. devoid
14. loaded 15. enhance 16. particularly 17. access 18. overall 19. drops
20. advocate

Chapter 2　　My Husband, the Outsider

Prereading Preparation (p. 23)

1. Answers will vary, but one definition of a *mixed marriage* is "a marriage between two people of different races, religions, or cultures."
2–4. Answers will vary.

A. Reading Overview: Main Idea, Details, and Summary (p. 28)

Main Idea:

Marian Hyun, a Korean-American woman, describes her experiences with her family's reaction to her dating and marrying a non-Korean man.

Details:

Marian: Marian wanted to marry a man of her own choice. She did not want to marry a traditional Korean man.

Marian's father: Her father wanted her to marry a Korean man. He wanted her to get married when she was 24. He wanted her to have a big wedding so he could invite many friends and relatives.

Marian's mother: Her mother wanted her to marry a Korean man. She wanted to help Marian choose a husband.

Marian's aunt: Her aunt wanted her to marry a Korean man. She wanted her to get married before she became too old. She didn't acknowledge that Marian was dating a non-Korean man.

The Korean doctor: He seemed to feel that Marian should behave as a native-born Korean and follow Korean traditions.

Marian's husband: Marian did not give us any information about her husband's opinion.

Summary

The narrator, Marian Hyun, describes her experiences with her family as she dated and got married. As an American-born Korean, she had many cultural conflicts with her parents, other relatives, and the Korean men she dated. In the end, she married a non-Korean man and had a small wedding.

B. Statement Evaluation (p. 30)

1. F 2. T 3. F 4. T 5. T 6. I

C. Reading Analysis (p. 31)

1. b **2.** b **3.** the husband of a person's daughter; a person's son through marriage
4. a. 2 b. 3 **5.** a. 3 b. 1 **6.** a. He hounded her for three months. b. 2 **7.** Because he hadn't realized how expensive a big wedding could be, and he changed his mind about wanting a big wedding for his second daughter.

D. Dictionary Skills (p. 33)

1. 3b: to take notice of 2. 4b: something that fully satisfies a wish: IDEAL 3. 3: strikingly, excitingly, or mysteriously different or unusual 4. 2a: incapable of association or harmonious coexistence

E. Critical Thinking Strategies (p. 36)

Answers will vary.

F. Questions for "Unwelcome in Chinatown" (p. 40)

1. She feels unwelcome in Chinatown because the Chinese waiters and salespeople treat her badly once they discover she does not speak Cantonese.

2. Yes, her experience as an American-born Chinese person seems like a typical experience because many of her American-born Chinese friends have had the same experience.

3. Answers will vary. Some possible responses include the following: (1) both Marian Hyun and Amy Wu were brought up in the United States as native-born Americans; (2) they both were raised speaking English, so that neither of them is fluent in their parents' native language.

4. Answers will vary.

G. Follow-up Activities (p. 41)

1–3. Answers will vary.
4. a. The highest percentage involves blacks marrying whites.
   b. The percent of black marriages that involve whites is higher than the percent of white marriages involving blacks.
   c. Asians have the lowest percentage of interracial marriages.

H. Topics for Discussion and Writing (p. 45)

Answers will vary.

I. Cloze Quiz (p. 46)

1. curious 2. exotic 3. disappointed 4. uproar 5. embarrassing 6. ignored
7. remember 8. preferred 9. acknowledge 10. once 11. snobby 12. lose face
13. reluctantly 14. violence 15. incompatibility 16. persistence 17. hounded
18. gave in 19. object 20. old maids

Chapter 3 **Beyond Rivalry**

Prereading Preparation (p. 49)

Note: A *sibling* is defined as "a person with the same parents as someone else, i.e., a brother or a sister." *Sibling rivalry* is defined as "competition between siblings."
1. Answers will vary.
2–6. Answers will vary.

A. Reading Overview: Main Idea, Details, and Summary (p. 54)

Main Idea:
Siblings are a major part of each other's lives as children, but they tend to drift apart as adults. However, as they become older, siblings often become closer again.

Details:
I. Social Connections
    A. Young Adult Siblings
        1. have careers
        2. get married
        3. have children
    B. Older Adult Siblings

        1. retire
        2. get divorced or become widowed
        3. children grow up and leave home
   II.   Effects of Critical Events in Siblings' Lives
        A. bring siblings closer together
        B. pull siblings further apart
   III. Feelings of Aging Siblings Towards Each Other
        A. 20 percent are hostile or indifferent
        B. majority feel lingering rivalry
        C. 53 percent increased contact
           1. more free time
           2. anxiety about sibling's health
           3. fewer friends and contacts
           4. need link to the past
   IV. Factors Affecting Contact with Siblings
        A. proximity
        B. having a sister
   V.   Factors Affecting Why Siblings Don't Ask Each Other for Help
        A. sibling is equally needy or frail
        B. sibling is a safety net or a last resort
        C. latent rivalry

Summary
Siblings may grow apart as adults because they become involved in their careers and get married and have children. However, as siblings become older, they retire, they may lose their spouse, and their children often leave home. At this time, siblings may become closer to each other or be pulled further apart by critical events in their lives, such as the illness or loss of a parent. Even when the siblings do have increased contact with each other, they tend not to ask each other for help for various reasons.

B. Statement Evaluation (p. 57)
1. F 2. F 3. T 4. NM 5. T 6. NM 7. F

C. Reading Analysis (p. 58)
1. a. 1 b. parental sickness; parental death **2.** a. 3 b. because the man hadn't spoken to his sister in 20 years **3.** b **4.** b **5.** a. decline b. a group of people who are with you c. 1 **6.** all the way in the past to the person's childhood **7.** a. 1 b. 3 **8.** proximity **9.** a. 2 b. loaning money, running errands, performing favors c. The phrase *such as* introduces examples.

D. Dictionary Skills (p. 60)
1. 4: a uniting or binding replacement or force: TIE
2. 1c: to bring to mind or recollection, to provoke memories
3. 2b: to manage to continue; definition 1 is too general.
4. 2: to support or corroborate on a sound or authoritative basis; definitions 1a, 1b, and 1c are all either legal or formal in nature.

E. Critical Thinking Strategies (p. 63)
Answers will vary.

F. Questions for "Middle Children and Their Position in the Family" (p. 66)
1. Middle children make friends faster than anyone else in the family. They tend to leave home first, and live farther away from the family than anyone else. They like to do their own thing, make their own friends, and live their own lives. Middle children are good mediators or negotiators. They learn the art of compromise. They are often the best-adjusted adults in the family.
2–3. Answers will vary.

G. Follow-up Activities (p. 66)
Answers will vary.

H. Topics for Discussion and Writing (p. 69)
Answers will vary.

I. Cloze Quiz (p. 70)
1. worse 2. drift 3. retirement 4. spouses 5. link 6. sibling 7. last 8. neighbors
9. marriages 10. generation 11. divorce 12. old age 13. events 14. rift
15. example 16. parent 17. close 18. hostile 19. relationships 20. estrangement

Unit 1 Review
J. Crossword Puzzle (p. 72)
Across Answers
2. solace 4. rift 7. case 9. access 12. debate 14. bilingual 15. concern 16. evoke
21. validate 23. exotic 24. last 25. incompatible 26. choice 27. bond
Down Answers
1. separation 3. exception 5. infer 6. spectrum 8. family 10. embrace 11. sibling
13. engagement 17. education 18. enhance 19. diminish 20. wedding 22. ideal

CNN Video Report: High-Tech Job Shortage (p. 74)
1. Answers will vary, but may include the fact that American schools have not prepared
   students for high-technology jobs; math and science are not emphasized in American
   schools as they are in other countries, technology has changed so fast in such a short
   time, and American schools have not kept pace with the changes.
2. A. T B. F C. T D. I E. I F. F
3. Answers will vary, but may suggest that the United States will continue to lose ground
   to other countries in the creation of IT jobs because they do not emphasize math and
   science education enough. Tougher standards and better training for teachers could
   improve the education system. Making technology education a higher priority for all
   children would help, but there is no panacea, no quick-fix solution to the problem.

Unit 2	Influences on Our Lives: Nature versus Nurture

Chapter 4	**Who Lives Longer?**

Prereading Preparation (p. 76)
1. Answers will vary. *Longevity* is defined as "length of life" or "a long lifetime."
2–4. Answers will vary.

A. Reading Overview: Main Idea, Details, and Summary (p. 80)
Main Idea:
Many factors influence how long we live. Some of these factors are fixed, but others, such
as physical lifestyle and psychosocial factors, are changeable.

Details:
Fixed Factors:
A. gender
B. race
C. heredity

Changeable Factors:
Health Measures:
(1) don't smoke
(2) drink moderately
(3) eat breakfast
(4) don't eat between meals
(5) maintain normal weight
(6) sleep eight hours
(7) exercise moderately

Psychosocial Factors:
(1) social integration
(2) autonomy
(3) stress and job satisfaction
(4) environment
(5) socioeconomic status

What you can do:
A. Institute sound health practices;
B. Expand your circle of acquaintances and activities

Summary

Our longevity is affected by many factors. Some of these factors, such as gender, race, and heredity, are fixed. However, other factors are changeable. We can take measures to improve our health—for example, get exercise and sleep eight hours every night. Psychosocial factors, such as our level of autonomy, the amount of stress in our lives, and the number of friends we have, also affect our longevity and are under our control.

B. Statement Evaluation (p. 82)
1. F 2. NM 3. T 4. T 5. NM 6. F 7. T

C. Reading Analysis (p. 83)
1. a. fallacies b. Scientists are separating two opposite ideas; the opposite of a fact is something that is not true, i.e., false—a fallacy. **2.** c **3.** b **4.** a **5.** cigarette smoking, drinking, and reckless driving **6.** c **7.** social integration, autonomy, stress and job satisfaction, environment, and socioeconomic status **8.** b **9.** stress and job satisfaction **10.** c **11.** a

D. Dictionary Skills (p. 85)
1. 3: an event or development that marks a turning point or a stage; definitions 1, 2a, 2b, and 4 all refer to physical structures.
2. 3a: characterized by intensity of feeling or quality
3. 3: a right or power to influence action or decision; definition 2 refers only to an opinion.
4. 3b: exhibiting or based on thorough knowledge and experience; 5: showing good judgment or sense; is also appropriate.

E. Critical Thinking Strategies (p. 87)
Answers will vary.

F. Questions for "More Senior Citizens, Fewer Kids" (p. 90)
1. The article discusses the declining birthrate and the increasing life expectancy in Taiwan.
2. In Taiwan, the proportion of elderly people to young people will increase steadily.
3. There will be a new set of social welfare needs such as nursing homes and day care programs for the elderly. There may not be enough young people to support older people. Because of the declining birthrate, there will be a dwindling population of working-age adults, which will slow economic growth.
4. The government promoted family planning campaigns. People are marrying later (at an older age), and some young people are opting to stay single.

G. Follow-up Activities (p. 91)
1. Answers will vary.
2. a. This chart shows life expectancy in the United States from 1940 to 1993.
   b. (1) about 75 years
      (2) about 67 years
   c. (1) 1940 to 1950; males gained almost four years
      (2) 1940 to 1950; females gained almost five years
      (3) Answers will vary. Explanations in general include medical advances, especially the introduction of antibiotics, specifically penicillin. The polio vaccine was also developed about this time.
   d. (1) Males gained about 11 years.
      (2) Females gained about 13 years.

3. a. This chart shows lifespan highs, lows, and averages by continent for people born in 1994.
    b. Answers will vary. Explanations might include widespread endemic diseases, general sanitation, air and water quality—factors that affect entire populations.
4–5. Answers will vary.

H. Topics for Discussion and Writing (p. 94)
Answers will vary.

I. Cloze Quiz (p. 95)
1. longer 2. separate 3. fallacies 4. ripe 5. longevity 6. birth 7. elements
8. changeable 9. heredity 10. reversed 11. influence 12. expectancy 13. shorten
14. evidence 15. ability 16. landmark 17. years 18. health 19. moderately
20. Maintain

Chapter 5   The Mindset of Health

Prereading Preparation (p. 97)
A doctor's *bedside manner* can be defined as a doctor's attitude and conduct in the presence of a patient. This is considered an important factor in the patient's care.

1–5. Answers will vary.

A. Reading Overview: Main Idea, Details, and Summary (p. 102)
Main Idea:
Our state of mind can positively or negatively affect how we respond to health issues. A mindful approach to illness can positively influence our health.

Details:
The Significance of Mindful Attitudes:
Context: We place our perception intentionally in a different context.

State of Mind: Our state of mind positively influences our state of body. For example, people who fasted for personal reasons were less hungry than people who fasted for external reasons, such as money.

The importance of context and mindfulness in handling illness:
1. Our interpretation of the events around us could be the first link in a chain leading to serious illness.
2. There are some diseases that were thought to be physiological and incurable. They may be more under our personal control than we believe.
3. Mindful or mindless reactions to disease (such as cancer) can influence its effects.
    a. There are probably people with undiagnosed cancer who feel healthy and may remain healthy.
    b. There are people with diagnosed cancer who go into a decline that is not directly related to the disease.

Research supporting the effects of mindfulness:
1. Patients have been successfully taught to tolerate pain by seeing how pain varies depending on context. These patients needed fewer pain relievers and left the hospital earlier than a comparison group of patients.
2. People in a nonsmoking context didn't suffer withdrawal symptoms, but they did experience cravings again when they returned to a context where smoking was allowed.

How to take a more mindful approach to illness:
1. Try to heal ourselves and not depend completely on doctors.
2. Get new information from our bodies and from books.
3. Work on changing contexts, both physical environment and emotional outlook.
4. Try to stay healthy rather than be made well.

How to positively influence our health:
1. Exchange unhealthy mindsets for healthy ones.
2. Increase a generally mindful state.

The Significance of Mindless Attitudes:

<u>Context</u>: We accept preconceived notions of the context of a particular situation.

<u>State of Mind</u>: We jeopardize our body's ability to handle a situation.

Summary

We may have mindful or mindless attitudes toward illness. If we have a mindless attitude towards an illness, we tend to accept preconceived notions about that illness, and we jeopardize our body's ability to handle the situation. If we have a mindful attitude towards illness, we can positively affect our body's ability to get well. There are several ways in which we can take a more mindful approach toward illness and positively influence our health.

B. Statement Evaluation (p. 105)
1. T 2. F 3. T 4. F 5. T 6. I 7. T

C. Reading Analysis (p. 106)
1. a. mindlessly b. 3 **2.** a. mindfully b. 2 c. 1 **3.** a. 1 b. an external reason
c. The subjects who were less hungry showed a smaller increase in free fatty acid levels.
4. b **5.** a. the source of pain b. The term is defined between the dashes. **6.** c **7.** a.
the health risks, the bad smell, the cost, others' reactions to smoking b. the relaxation,
the concentration, the taste, the sociable quality c. 3 **8.** b

D. Dictionary Skills (p. 108)
1. 4b: the main part of a literary or journalistic work: TEXT. All of definitions 1, 2, 3, and 6, as well as 4a and 4c, refer to physical objects; 5a and 5b refer to groups of people.
2. 2b: something pledged. Definition 2a is too specific; 2c implies an obligation to another; all of 1 refers to legal or formal matters.
3. 3c (1): progression through a development or period or a series of acts or events.
4. 1a (1): an individual's conception or impression of something known, experienced, or imagined. This most clearly describes a notion as a personal idea.

E. Critical Thinking Strategies (p. 110)
Answers will vary.

F. Questions for "How to Behave in a Hospital" (p. 113)
1. She suggests that we act submissive, humble, grateful, and undemanding. In other words, she suggests that we be completely passive.
2. We should act as if it may be our fault, and never suggest that it might be the fault of anyone working in the hospital.
3. Gloria Emerson suggests that we take no active role in our treatment and that we do not ask questions when we don't understand. In contrast, Ellen Langer says that we should be active and ask questions to understand our medication and treatment.

G. Follow-up Activities (p. 114)
Answers will vary.

H. Topics for Discussion and Writing (p. 115)
Answers will vary.

I. Cloze Quiz (p. 116)
1. separate 2. essential 3. physical 4. problems 5. split 6. influences
7. perceptions 8. automatically 9. intentionally 10. fast 11. external
12. experiment 13. hungry 14. body 15. research 16. system 17. link 18. illness
19. control 20. between

Chapter 6   Small Wonders

Prereading Preparation (p. 118)
A prodigy is defined as "a genius, someone of great ability."
1–3. Answers will vary.

A. Reading Overview: Main Idea, Details, and Summary (p. 123)

Main Idea:

Prodigies are children who by age 10 display a mastery of a field usually undertaken only by adults. Prodigies display a single-minded drive to excel. Recent discoveries have shown a significant difference in the activity of the brain of a prodigy versus that of an average child.

Details:

Name of Prodigy: Nguyen Ngoc Truong Son
How this child excels: He is gifted at playing chess. At 12 he is Vietnam's youngest champion and a grand master in the making.

Name of Prodigy: Abigail Sin
How this child excels: She is Singapore's most celebrated young pianist at age 10.

Organization or Profession: Author and Psychologist
Name of Spokesperson: Ellen Winner
Does this person believe prodigies are born, made, or both? Prodigies are born.
Arguments or Evidence: Prodigies are exotic creatures whose standout accomplishments are obvious. Prodigies demonstrate a "rage to learn."

Organization or Profession: Director, University of Melbourne's Morgan Center
Name of Spokesperson: Michael O'Boyle
Does this person believe prodigies are born, made, or both?: Prodigies are born.
Arguments or Evidence: Compared with average kids, children with an aptitude for numbers show six to seven times more metabolic activity in the right side of their brains. Scans also showed heightened activity in the frontal lobes, believed to play a crucial "executive" role in coordinating thought and improving concentration. O'Boyle believes prodigies also can switch very efficiently between the brain's left and right hemispheres, utilizing other mental resources and perhaps even shutting down areas that produce random distractions. Prodigies seem to be able to focus better—to muster the mental resources necessary to solve problems and learn.

Organization or Profession: Creator of the Suzuki Method
Name of Spokesperson: Shinichi Suzuki
Does this person believe prodigies are born, made or both?: Prodigies are made.
Arguments or Evidence: "There is no inborn talent for music ability." Even those who believe certain talents are innate agree that a child's upbringing has a big impact on whether a gift is developed or squashed.

Organization or Profession: National Taiwan Normal University
Name of Spokesperson: Wu Wu-tien
Does this person believe prodigies are born, made, or both?: Half born, half made.
Arguments or Evidence: Found more than three-quarters of the 32 outstanding physics and chemistry students were the eldest child in small, dual-income households—families with relatively high socioeconomic status.

Summary

Child prodigies show remarkable abilities from a young age. They are also characterized by an unstoppable drive to use their exceptional abilities. Many experts maintain that these children are born this way, and studies have shown that their brains operate differently than those of average children.

B. Statement Evaluation (p. 126)

1. I 2. T 3. F 4. F 5. F 6. T 7. I

C. Reading Analysis (p. 127)

1. a. 2 b. 1 **2.** a. 2 b. chess c. 1 **3.** a. wunderkind b. 2 **4.** A *prodigy* is a child who by age 10 displays a mastery of a field usually undertaken only by adults.
5. "rage to learn," unstoppable urge **6.** a **7.** a. inborn b. 4 c. 2

D. Dictionary Skills (p. 129)

1. 1: a subtle distinction or variation
2. 2b: a level (as of intelligence) typical of a group, class, or series

3. 7a: an urgent, basic, or instinctual need
4. 2a (1): painfully affecting the feelings

E. Critical Thinking Strategies (p. 131)
Answers will vary.

F. Questions for "Reading at 8 Months? That Was Just the Start." (p. 135)

1.
Accomplishments	Age
Began reading words	8 months old
Finished her elementary education	5 years old
Traveled to middle school for eighth-grade math	2nd grade
Began college at Stony Brook	10 years old
Will earn her undergraduate degree	13 years old

2. *Problem:* Alia had trouble finding a school that was appropriate for her level of education because of her age. By fourth grade, neither public nor private schools could accommodate her. Colleges would not accept her at such a young age.
    Solution: She attended State University at Stony Brook, a public college.
    Problem: Alia had trouble making friends her own age because she was not in school with young people.
    Solution: Mrs. Sabur helped Alia find friends her age. She signed Alia up for art classes and a lunch group.

G. Follow-up Activities (p. 136)
Answers will vary.

H. Topics for Discussion and Writing (p. 138)
Answers will vary.

I. Cloze Quiz (p. 139)
1. inborn 2. pondering 3. nuance 4. naturally 5. prodigy 6. probe
7. wunderkinder 8. brains 9. startlingly 10. average 11. giftedness 12. ethnicity
13. definition 14. drive 15. functioning 16. differentiate 17. previous
18. mathematics 19. nurture 20. music

Unit 2 Review

J. Crossword Puzzle (p. 141)
Across Answers
2. say 8. notion 9. landmark 10. key 11. innate 13. ponder 14. fixed 16. course
18. toddler 19. up 22. sound 23. yes 24. got 25. shift 26. master 27. coronary

Down Answers
1. hypothesis 3. prodigy 4. add 5. fast 6. probe 7. keep 12. differentiate
15. drawback 16. connection 17. commitment 20. profound 21. nurture

CNN Video Report: Michael Kearney, Child Prodigy (p. 143)
1. Answers will vary, but may include the following: parents of child prodigies should allow them to go to a university to keep them from being bored; *or* parents of child prodigies should not put them in schools with older children, outside their peer group.
2. A. Michael is ordinary in some ways: he loves video games, he squabbles with his kid sister, he takes tennis lessons. He is extraordinary for being a 10-year-old college graduate.
   B. Michael was reading at 8 months old. Most children learn to read between ages 5 and 7. Answers will vary when students discuss at what age they learned to read.
   C. Michael felt very small in college, like a munchkin. He had different interests from the other students and was not at the same stage of social development.
   D. Michael's parents were confused about what to do: they knew the best thing for his intellectual level was send him to college, but the best thing for his social level would have been to enroll him in kindergarten.

E. Michael majored in anthropology. He is planning on pursuing commercial endorsements in Japan. Answers will vary as to whether students believe Michael will be successful in Japan.

3. Answers will vary, but may include the following: Michael's intelligence is due to "nature," he was born with an exceptional brain; Michael's intelligence is due to "nurture," his parents gave him classic literature at an early age and helped propel his intelligence and drive by nurturing him. Answers will vary as to whether inheritance played a role in his development, and if so, what kind of role.

Unit 3 — Technology and Ethical Issues

Chapter 7 — Assisted Suicide: Multiple Perspectives

Prereading Preparation (pp. 146-147)

1. Answers will vary, but may include a list such as: Politicians, Religious leaders, Family members, Spouses, Sick people /Terminally ill patients, Doctors and health care providers
2. Answers will vary. (See Dr. Quill's answers on the top of page 147.)
3. Answers will vary. (See Dr. Quill's answers on the top of page 147.)
4. Answers will vary, but may include such points as: Some doctors might argue, like Dr. Quill, that every person should have the right to choose his own quality of life and to not suffer once the pain is too much, particularly when there is little hope for a cure. Other doctors might believe that there is always hope that a cure will be discovered, even for a disease that the patient will die from very soon. These doctors might argue that patients should always have hope, even if it is only a small amount, and therefore should not end their lives prematurely.
5. Answers will vary, but may include: Both doctors have considered this question in relation to real cases, like those of their own patients. These doctors conclude that the idea of assisting somebody to die when they are terminally ill is a complicated decision to make. A doctor and family member must consider many factors before coming to a conclusion. They feel that doctors and ethicists in the medical community should discuss such issues carefully before making these difficult decisions.

A. Reading Overview: Main Idea, Details and Summary (p. 150)

Main Idea:

Dr. Moore, who has been practicing medicine all his life, describes two very ill patients he treated differently. He concludes that the decision to help end a patient's life requires strong judgment and long experience.

Details:

The Dilemma: For doctors with terminally ill patients, the dilemma is whether to actively help these patients die.

Case #1: A former nurse who had sustained a fractured pelvis. Her condition was serious: her lungs filled up; her urine stopped, her heart developed dangerous rhythm disturbances. She was on life support equipment. Her family requested that the doctor take her off the machines.

Dr. Moore's Decision: He decided not to take her off the machines.

Outcome: She recovered and left the hospital.

Case #2: An 85-year-old woman whose hair caught fire. Her condition: she had a deep burn; her condition was probably fatal.

Dr. Moore's Decision: They backed off treatment; they gave her plenty of morphine.

Outcome: She died peacefully in the hospital.

The Lesson of Dr. Moore's Experience: As a reasonable physician, you should do what you would want done for you. Assisting people to die requires strong judgment and long experience to avoid its misuse.

Summary

Dr. Moore, 81, has practiced medicine all his life. He describes two very ill patients he treated differently. One he refused to let die; the other he did help to die. He brought up the second patient's case at an ethics seminar where the participants were surprised that he discussed a real case taking place in the present day. In both cases, he feels he made the right decision. He believes that the decision to help end a patient's life requires strong judgment and long experience.

B. Statement Evaluation (p. 153)

1. F 2. I 3. T 4. I 5. I

C. Reading Analysis (p. 154)

1. a. 2 b. 3 c. if and when to help a patient die   d **2.** a. giving terminal cancer patients heavy medication to help them to die without pain   b. 1 c. 2 **3.** b **4.** b
5. a. It means that patients can recover from a serious condition quickly, too.   b. an electrical device that maintains a person's heartbeat   c. It is described in lines 12–13.
6. the former nurse who sustained a fractured pelvis in a car accident, the wife and mother of the two men **7.** c **8.** a. 3 b. 1 **9.** c

D. Dictionary Skills (p. 156)

1. 2c: the principles of conduct governing an individual or a group
2. The second full entry: 1a; the past participle of *fracture* used as an adjective to describe something broken.
3. 1: to keep in an existing state; or 4b: SUSTAIN. Both definitions are appropriate, given the context of sustaining life.
4. 6b: SUFFER, UNDERGO. In this context, *suffered* is a synonym for *sustained.*

E. Critical Thinking Strategies (p. 158)

Answers will vary.

F. Questions for "Should Doctors Be Allowed to Help Terminally Ill Patients Commit Suicide?" (p. 162)

1. a. Humphry believes that death is part of medicine and that doctors should be able to help terminally ill people die if their suffering becomes unbearable.
   b. Depressed people should be counseled and helped to live.
2. Answers will vary. Humphry's wife might have asked her doctor to help her end her life and the doctor might have done so because Humphry stated that there was nothing *else* they could do.
3. Callahan believes that doctors should never help terminally ill people die. If they want to die, they can commit suicide without a doctor's assistance.
4. He worries that people will be pushed to suicide by a doctor's suggestion. He also worries that people will be pushed by their families to consider suicide because of the medical expenses and the burden to their families.

G. Follow-up Activities (p. 163)

Answers will vary.

H. Topics for Discussion and Writing (p. 164)

Answers will vary.

I. Cloze Quiz (p.165)

1. internship 2. medication 3. essential 4. describe 5. fractured 6. maintained
7. their 8. machines 9. respected 10. lethal (*fatal* is acceptable here) 11. sick
12. awoke 13. smoking 14. fatal (*lethal* is acceptable here) 15. ethics 16. problem
17. case 18. in retrospect 19. students 20. reality

Chapter 8   Sales of Kidneys Prompt New Laws and Debate

Prereading Preparation (p. 167)
1–3. Answers will vary.

A. Reading Overview: Main Idea, Details, and Summary (p. 173)

Main Idea:

In an effort to control the sale of organs for transplant, Britain and other countries have passed laws prohibiting the sale of organs. Some people fear that these laws may lead to fewer available organs for transplant.

Details:

Laws about organ donation:

Britain: It is a criminal offense to sell or buy organs.

World Health Organization: It does not make laws governing the sale of organs.

U.S.: The sale of human organs is unlawful.

Belgium: According to law, organ donation is automatic upon death unless specifically requested otherwise.

Opinions about sales of organs:

Britain: It is a controversial issue in Britain.

World Health Organization: It has condemned the practice and has asked member nations to take appropriate measures, including legislation, to prohibit trafficking in human organs.

U.S.: Ethicists and policy analysts have suggested that paying donors or their estates may be an effective way to increase the supply of available organs.

Belgium: We have no information about Belgian opinions.

Arguments in favor of a law prohibiting the sale of organs:
1. Legislation should make organ donation automatic at a person's death, in order to increase organ availability.
2. People in desperate circumstances have, and would, sell their organs, even martyr themselves, in order to save their families.
3. Some people would sell an organ for frivolous reasons.

Arguments against a law prohibiting the sale of organs:
1. People should be able to do whatever they wish with their bodies, if it's of their own free will.
2. Financial compensation for organs could stimulate an increase in organs and tissues available for transplantation and research.
3. The law could scare off donors because it might create the impression that all donations are improper.

Summary

Because many people, especially poor people, have been selling their organs for transplants, Britain, the United States, and other countries have passed laws prohibiting the sale of organs. However, some people fear that such laws may lead to the decrease of available organs for transplant.

B. Statement Evaluation (p. 175)
1. F 2. F 3. T 4. T 5. NM 6. F 7. NM 8. T

C. Reading Analysis (p. 176)
1. a. 2 b. 1 **2.** a. selling human organs for transplant b. 2 **3.** c **4.** a. Britain's National Health Service b. 1 **5.** a. 1 b. 3 **6.** a **7.** c **8.** a. 1 b. to buy Porsches (i.e. expensive luxury cars) or take a girlfriend on a holiday c. 2

D. Dictionary Skills (p. 178)
1. 2b: to deal with, TREAT; 2a: to direct the efforts or attention, is also appropriate
2. 2c: to make known or public. This is appropriate in view of "headlines."
3. a. 1a: actual performance or application b. 3a: the continuous exercise of a profession
4. The second full entry; 2: TRADE, BARTER

E. Critical Thinking Strategies (p. 181)

Answers will vary.

F. Follow-up Activities (p. 182)

1. Answers will vary.
2. a. This graph compares the number of heart, kidney, lung, liver, and pancreas transplants in the United States for the years 1982 and 1995.
    b. (1) kidney
       (2) kidney
       (3) Kidney transplants are the most frequent because people have two kidneys. Two kidneys are available from a cadaver. In addition, kidneys are more available from living donors as well as from cadavers because people can live with one kidney. Demand for kidneys is very high.
    c. (1) kidney
       (2) liver
3. Answers will vary.

G. Topics for Discussion and Writing (p. 185)

Answers will vary.

H. Cloze Quiz (p. 186)

1. transplant 2. disclosed 3. organ 4. banning 5. sale 6. supply 7. impoverished 8. possible 9. kidneys 10. law 11. dead 12. recipient 13. Punishment 14. practice 15. traffic 16. hospitals 17. pick 18. waiting 19. countries 20. cadaver

Chapter 9 The Gift of Life: When One Body Can Save Another

Prereading Preparation (p. 188)

1–2. Answers will vary.

A. Reading Overview: Main Idea, Details, and Summary (p. 193)

Main Idea:

Faced with the terminal illness of their daughter, the Ayala family decided to have another child in order to provide a compatible donor. The Ayalas' decision generated considerable controversy regarding the ethical and moral issues involved in their case and similar ones.

Details:

The Ayalas' Dilemma: Their daughter Anissa was terminally ill; her only brother's marrow was incompatible with hers.

The Ayalas' Decision: They decided to reverse Abe Ayala's vasectomy and to have another child to serve as donor for Anissa.

Arguments Supporting the Ayalas:
(1) They would be able to save their daughter's life.
(2) It makes just as much sense to have a child to save another as it does to have a child for any other reason.
(3) They will love the second daughter, and would not have aborted her even if she had not been a suitable donor.

Arguments Opposing the Ayalas:
(1) It is not ethical to bring a baby into the world to serve as a biological resupply vehicle.
(2) The baby did not consent to be used as a donor.
(3) The parents created a new life and used it for their own purposes.

The Larger Dilemmas:
(1) Today, life is being tapped to save life.
(2) What is the morality involved if a couple conceives a baby for such a purpose and the fetus's tissue is incompatible? Do they abort the fetus and try again?

(3) Is the risk for living donors worth the chance of saving another's life?

(4) Could the body be turned into a commodity if compensation is offered for organs?

Summary

The Ayalas' decision to conceive a child as a donor for their daughter has caused concern and controversy. Ethical concerns include the morality of giving life to a child who will serve as a donor without giving its consent, the issue of abortion if the fetus proves to be an incompatible donor, the issue of living donation and the risks to the donor, and the debate over compensation for organ donation.

B. Statement Evaluation (p. 196)

1. F 2. T 3. F 4. I 5. I 6. T 7. F

C. Reading Analysis (p. 197)

1. b **2.** a **3.** a. 2 b. in cases of leukemia **4.** a. 2 b. 2 c. 1 **5.** a. when the baby was old enough and strong enough to donate bone marrow safely b. 1 **6.** agree **7.** a **8.** b **9.** a driving safety laws b. Fewer people die in driving accidents due to these driving safety laws. Therefore, there are fewer cadaver organs available. **10.** a. 3 b. 1 **11.** a

D. Dictionary Skills (p. 200)

1. 1b: a state of inability to perform a natural function
2. *vt,* 1: to find a fault in
3. The second full entry: *vt:* 2: to originate or take part in the development of
4. 3a: characterized by intensity of feeling or quality

E. Critical Thinking Strategies (p. 202)

Answers will vary.

F. Questions for "Two Parents Offer Their Daughter the Breath of Life—to No Avail" (p. 204)

1. a. two
   b. Yes. The two lung transplants were successful. However, Alyssa died of heart failure.
2. Because either or both of his parents risked dying from their partial lung transplants.
3. a. Cindy still experiences pain. Roger suffers from muscle weakness.
   b. No, they don't. They say they would do it again if given the chance.

G. Follow-up Activities (p. 205)

Answers will vary.

H. Topics for Discussion and Writing (p. 208)

Answers will vary.

I. Cloze Quiz (p. 209)

1. surgeon 2. marrow 3. rejection 4. launched 5. denouement 6. unless 7. donor 8. failed 9. sibling 10. incompatible 11. success 12. pregnant 13. optimum 14. safely 15. radiation 16. disturbed 17 consent 18. life 19. transplant 20. frivolous

Unit 3 Review

J. Crossword Puzzle (p. 211)

Across Answers

2. excerpt 6. put 7. pacemaker 10. optimum 14. fatal 17. controversial 18. organs 20. denouement 22. impoverished 23. martyr 25. retrospect 26. disclose

Down Answers

1. up 3. catheter 4. deem 5. frivolous 8. essential 9. donor 11. marrow 12. maintain 13. cadaver 15. case 16. automatic 19. address 21. ethics 24. us

CNN Video Report: Baby Donor (p. 213)
1. Answers will vary.
2. A. T
   B. T
   C. NM
   D. F
   E. T
3. Answers will vary, but may include the ethical issues ranging from issues of consent, propriety of harvesting marrow from a toddler, and decisions about whose life is more important. Answers will vary when considering whether couples should be prohibited from having babies to harvest their marrow or organs—those who agree may say that it is wrong to have a child solely to use parts of its body for others, those who disagree may say that people have children for many different reasons. Answers will vary on the issue of patient's consent—some may say it is always necessary, others may say there are cases that are exceptions. Answers will vary on the issue of parental consent—some may say that parents always know what's best, and others may say that parents should not have life or death power over their children.

Unit 4   The Environment

Chapter 10   Playing with Fire

Prereading Preparation (p. 216)
1. The phrase "playing with fire" can be defined in its figurative sense as "doing something enjoyable, but dangerous."
2. A rain forest can be defined as a forest with a daily rainfall and very thick growth of trees and other plants.
3. Answers will vary.

A. Reading Overview: Main Idea, Details, and Summary (p. 221)
Main Idea:
The Amazon rain forests in Brazil are being destroyed at an alarming rate. This destruction is negatively affecting the environment and may reach a point where deforestation cannot be reversed.

Details:
I. The Destruction of the Amazon Rain Forests
    A. by loggers, who cut down trees
    B. by builders of dams, which flood the land
    C. by gold miners, who poison rivers with mercury
    D. by farmers, who burn sections of the forest for farming
    E. by the government, which is clearing land for highways
II. Effects of the Disappearance of the Rain Forests
    A. Over one million species of animals and plants will vanish.
    B. It may change global weather patterns.
    C. Burning the forest sends huge amounts of CO_2 into the atmosphere.
III. Overview of How Brazilian Rain Forests Became Endangered
    A. Brazil built the Trans-Amazon Highway to help settle the country's interior.
    B. Settlers cleared the land and planted crops.
    C. The poor soil failed in a few years.
IV. Advantages of Maintaining the Rain Forests
    A. The market value of jungle produce will yield more income than cattle ranching or lumbering.
    B. Rain forests are a potential food source.

C. Rain forests are a source of alternative, natural pesticides.

D. Many jungle chemicals may be effective drugs in treating diseases such as cancer.

Summary

In an effort to settle its vast interior, the Brazilian government built a highway to encourage people to move to and farm vast areas. However, the farmers and ranchers burned the rain forest to clear land. The poor soil eventually failed, and people have continued to clear land and destroy the rain forest. Environmentalists are concerned that the deforestation is creating serious environmental problems and may lead to the permanent, irreversible destruction of the Amazon rain forest.

B. Statement Evaluation (p. 223)

1. T 2. T 3. I 4. F 5. I 6. T 7. I

C. Reading Analysis (p. 224)

1. a. 2 b. because of the thousands of fires in the rain forests **2.** b **3.** a **4.** a. 2 b. 2 c. because loggers, dams, mercury pollution, and cocaine farming all endanger the rain forest **5.** c **6.** a **7.** a. the trapping of heat by atmospheric CO_2 b. carbon dioxide **8.** b **9.** c **10.** a **11.** a British journal

D. Dictionary Skills (p. 226)

1. 3a (1): experienced, made, or received newly or anew; also 3d: newly or just come or arrived

2. *vt:* 4a: to lay level with or as if with the ground

3. The first full entry: 1: to move to action: INCITE.

4. 2d (1) because it describes the three-year analysis; 2d (2) more appropriately describes what Charles Peters actually published

E. Critical Thinking Strategies (p. 228)

Answers will vary.

F. Questions for "Taking Two Steps Back" (p. 232)

1. (1) Smoke blocked out the sky for hundreds of miles; (2) many people developed bronchial problems and had to be hospitalized; (3) the smoke blinded motorists and caused highway accidents.

2. Mendes was a union leader and environmentalist who protested against land-clearing ranchers. He was probably murdered to stop the protests and to frighten other people who were concerned about the environment.

3. a. As a result of the Earth Summit in 1992, Brazil backed, or supported, treaties designed to protect the environment. In addition, because of a weaker, or souring, economy, ranchers did not have the money to expand.

   b. Because Brazil's economy has become much stronger (has rebounded) recently, farmers are beginning to expand again. Another reason is that a drought has made it easier to set fires and keep them going.

4. a. The government claims that the newspapers have exaggerated the extent of the fires, and that the headlines are way out of proportion.

   b. The author disagrees with the Brazilian government's explanation because he says that "only now has Brasilia come up with $2.4 million for a detailed survey of the last three years' damage." He implies that the government wasn't interested before.

G. Follow-up Activities (p. 233)

1. Answers will vary.

2. a. This chart illustrates the destruction of the world's rain forests from 1700 through 2100.

   b. There were 1,200 million hectares.

   c. None

   d. (1) It means the rate of destruction that will probably occur in the future.

      (2) It is based on the actual rate of destruction since 1950.

      (3) We can change this rate by limiting further destruction of the world's rain forests.

3–4. Answers will vary.

H. Topics for Discussion and Writing (p. 235)
Answers will vary.

I. Cloze Quiz (p. 236)
1. River 2. danger 3. level 4. forests 5. disappear 6. Moreover 7. climactic
8. recycles 9. evaporation 10. roads 11 encourage 12. cutting 13. rain
14. deforestation 15. survival 16. study 17. products 18. burning 19. irreversible
20. world

Chapter 11 Wilder Places for Wild Things

Prereading Preparation (p. 239)
1. Traditional zoos can be described as smaller facilities that have animals in cages. Long ago, a traditional zoo was a *menagerie,* defined as a group of animals held in captivity. A modern zoo is often situated on a more extensive land area, with animals living in environments created to resemble their natural habitats.

2–4. Answers will vary.

A. Reading Overview: Main Idea, Details, and Summary (p. 244)
Main Idea:
As many species of animals are being threatened with extinction, the role of zoos has become more important. This role includes preserving endangered animals and providing naturalistic settings to encourage the animals to reproduce.

Details:
I.   Examples of Animal Behavior in Naturalistic Settings
   A.   Beavers cut down trees for their winter food supply.
   B.   Chimpanzees work for food by manipulating tools.
   C.   Gorillas mate and form families.
II. Zoos Re-create Animals' Natural Environment
   What zoos do: reproduce sights, sounds, smells, and feel of the wild.
   Examples: rainstorms, cliffs, trees, plants, jungle vines, waterfalls, natural sounds, natural foods, artificial day and night
   Results: Animals mate, raise young, and develop survival skills.
III. Species-Survival Programs (SSPs)
   A.   Purpose of the SSPs
      1. To pair up males and females from different zoos
      2. To breed endangered species
      3. To inform and excite the public about zoos and animals
   B.   Examples of Successful Animal Releases into the Wild
      1. The return of condors to the Andes
      2. The release of golden lion tamarins into a reserve in Brazil
      3. The return of oryxes to Oman, Jordan, and Israel

Summary
The role of zoos has become increasingly important as more animals are threatened with extinction. Zoos have begun providing more naturalistic settings, which encourage animals to reproduce, and exchanging animals for breeding purposes. Zoos preserve endangered animals and sometimes even return them to their natural environments.

B. Statement Evaluation (p. 246)
1. F 2. T 3. O 4. F 5. T 6. T 7. O

C. Reading Analysis (p. 247)
1. a. their food b. 1 **2.** mating and forming a family **3.** b **4.** c **5.** a. because the animals' environment is not really natural, it is man-made b. 1 c. lion-tailed macaques
6. a. elephants b. 2 **7.** species-survival program **8.** a 9 c **10.** a. 1 b. 2

D. Dictionary Skills (p. 249)

1. The second full entry: 1b: something serving as a signal or hint
2. 2: ENGROSS, ABSORB
3. The third full entry: 3: SIMULATE. Definitions 1 and 2 refer to physical actions, but *simulate* is a synonym for *mimic* in this context.
4. 2b: to do a favor for

E. Critical Thinking Strategies (p. 251)

Answers will vary.

F. Questions for "Predators on the Prowl" (p. 254)

1. Iris Kenna was killed by a mountain lion.
2. a. Californians must decide on a law to permit mountain-lion hunting.
   b. The purpose of the law is to control the mountain-lion population, which in California is now 6,000 animals.
   c. Some people are against the proposed law because they think the animals should be protected.
3. The mountain-lion problem has increased because hunting of mountain lions has been banned since 1972. In addition, the human population has increased greatly, and people have taken over mountain-lion territory.
4. Most people in Colorado believe that development in mountain-lion territory should be restricted.
5. Answers will vary. The authors are probably in favor of restrictions on land development. They state that people "usurped" (a negative term) wild animal territory, and that cougars are "majestic" (a positive term).

G. Follow-up Activities (p. 256)

1–3. Answers will vary.

H. Topics for Discussion and Writing (p. 257)

Answers will vary.

I. Cloze Quiz (p. 258)

1. replace 2. beavers 3. reproduce 4. work 5. hide 6. mated 7. smaller
8. visitors 9. extinct 10. vanish 11. role 12. construction 13. habitats 14. sounds
15. natural 16. weather 17. behaviors 18. elephants 19. mimic 20. cues

Chapter 12   A Nuclear Graveyard

Prereading Preparation (p. 261)

Nuclear power can be defined as "power generated by the splitting of the atom." The waste generated by this process is radioactive, which means it emits waves that are lethal to humans.

1. a
2. (1) Earthquake! Movement in the earth's crust. (2) Groundwater wells up suddenly, flooding the repository. (3) Nuclear poisons seep into underground water that flows into Death Valley. (4) Insects, birds, and animals drink at the valley's contaminated springs. (5) Radioactivity spreads into the biosphere. (6) Disaster!
3. Answers will vary.

A. Reading Overview: Main Idea, Details, and Summary (p. 267)

Main Idea:

The U.S. government has selected Yucca Mountain in Nevada as a possible site for a nuclear waste depository. This choice has created considerable controversy.

Details:

Arguments Against Using This Site:

(1) The landscape shows evidence of earthquakes and volcanoes.
(2) Earthquakes disrupt the water table.
(3) Water corrodes storage canisters and hastens the escape of radioactive particles through the rock.
(4) Scientists cannot know absolutely whether groundwater will well up under the Yucca Mountain during the next 10,000 years.

(5) If poisons escaped from the site, there could be a major disaster.
(6) If the water table has risen in the past, it is likely to do so again, especially over 10,000 years. Szymanski pointed out geological evidence to support this theory.
(7) The federal government has made mistakes in the past with regard to storing nuclear waste.

Arguments in Favor of Using This Site:
(1) Geologists believe that shock waves from an earthquake could not rupture the repository. They also believe that eruptions from small volcanoes probably wouldn't threaten the repository because the flows would be small and localized.
(2) Underground nuclear explosions at the nearby test site have shown that tunnels can withstand forces even greater than those produced by earthquakes.
(3) The site is very remote. It is very far from civilization.
(4) The water table is unusually deep. Nuclear waste could be buried far beneath the ground yet still rest safely above the groundwater.
(5) A panel of researches, convened by the National Academy of Sciences to evaluate the risks associated with ground water, disagree with Szymanski's findings.

Summary
The U.S. government's possible plan to build a nuclear waste repository in the Yucca Mountains in Nevada has created considerable controversy among Nevadans—who don't want the site in their state—the Department of Energy, and the National Academy of Sciences' panel of researchers, geochemists, and geologists. These groups have debated the available geological evidence, and so far no one has agreed to host the site.

B. Statement Evaluation (p. 269)
1. T 2. F 3. T 4. T 5. F 6. I 7. I

C. Reading Analysis (p. 271)
1. an earthquake causing water contamination that will poison life **2.** a. 1 b. people who live in the state of Nevada; residents of Nevada **3.** a. 2 b. There is only a trace of a dirt road; obviously, almost no one lives in that area. c. dryness **4.** b **5.** refuse
6. a. 1 b. 2 **7.** c **8.** rain (rainwater) **9.** a. upwelling of magma b. 1 **10.** a. 2
b. Workers in a coal mine below a Chinese city did not feel any tremors when a devastating earthquake hit the city. **11.** a. to find a state or an Indian tribe willing to host the nuclear waste depository b. 3 **12.** a. Incentives include offers to build highways, airports, or schools and to pay for harbor cleanups. b. The assurances include promises of local participation in deciding how the facility is operated and the freedom to back out of the evaluation process at any time. c. 2 d. 1 e. 1 f. 3

D. Dictionary Skills (p. 273)
Part 1
1. 2b: to deal with; 2a: to direct the efforts or attention of, is also appropriate.
2. 1: devoid of inhabitants and visitors *or* 3b: BARREN, LIFELESS
3. The third full entry: 1b: in the sense of providing a facility, but not for an event or a function.
4. 1b: exhausted of active or required components or qualities often for a particular purpose; also 2: drained of energy or effectiveness
Part 2
5. the third full entry: 1: very small: INFINITESIMAL
6. the second full entry: 1: the worthless or useless part of something: LEAVINGS

E. Critical Thinking Strategies (p. 277)
1. Answers will vary. However, she probably doesn't think it's a poor location because in the first sentence of the continued article, she describes the potential disaster as a "scary scenario," which implies exaggeration. She also says, "In fact, the risk to Nevadans may be overstated." The overall tone of the article seems biased in favor of the site.
2–4. Answers will vary. For Question 3, possible responses might include that the people designing the repository, as well as the U.S. government, have a sense of responsibility for people who will live in the near and distant future. The government might be concerned about legal consequences if the site contaminated water in the foreseeable future, for instance, the next 100 or even 200 years.

F. Questions for "A Nuclear Graveyard" (excerpt) (p. 280)

1. The site was chosen for political reasons. The author means that Nevada, because it has a small population and, consequently, few delegates in Congress, did not have the political power to influence the decision to locate the repository in Nevada.
2. Nevadans are concerned about the Department of Energy's horrible environmental record and long-standing culture of secrecy. Furthermore, the DOE's efforts to clean up secret dumps have failed abysmally. Nevadans are worried that the same thing might happen to them.
3. The Yucca Mountain project will have many layers of external oversight and will not be kept secret.
4. Nevada's economy depends upon gaming (gambling, as in Las Vegas) and tourism. The nuclear repository might keep tourists away from Nevada.

G. Follow-up Activities (p. 281)

1. Answers will vary.
2. B, C, E, A, D
3. Answers will vary.

H. Topics for Discussion and Writing (p. 284)

Answers will vary.

I. Cloze Quiz (p. 285)

1. refuse 2. nuclear 3. site 4. radioactive 5. water 6. remoteness 7. road
8. government 9. earthquakes 10. repository 11. years 12. poisonous 13. buried
14. geologist 15. Nevada 16. finding 17. host 18. incentives 19. lure
20. assurances

Unit 4 Review

J. Crossword Puzzle (p. 287)

Across Answers

1. all 4. yes 6. lure 8. movement 10. scour 12. repository 15. cue 16. fresh
18. remote 21. cougar 22. mimic 23. study 24. proliferate 25. desolate
26. inattention 27. donate

Down Answers

1. assurance 2. level 3. prompt 5. immerse 7. pachyderm 9. off 11. deforestation
13. spent 14. overstate 17. imminent 19. incentive 20. hype

CNN Video Report: Ivan the Gorilla (p. 289)

1. Answers will vary, but may include that modern zoos are meant to educate and entertain the public, as well as preserve endangered species. Some ways that modern zoos differ from traditional ones include the following: modern zoos put the animals in larger spaces, and modern zookeepers go to extraordinary lengths to recreate the conditions found in the wild in terms of sounds, lighting conditions, daily routines, food, and terrain.
2. A. F
   B. T
   C. T
   D. O
   E. F
3. Answers will vary.

Topics for Today
VIDEO SCRIPTS

CNN Video Report: High-Tech Job Shortage
Running Time 01:41

Video Vocabulary
marketable: capable of being sold
acute: severe
Industrial Revolution: the rapid development of power-driven machines that spurred a major change in the U.S. economy in the late 19th century
lo and behold: interjection used to express wonder or surprise

Video Script
Reporter: Eighth graders at the Bilingual and Bicultural Middle School in Harlem are learning how math can be useful online.

Male Teacher: O.K., we're going to do eBay. It's worth $65.69 each. That's a lot.

Zulma Rivas (Educational Coordinator): We're here to make them marketable. We want to make children able to go out to the workforce and be able to use the technology that's available to them.

Reporter: Combine technology skills with a math and science background and these students will find more jobs than they ever dreamed possible. The reason: an acute shortage of workers specializing in information technology.

Harris Miller (IT Expert): We have a dramatic shortage of skilled IT workers. It's like running out of iron ore in the middle of the Industrial Revolution.

Reporter: Of the 1.6 million technology jobs created in the United States this year, computer specialists say half remain empty. A problem that will only get worse before it gets better. What's more, the U.S. school system has not been able to keep up with the Internet explosion. In fact, the U.S. is barely staying afloat. One study shows, when it comes to math, American eighth graders don't even rank in the top ten countries.

Mathew Gandal (IT Researcher): What we've found in these other countries is that, from the beginning, they expect students to learn more. They give them much more challenging courses and curriculum. The teachers are trained based on much more challenging standards and, lo and behold, the students achieve.

Reporter: Which is why the U.S. has had to import more than 100,000 computer specialists every year. Experts warn that though the economy is doing well now, the United States could lose ground and they encourage the business community, the government, and educators to do more to train students in math and science, beginning as early as kindergarten.

Deborah Feyerick, CNN, New York.

CNN Video Report: Michael Kearney, Child Prodigy
Running time 03:10

Video Vocabulary
anthropology: the study of humans and their cultures
accelerated: speeded up, moved faster

munchkin: a person who is notably smaller than others
endorsement: approval of a product for advertising purposes
primates: members of the highest order of animals, including humans and apes
linguistics: the study of the nature and structure of languages

Video Script

Reporter: He looks like your *average* 11-year-old. He loves video games, has a typical relationship with his kid sister, and takes tennis lessons.

Tennis Instructor: There we go!

Reporter: But despite his ordinary appearance, Michael Kearney is rather extraordinary.

Michael: I started my entire education when I was three, when I went to kindergarten. Then went to high school at, I believe, five, graduated high school at six, entered college at six, graduated from Santa Rosa Junior College at eight, went to the University of South Alabama at eight, graduated from the University of South Alabama, June 5th, 1994 at ten.

Reporter: Hard to believe, but true. Last June, Michael Kearney became the world's youngest college graduate, earning a degree in anthropology. Even as an infant, he was ahead of his time.

Cassidy Kearney (Mother): Michael started reading at eight months and then by the time he was three, y'know, he was reading *Treasure Island* and *The Count of Monte Cristo.*

Reporter: Although Michael's parents didn't realize at first how gifted he was, once they did, they felt an accelerated education was best for him. And how did he feel about going to college when most kids are in grade school?

Michael: It made me feel very small. I felt like a munchkin. I made a lot of friends in college, but really had absolutely nothing in common with them, except school. They were going off to bars and going to drink, they were dating, doing all that and I'm like, "Uh, do you guys watch Power Rangers?"

Reporter: Often criticized for robbing their son of his childhood, Michael's parents have mixed feelings about his fast-track education.

Cassidy Kearney: Michael is the kind of person, if he has nothing to study or something to do in education, um, he withdraws. And so we think it's more painful for him, so we've let him go ahead. But the problem that we have is that Michael should have gone to kindergarten. Instead we put him in college.

Kevin Kearney (Father): I don't advocate raising children like this; I think you do it because you have to.

Reporter: And now this kid is something of a celebrity, having been on television and in the *Guinness Book of World Records.* Since graduation, Michael's life has been a whirlwind. Last November, he headed to Los Angeles.

Michael: To pursue my dream of being a game-show host.

Reporter: He wasn't there very long. His family has now gone to Japan where they hope to make money from commercial endorsements to help Michael pay for graduate school.

Michael: I'm going to be probably doing visual anthropology. We watch videos of primates and such, and then we try to figure out their linguistics.

Reporter: In the meantime, he hopes to add "author" to his list of accomplishments by writing a book on a subject he knows a lot about: the life of a child prodigy named Michael Kearney.

Kathleen O'Connor, CNN Newsroom, Burbank, California.

Unit 3 Technology and Ethical Issues

CNN Video Report:
Baby Donor
Running time 02:00

Video Vocabulary

anesthetize: to administer a substance used by doctors to prevent a patient from feeling pain

bone marrow: a soft jellylike substance inside bones that makes new blood cells

leukemia: cancer of the white blood cells, often leading to death

vasectomy: surgery on a man's reproductive organs to prevent him from having children

Video Script

Reporter: This is the little girl who was born for a specific reason: to save her older sister's life.

Mary Ayala (Mother): She's everything to us.

Reporter: Just one day after being anesthetized and having a needle inserted into her hip, fourteen-month-old Marissa Ayala appears to be suffering no ill effects. Some of her bone marrow was removed and transplanted into her 19-year-old sister, Anissa. The transplant operation was the only hope of survival for Anissa, who has a form of leukemia that, unless treated, is almost always fatal.

Mary Ayala: Anissa was doing real good this morning. She was in good spirits and, uh, she was just waiting for somebody, she was just waiting for someone to get there to be with her.

Reporter: The Ayala family became the focus of international attention when Anissa's parents publicly acknowledged they conceived a child in hopes it would have matching marrow for the transplant operation. Unable to locate a donor outside of the family, Anissa's 45-year-old father had his vasectomy reversed and six months later

43-year-old Mary Ayala conceived. The couple prayed the new child would beat the one in four odds of having matching marrow. Their prayers were answered. Now they're more optimistic than ever following a successful operation.

Mary Ayala: She'll do good. I know she will. She's my daughter and she's fought some pretty hard battles in her life and this is going to be the hardest, but she's going to come through it.

Reporter: Anissa isn't out of the woods yet, however. Her body may reject the new bone marrow and there is a high risk of infection until the new marrow begins to grow.

Brother: It's hard. I don't even really think about it; I just know she's going to make it, and then I think of the future and how it's going to be after, so everything's going to be great. She'll pull through.

Reporter: Doctors say Anissa will be hospitalized for at least seven weeks. The next six months, they say, will be critical. But, that 80% of bone marrow recipients with Anissa's form of leukemia survive. Marissa doesn't yet know how important she has become. Hopefully, her older sister will have the rest of her life to tell her.

Greg LaMotte, CNN, Los Angeles

Unit 4	The Environment

CNN Video Report: Ivan the Gorilla
Running time 02:12

Video Vocabulary
red-eye: a late-night airline flight
silverback: an adult male gorilla with gray or whitish hair on its back
cavorted: ran around and jumped in a happy way, frolicked
priming: making something ready, preparing
hordes: masses of people, crowds
gawking: looking at something with the mouth open in wonder
Turnabout is fair play: an expression meaning "It's fair to do to someone what they did to you."

Video Script
Zookeeper: Good!

Reporter: Ivan the gorilla has arrived. Settling in with a soft drink at his new home—Zoo Atlanta.

Mitchell Fox (Animal Advocate): Ivan is where he belongs now. Although Ivan is 33 years old, I consider this to be his second birthday because he has a real life ahead of him now.

Reporter: Ivan was captured from the wild as a baby. He spent the last three decades behind a glass enclosure in a concrete cage at a shopping mall in Tacoma, Washington.

Dave Towne (Director, Woodland Park Zoo): That was not an unusual thing, but of course standards and concerns and knowledge have changed substantially.

Reporter: When the owners of the shopping mall filed for bankruptcy, a search began for Ivan's new abode. Tuesday he popped a Valium prescribed by his vet, hopped on the red-eye from Tacoma and arrived at Zoo Atlanta in top form. This is a zoo with firsthand experience in guiding a gorilla through the transformation of total confinement to the freedom of a natural habitat. The Zoo's prime attraction is a showy silverback named Willy B. He too lived a solitary life behind bars. But after 27 years he emerged, cavorted with his own kind, and earlier this year became a father. This is his daughter, Kudzu. Ivan's keepers are priming him for similar good fortune, sending him off with a customized care package.

All part of the plan to maintain Zoo Atlanta's reputation as one of the largest and most successful captive breeding colonies in the country.

Terry Maple (Director, Zoo Atlanta): All things are possible for Ivan under these conditions—he'll feel grass under his feet, the wind in his hair—and smell and see things he's never seen or smelled before.

Reporter: For years, Ivan has endured hordes of humans on the outside looking in. After a brief quarantine, he'll join Willy B. in exploring the great outdoors while gawking back at zoo visitors corralled inside behind a glass wall. Turnabout's fair play.

Pat Etheridge, CNN, Atlanta.

Topics for Today
A S S E S S M E N T

Chapter 1 Review—Hop, Skip . . . and Software?

Focus: Information Recall

Read the questions first. Then read the passages on Student Book pages 3–6 and 16–17 again. Close your book and answer the questions without looking at the passages.

1. What is the Alliance for Childhood's position on computers in elementary schools?

   _____

2. In Educational Testing Service's study, did all the students who had used computers in math class do better on standardized tests? Explain.

   _____

3. Are students attending urban schools more likely or less likely to use computers?

   _____

4. What do educators at the Waldorf School think is most important for young children?

   _____

5. What will the Free Pad computers replace in Arkansas?

   _____

Focus: Vocabulary Cloze

Read the passage below. Choose the best word for each blank from the box. Use each word once.

advocate	concerned	debate	educators	embraced
enhance	exceptions	introduction	spectrum	technology

There is great controversy among (1) _____ about the use of computers in elementary schools. On one side of the (2) _____, people who think computers (3) _____ and enrich learning want more application of (4) _____ in classrooms. At the other end of the (5) _____, teachers and parents are (6) _____ that introducing computers during early childhood may interfere with healthy development. They (7) _____ a structured, gradual (8) _____ of computers at older ages so that young children have a chance to experience things first-hand and develop good social interaction skills. However, with a few (9) _____, most elementary schools have (10) _____ computers as an effective learning tool for young children.

Name: _____ Date: _____

Chapter 2 Review—My Husband, the Outsider

Focus: Information Recall

Read the questions first. Then read the passages on Student Book pages 25–27 and 38–39 again. Close your book and answer the questions without looking at the passages.

1. What is "mixed" about Marian's marriage? Explain.

   _____

2. Why were Marian's relatives unhappy that she had a small wedding?

   _____

3. Why did the Korean doctor keep asking Marian for dates?

   _____

4. By what age are Korean women expected to marry?

   _____

5. Who is treated better in Chinatown—tourists or American-born Chinese? Why?

   _____

Focus: Vocabulary Cloze

Read the passage below. Choose the best word for each blank from the box. Use each word once.

acknowledging	curious	disappointed	dream	exotic
hounded	incompatible	reluctantly	persistence	preferred

Marion Hyun's father disagreed when she dated people she liked instead of the Korean men her

father (1) _____. When she started college, she dated a brilliant American-born Korean, her

father's (2) _____ son-in-law. When they broke up, her father had a hard time (3) _____

that the relationship was over.

Later, Marian's mother asked her to go on a date with her friend's son, a Korean doctor.

(4) _____, she agreed to the first date; however, she refused to continue dating him after discover-

ing they were (5) _____. Strangely, he (6) _____ her for months, but his (7) _____

didn't pay off.

Just when Marian's family thought she'd never marry, she finally did. When Marian and her

husband-to-be announced their engagement, their friends and families were (8) _____ about the

wedding ceremony. They thought it would be an (9) _____ celebration, an occasion that would

reflect the couple's very different backgrounds. As it turned out, they were (10) _____.

Chapter 3 Review—Beyond Rivalry

Focus: Information Recall

Read the questions first. Then read the passages on Student Book pages 50–53 and 64–65 again. Close your book and answer the questions without looking at the passages.

1. What does *sibling rivalry* mean?

   _____

2. Why will late-life sibling bonds be especially important to Baby Boomers?

   _____

3. According to Dr. Antonucci, what happens to our "convey of people" as we age?

   _____

4. Name two reasons why siblings don't turn to each other for instrumental help.

   a. _____

   b. _____

5. Why is a middle-born child's peer group so important to them?

   _____

Focus: Vocabulary Cloze

Read the passage below. Choose the best word for each blank from the box. Use each word once.

bond	closer	drift	estranged	evoke
generation	link	parent	rift	spouses

Brothers and sisters sometimes fight during childhood and then (1) _____ apart as young adults. Marriage and their own families occupy much of their attention. Adult siblings can also become (2) _____ when their (3) _____ don't get along. This type of tension can even create a (4) _____ between siblings that were previously close.

Later in life, siblings often become (5) _____. Sometimes this is due to experiencing a common loss such as the death of a (6) _____. The sibling (7) _____ is an especially strong relationship because brothers and sisters of the same (8) _____ share a common (9) _____ to their early family life. Talking and reminiscing about family can (10) _____ positive feelings and happy memories.

Chapter 4 Review—Who Lives Longer?

Focus: Information Recall

Read the questions first. Then read the passages on Student Book pages 77–79 and 88–89 again. Close your book and answer the questions without looking at the passages.

1. Who typically lives longer—men or women? By how many years?

   _____

2. Name three health practices that can improve your longevity.

   a. _____

   b. _____

   c. _____

3. According to Dr. Byung Yu, what is the most important thing you can do to increase your longevity?

   _____

4. Is all stress bad for you? Explain.

   _____

5. What are two factors influencing Taiwan's changing population?

   a. _____

   b. _____

Focus: Vocabulary Cloze

Read the passage below. Choose the best word for each blank from the box. Use each word once.

birth	changeable	demands	declining	expectancy
heredity	landmark	longevity	population	profound

    What is the secret of living longer? A (1) _____ study shows that there are seven health habits that can improve your (2) _____. Some genetic factors are fixed by (3) _____, but by contrast, the seven habits are (4) _____. If you adopt these habits, they are likely to have a (5) _____ impact on your life span.

    In Taiwan, sociologists are studying important changes in the (6) _____. The (7) _____ rate, the number of new births per thousand people, is (8) _____ every year. At the same time, life (9) _____ is rising, resulting in a growing proportion of elderly people. Social scientists predict this trend will put new (10) _____ on society.

157

Chapter 5 Review—The Mindset of Health

Focus: Information Recall

Read the questions first. Then read the passages on Student Book pages 99–101 and 111–112 again. Close your book and answer the questions without looking at the passages.

1. Ellen Langer states that we learn to do what from a very early age?

   _____

2. What one factor can influence our tolerance of pain?

   _____

3. In the experiment with smokers, did they have strong desires to smoke in nonsmoking situations? Explain.

   _____

4. According to Gloria Emerson, what two things do hospital patients want?

   _____

5. Give an example of *institutional loyalty* from the second reading.

   _____

Focus: Vocabulary Cloze

Read the passage below. Choose the best word for each blank from the box. Use each word once.

bodies	control	experiments	influence	mindful
mindlessly	mental	physical	separate	system

Most people tend to see their minds and bodies as (1) _____ elements instead of as one integrated (2) _____. In fact, we go to one kind of doctor for (3) _____ illnesses and to another for mental problems. However, recent (4) _____ indicate that our (5) _____ attitude can (6) _____ how our bodies physically respond to stimuli. If we intentionally try to be (7) _____ of the context of certain situations, we have more (8) _____ over our health than if we behave (9) _____. Can we use our minds to help us keep our (10) _____ healthy?

Chapter 6 Review—Small Wonders

Focus: Information Recall

Read the questions first. Then read the passages on Student Book pages 120–122 and 133–134 again. Close your book and answer the questions without looking at the passages.

1. How did Nguyen Ngoc Truong Son learn to play chess?

   _____

2. What is the standard definition of a *prodigy?*

   _____

3. How are Abigail Sin and her twin different?

   _____

4. What part of the brain plays an important role in coordinating thought and improving concentration?

   _____

5. Name three of Alia Sabur's qualities, beyond her extraordinary mind, that her professors say make her special.

   a. _____

   b. _____

   c. _____

Focus: Vocabulary Cloze

Read the passage below. Choose the best word for each blank from the box. Use each word once.

average	brains	differentiates	drive	function
gifted	nurture	startling	toddler	wunderkinder

Prodigies show that they are different from (1) _____ children at an early age. These

(2) _____ children display special talents when they are only (3) _____. When parents rec-

ognize that their child is unusual, they provide extra (4) _____ and care. Often (5) _____

show a strong (6) _____ to learn music or mathematics, although some child prodigies display a

mastery of skills in other fields.

Neurological experiments on prodigies have shown (7) _____ results. Their

(8) _____ seem to (9) _____ quite differently than ordinary children's do. Researchers are

beginning to think that it is this difference in brain function that (10) _____ prodigies from aver-

age children.

Chapter 7 Review—Assisted Suicide: Multiple Perspectives

Focus: Information Recall

Read the questions first. Then read the passages on Student Book pages 148–149 and 160–161 again. Close your book and answer the questions without looking at the passages.

1. How would doctors in Dr. Moore's generation help terminally ill patients die?

   _____

2. What was the injured nurse's attitude toward being maintained by machines?

   _____

3. Why were the students in the medical ethics seminar shocked?

   _____

4. What happened to Derek Humphry's wife?

   _____

5. Who are the people Daniel Callahan thinks would want to commit suicide?

   _____

Focus: Vocabulary Cloze

Read the passage below. Choose the best word for each blank from the box. Use each word once.

cases	controversy	fatal	fractured	internship
lethal	medication	recovered	respected	treatment

Dr. Moore, a (1) _____ 81-year-old physician, said that helping patients die is not new.

During his (2) _____ decades ago, doctors gave large amounts of heavy (3) _____ to

patients with hopeless diseases or illness. Dr. Moore said it was done quietly, without (4) _____,

because doctors felt it was essential.

In his book *A Miracle and a Privilege,* Dr. Moore describes two medical (5) _____. The first

patient was on life-support machines because of complications that had developed after she

(6) _____ her pelvis. Her family urged the doctor to let her die peacefully. He didn't stop treatment

and the patient later (7) _____ and regained full health. The other patient had (8) _____

burns. When the patient showed no signs of progress, Dr. Moore stopped (9) _____ and gave her

(10) _____ doses of morphine to help her pain. She died peacefully. Dr. Moore feels that these

decisions required strong judgment and a lot of experience.

Name: _____ Date: _____

Chapter 8 Review—Sales of Kidneys Prompt New Laws and Debate

Focus: Information Recall

Read the questions first. Then read the passages on Student Book pages 167–168 and 169–172 again. Close your book and answer the questions without looking at the passages.

1. Name three parts of the body that a living person can sell.

   a. _____

   b. _____

   c. _____

2. When did the British Parliament outlaw the sale of human organs?

   _____

3. What is the World Health Organization's position on organ sales?

   _____

4. Why does Dr. John Newman think that government payment for kidneys is cost effective?

   _____

5. Why doesn't Belgium's automatic organ donation program work?

   _____

Focus: Vocabulary Cloze

Read the passage below. Choose the best word for each blank from the box. Use each word once.

banning punished	cadavers recipients	donors supply	impoverished trafficking	organs waiting

There are many more sick people (1) _____ for transplant organs than there are

(2) _____. The short (3) _____ of available organs has led some (4) _____ people to

sell one of their kidneys. Other (5) _____ such as hearts, livers, and pancreases have to come from

(6) _____, the bodies of dead people. Health authorities are worried that without laws restricting

the sale of body parts, very poor people will continue to be tempted to sell their organs. Therefore, many

governments have passed laws (7) _____ organ (8) _____. People who take part in this

practice are either (9) _____ with fines or sent to prison. Although this is sure to limit the black

market trade of body parts, this does not make more organs available to potential (10) _____ who

desperately need a transplant.

Topics for Today, Book 5, Assessment

Name: _____ Date: _____

Chapter 9 Review—The Gift of Life: When One Body Can Save Another

Focus: Information Recall

Read the questions first. Then read the passages on Student Book pages 190–192 and 203 again. Close your book and answer the questions without looking at the passages.

1. Why couldn't Anissa Ayala's brother, Airon, donate bone marrow to her?

   _____

2. What were the odds of Marissa's bone marrow matching her sisters?

   _____

3. Why do seat-belt and motorcycle helmet laws result in a shortage of organ donors?

   _____

4. Why has Dr. Thomas Starzl stopped performing live-donor transplants?

   _____

5. How do the Plums feel about trying to save their daughter? Explain.

   _____

Focus: Vocabulary Cloze

Read the passage below. Choose the best word for each blank from the box. Use each word once.

donor **profoundly**	**compatible** **radiation**	**launched** **rejection**	**marrow** **sibling**	**pregnant** **surgeon**

When parents have a (1) _____ ill child, they sometimes take extreme measures to help save the child's life. Anissa Ayala had a serious form of leukemia and needed a bone (2) _____ transplant. The problem was that the tissue had to come from someone whose tissue was (3) _____ with hers. Doctors told the Ayala family that Anissa's best hope was to receive bone marrow from a (4) _____. After the family found out her brother could not donate his marrow, they (5) _____ a nationwide search to find a (6) _____. When that didn't produce results, they decided to have another child in hope that this child's bone marrow would match Anissa's. Anissa's mother became (7) _____ at age 43.

When Marissa Ayala was 14 months old, a (8) _____ operated on her to draw marrow for Anissa. Doctors prepared Anissa by giving her (9) _____ treatments to reduce the chance of (10) _____ of the transplant. Fortunately, the operation was a success and now the sisters are very close.

Chapter 10 Review—Playing with Fire

Focus: Information Recall

Read the questions first. Then read the passages on Student Book pages 217–220 and 230–231 again. Close your book and answer the questions without looking at the passages.

1. Who are the two groups in the confrontation over rain forests?

   a. _____

   b. _____

2. Besides Brazil, how many countries does the Amazon stretch into?

   _____

3. Why did Brazil build the Trans-Amazon Highway in the 1970s?

   _____

4. Name two natural products that can be harvested from the Amazonian jungle.

   a. _____

   b. _____

5. What happened to environmentalist Francisco Alves Mendes?

   _____

Focus: Vocabulary Cloze

Read the passage below. Choose the best word for each blank from the box. Use each word once.

climate	**deforestation**	**disappears**	**evaporates**	**heat**
irreversible	**recycles**	**River**	**survival**	**world**

People throughout the (1) _____ are worried about the future of the Amazon. The huge expanse that makes up the Amazon (2) _____ and rain forest is important for the (3) _____ of the whole Earth. Moisture (4) _____ from the forest and (5) _____ into rain, returning the water to the ecosystem. In the process, harmful carbon dioxide changes into oxygen. If the forest (6) _____ forever, how will this affect the planet? Some scientists think the carbon dioxide will hold in (7) _____, contributing to the Greenhouse Effect.

Now the main dangers to the (8) _____ of the rain forest are burning fires and cutting wood for timber. Both of these cause (9) _____. Environmentalists say these practices should be reduced before (10) _____ damage occurs.

5 · ASSESSMENT

Name: _____ Date: _____

Chapter 11 Review—Wilder Places for Wild Things

Focus: Information Recall

Read the questions first. Then read the passages on Student Book pages 240–242 and 252–253 again. Close your book and answer the questions without looking at the passages.

1. Why do zookeepers provide activities for beavers, chimpanzees, and other animals?

   _____

2. When was the first naturalistic zoo opened in the United States?

   _____

3. Name three ways that zoo curators try to recreate natural environments.

   a. _____

   b. _____

   c. _____

4. Why does the American Association of Zoological Parks and Aquariums keep a studbook?

   _____

5. What did the states of Oregon, Arizona, and Colorado change? Why?

   _____

Focus: Vocabulary Cloze

Read the passage below. Choose the best word for each blank from the box. Use each word once.

behaviors	constructed	cages	curators	habitats
immersed	mimic	natural	reproduce	vanished

    If you had visited a zoo a century ago, you would have seen many unusual animals, but they all would have been kept in (1) _____. You could have gotten quite close to them to watch them carefully, but you wouldn't have seen many animals display natural (2) _____. This is because a cage is not a natural environment.

    Modern zoos try to create settings for animals that (3) _____ their natural environments. In many modern zoos, cages have (4) _____. In their place are large areas (5) _____ so that you don't see how the animals are kept in place. Creative (6) _____ try to make the zoo (7) _____ seem like home to the animals with (8) _____ plants, landscapes, sounds, and things to do. Creating such an environment has several positive effects. Not only are the animals healthier and happier, but they are more likely to mate and (9) _____. In addition, visitors become (10) _____ in the animals' environments and hopefully realize the importance of preserving natural habitats in the wild.

Topics for Today, Book 5, Assessment

Chapter 12 Review—A Nuclear Graveyard

Focus: Information Recall

Read the questions first. Then read the passages on Student Book pages 263–266 and 278–279 again. Close your book and answer the questions without looking at the passages.

1. What is the source of most nuclear waste?

   _____

2. What are the "twin virtues" of the Yucca Mountain site?

   _____

3. What is Jerry Szymanski's idea about groundwater in the past? Where does he think the water came from?

   _____

4. Some scientists think Jerry Szymanski's idea is wrong. Why? Where do they believe the water came from?

   _____

5. Why do Nevadans feel Congress ordered the DOE to focus on Yucca Mountain? Explain.

   _____

Focus: Vocabulary Cloze

Read the passage below. Choose the best word for each blank from the box. Use each word once.

assurances	**buried**	**desolate**	**earthquakes**	**government**
Nevada	**radioactive**	**refuse**	**repository**	**site**

For many years, there has been a disagreement between the federal (1) _____ and citizens in the state of (2) _____ about storing nuclear wastes in Yucca Mountain. Nuclear power plants eventually use up the fuel rods that create energy. However, these nuclear wastes remain (3) _____ for thousands of years. Government officials believe that the safest way to dispose of this (4) _____ is to bury it deep underground. The burial site should be a (5) _____ and isolated place far from where people live. The remote (6) _____ they have chosen is Yucca Mountain.

The government has given the citizens of Nevada (7) _____ that the (8) _____ nuclear waste will be safe. Some geologists and scientists are worried that the (9) _____ could be damaged by a rise in underground water levels. These scientists claim that (10) _____ and volcanoes can affect the water table. The government says that this is unlikely.

5 · ASSESSMENT